Praise for *The Face-to-Face Book*

"A timely reminder from two of the most influential minds in business that creating real relationships requires more than counting likes and shares. For brands that want to avoid chasing the latest social media trend and harness the power of a face-to-face relationship, this book will give you the inspiration and tools to do it!"

—Rohit Bhargava, SVP of Social@Ogilvy and author of *Likeonomics*

"Ed Keller and Brad Fay are at the very front edge of the industry conversation about how to get consumers talking, and they are creating new wisdom on the subject every day. *The Face-to-Face Book* is a must-read for anyone looking for inspiration to drive buzz in new ways, as we have been doing at NBCUniversal."

—Tony Cardinale, EVP Brand Planning and Strategic Insights at NBCUniversal

"*The Face-to-Face Book* presents cutting-edge thinking in a great book. With the explosion of digital marketing and the increasing hype of social media we tend to forget that a table and several chairs is still a favorite way for word of mouth to spread. If you want to understand the true impact of your marketing, pick up this book. You are in for a great ride!"

—Ekaterina Walter, social media strategist, Intel

"*The Face-to-Face Book* is incredibly useful for anyone in marketing. Keller and Fay's research covers the broadest spectrum of brand-relevant conversations, which then lays the groundwork for communication strategies that are 'social by design' instead of simply social as a channel. At SMG we have found that more meaningful conversations about brands will lead to the more meaningful human experiences that truly drive long-term marketplace success."

—Kate Sirkin, EVP, Global Research, Starcom MediaVest Group

"Charles Handy once said, 'measuring more is easy, measuring better is hard'—that's what this book is about. Keller and Fay have cracked the code on providing a complete assessment of the origins and impact of word of mouth, its multiplier effect, and the ultimate in earned media."

—Artie Bulgrin, SVP Research and Analytics, ESPN, Inc.

*f*P

The Face-to-Face Book

WHY REAL RELATIONSHIPS RULE IN A DIGITAL MARKETPLACE

Ed Keller *and* Brad Fay

FREE PRESS

NEW YORK   LONDON   TORONTO   SYDNEY   NEW DELHI

*f*P

FREE PRESS
A Division of Simon & Schuster, Inc.
1230 Avenue of the Americas
New York, NY 10020

First Free Press hardcover edition May 2012

FREE PRESS and colophon are trademarks of
Simon & Schuster, Inc.

For information about special discounts for bulk purchases,
please contact Simon & Schuster Special Sales at
1-866-506-1949 or business@simonandschuster.com.

Designed by Julie Schroeder

Manufactured in the United States of America

1   3   5   7   9   10   8   6   4   2

Library of Congress Cataloging-in-Publication Data
Keller, Ed.
The face-to-face book : why real relationships rule in a
digital marketplace / Ed Keller and Brad Fay.
p. cm.
Includes bibliographical references and index.
1. Word-of-mouth advertising. 2. Social marketing. 3. Marketing—
Social aspects. I. Fay, Brad. II. Title.
HF5827.95.K45 2012
658.8'72—dc23
2012001413

ISBN 978-1-4516-4007-6
ISBN 978-1-4516-4008-3 (ebook)

To Bud Roper, for bringing us
together and starting us talking about word of mouth
before it was in vogue.

And to Jay Wilson,
for helping us to keep the conversation going.

Contents

Introduction

_____

THE SOCIAL MEDIA GOLD RUSH

When the history of the early twenty-first century is written, will textbooks observe that Internet users spent billions of dollars on "virtual" animated online farm creatures during the worst economic slump since the Great Depression?

Much of history has been built on a series of gold rushes, not only for precious metals, but also for stocks, real estate, even tulips during the Dutch "tulip mania" of 1637. Could social media be the next big bubble? Is the rush to do business with Facebook, Twitter, and Zynga—the creators of the online farm game FarmVille—overheated?

During the American Gold Rush of 1848–1853, more than a quarter-million people flocked to California to exploit the new state's golden bounty. That migration built proud cities like San Francisco and Sacramento and helped to fuel the great westward expansion of a young nation, with enormously important consequences for America. In today's dollars, tens of billions' worth of gold were discovered. But the vast majority of those Forty-niners, as they were called, became no richer for their journey and hard work.

We believe that social media today represents the latest gold rush, with too many businesses and marketers in search of Facebook and

Twitter gold dust that they hope will rub off on them, chasing an immense social wave that is not yet fully understood. Missed in the frenzy is a far bigger opportunity with much greater impact to connect with people—consumers, voters, supporters—in important new ways. While the growth of social networking sites is impressive, the largest social gold mine is literally right beneath our noses: in the word-of-mouth conversations that happen in our kitchens and living rooms, in our churches and synagogues, next to the office water cooler, on the sidelines of youth soccer and baseball games, powered by the intimacy of face-to-face communications.

More than 90 percent of the conversations about products, services, and brands that take place every day in America happen offline, according to research that will be revealed in the chapters of this book.[1] This adds up to billions of brand-related conversations and recommendations each and every week in America that take place face-to-face, or in real life (IRL), as it is known in Internet circles. Only a small percentage takes place online, whether through the multitude of social networking sites that we think of as social media, or through other online channels such as texting or email. Social media is big and growing, but it is still dwarfed by the analog world in which people live and interact.

That's why this is *The Face-to-Face Book*. It is the story of how the decisions we make are based on true interpersonal influence: social influence, which happens most often, and most powerfully, face-to-face.

Make no mistake: there is a hugely important social wave rolling

---

1.   Throughout this book, statistics from the Keller Fay Group's TalkTrack® research service are quoted. This research program began in 2006 and involves continuous tracking of the word-of-mouth conversations of the American people, including those that take place offline as well as online. Unless otherwise mentioned, those statistics will be based on survey data collected during the twelve months ending June 2011, during which time more than 37,000 interviews were conducted online among a nationally representative sample of Americans age 13 to 69. For more information about TalkTrack and its methodology, see the notes.

across the world of business today, based on the very belated insight that we humans are fundamentally social beings, for whom social influence determines nearly every decision we make. It's an insight that was first observed and discussed decades ago, in the 1950s and 1960s. But with the rise of the golden age of television, it was largely ignored in favor of the glitz of that era's revolutionary new medium. The opportunity was there, though almost entirely missed by the world's marketers and entrepreneurs, until Mark Zuckerberg, the founder of Facebook, proved to everyone that there's gold in them thar hills. Yet too many people are attempting to mine only one vein of social opportunity, following the path blazed most successfully by Zuckerberg. It's as if those gold-seeking Forty-niners were crowding together in pursuit of gold only at the original site of Sutter's Mill in Coloma, California, where James W. Marshall found those first nuggets of gold in 1848.

The opportunities of the Gold Rush were not limited to the Sutter's Mill property, but spread across much of the Sierra Nevada mountain range. And the opportunity, ultimately, was not just to find gold. California turned out to be a place of many other bounties—agriculture, trade and commerce, tourism, and invention—all of which were helped by the explosion of population and discovery induced by the gold rush. It was that same spirit of invention and discovery that brought Zuckerberg to the Golden State from the ivory towers of Cambridge, Massachusetts, in the famous early days of Facebook.

This is neither a book against Facebook nor against social media in general. In certain respects, Mark Zuckerberg is the James W. Marshall of today's social wave. The man and his company tapped into a mother lode that was there all along but ignored by many. He proved the power of social connections to the world. As of this writing, Facebook is approaching one billion users, one in seven of the world's population, and the largest audience for a single media platform in the history of humanity. It is an awesome achievement, but the successes of Facebook—and its social media kin—are the *result* of a tremendous social opportunity, and not its cause or source. People flock to Facebook because it meets a social need that was previously underserved online. But people's desire to be social manifests itself in many other places as well, creating multiple opportunities for businesses that wish to participate.

We believe in a marketplace that is highly social, but not because of particular platforms or technologies. The most successful businesses in the future will be the ones that embrace a model that puts people—rather than technology—at the center of products, campaigns, and market strategies. They will recognize that people have a far greater impact on each other than we previously realized, and that consumers are not just a collection of individuals. It's an insight that applies as well to politics, which is increasingly impacted by socially driven movements such as the Tea Party, the "Occupy" protests, and peer-to-peer movements that are reshaping politics across the Middle East. New communications opportunities are being revealed by a rapidly growing "science of social" that is gathering momentum. Those who achieve the greatest success will recognize that there are many ways to tap into the power of today's social consumer. Social media sites are just one way, and still a relatively limited one at that.

In the chapters of this book we will share with you our perspective on how you can think holistically about social influence in business, marketing, and politics. We rely heavily on insights from research about social influence by our firm, the Keller Fay Group, and others. So there is a solid, research-based foundation for everything we describe. But while the foundation is built on research, this is not a book that is dominated by numbers. We have interviewed top executives of companies that are going about things in smart, new ways—ways that are consistent with the facts and not just the hype—and we have endeavored to let their stories take the lead role, with the data in a largely supporting role. These companies include Audi, Best Buy, Dell, Domino's, General Mills, Kimberly-Clark, Kraft, MillerCoors, Procter & Gamble, Toyota, and Zappos, among others.

But social marketing is not only the domain of large companies, so we feature the stories of some small companies that are thinking creatively about how best to create social businesses offline and on-line. And outside of business altogether, we look at how recent presidential campaigns have tapped into social marketing strategies. We hope we have been able to strike the right balance for those readers who understand things best through stories, and those who take comfort in the facts that come from research.

As we describe the history, present, and future of social marketing, you'll learn what motivates people to talk about brands and companies and about the influencers who are at the center of the conversation. We write about the important role of advertising and other forms of traditional marketing in sparking conversations, and how media can be planned more effectively to maximize consumer advocacy and word of mouth. We also recommend how to use social media in smart and meaningful ways, and give examples where brands have taken the bait and have been misled. We will share examples of how word of mouth can be not only a goal and a strategy that drives business forward, but also how it can be used as a primary channel unto itself. And we look at the mix of positive and negative word of mouth with some facts that will surprise you and help you to realize the good that can come from negative word of mouth when it's properly managed. We conclude with a discussion of companies that have changed the way their organizations operate to deal successfully with the social era in which they operate today, and that will continue to define the marketplace in the decades ahead.

There are many pathways to tap the power of people's social connections and their desire to share and learn from each other. Some businesses recognize this and are responding appropriately. We applaud and celebrate them. But those marketers who are mining only one vein—namely, social networking tools and technologies—are not seeing the full scope of an enormous social opportunity. And if history and research prove true, they will ultimately lose business because of it. The great social wave is an opportunity that no business can afford to ignore or look at myopically. It's happening all around us, mostly in the real world, face-to-face.

1

The Science of Social

The California Gold Rush was about putting everything on the line to chase a dream, find a new life, and have a chance for riches beyond imagination. Hundreds of thousands of ordinary Americans did just that in 1849 and for a year or two afterward—the Forty-niners, they were called. Some struck it rich, but most did not. The truth, though, is that most of the people who took the risk had little to lose. They lacked property and had few possessions and few economic prospects back east or in their home countries. So why not "go west, young man," as the popular columnist Horace Greeley advised, in search of fame and fortune?

In this day and age, an established and successful $17.5 billion consumer products company would never take that sort of "all-in" risk. Or would it?

The beverage and snack giant PepsiCo provides the most dramatic example of a company that succumbed to the social media gold rush mentality. In 2010 the company sharply pulled back its spending on traditional media, especially on television, and most symbolically on its much anticipated commercials during the 2010 Super Bowl. Instead Pepsi placed a very large bet on social media as the smart, new way to engage its consumers and drive sales. Launching a campaign it called the Pepsi Refresh Project, the brand engaged 87 million consumers through Facebook and other social media in an effort to distribute $20 million in charitable contributions to local causes as an alternative to traditional advertising.

The campaign's ambitions were impressive and aligned with the times—a transformative communications model that was based on creating community, engaging consumers, and, of course, leveraging a wide range of new online social networking tools. The advertising industry trade publication *Advertising Age* offered a prophetic headline in February 2010, announcing the Refresh campaign: "Pass or Fail, Pepsi's Refresh Will Be a Case for Marketing Textbooks."

Though ours is not a textbook, we use Pepsi's Refresh as a case nonetheless. Pepsi's big bet on social media did not come close to achieving the pay dirt it intended. While Pepsi's Refresh Project deservedly won praise for being innovative and for the public good that it offered, the strategy did not meet the company's core goal: selling soft drinks.

In March 2011 the trade publication *Beverage Digest* announced that for calendar year 2010 Diet Coke had surpassed Pepsi as the number-two soft drink, behind the Coca-Cola Classic brand. Pepsi sales in 2010 were down 6 percent in a category that declined 4.5 percent overall. In a tacit admission of error, Pepsi announced in early 2011 that it was raising traditional ad expenditures by 30 percent and returned to the 2011 Super Bowl after just a one-year absence. Several months later Pepsi executives were telling the *Wall Street Journal* about plans for a new ad campaign for the flagship Pepsi brand and about their decision to sign on as a lead sponsor for *The X Factor,* Simon Cowell's TV music competition (in the mold of *American Idol*), which launched in the United States in the fall of 2011. The reported cost of Pepsi's campaign was $60 million for the first season. Big-time advertising and sponsorship was back at Pepsi.

"We need television to make the big, bold statement," Massimo d'Amore, CEO of PepsiCo Beverages North America, admitted to the *Journal*. Pepsi learned the hard way that traditional mass media is still a powerful weapon for driving social engagement and sales. The mistake Pepsi made when it withdrew advertising in favor of the Refresh campaign—whatever its social benefits—was thinking that it could replace rather than supplement a large and sophisticated media strategy that had been refined over decades. PepsiCo believed in the social media hype to its detriment.

Pepsi was right about the potential benefit of social interaction, but it was overly focused on online social networks. Our research at the Keller Fay Group shows that Pepsi does in fact sell soft drinks because of social interactions, but not necessarily because of *online* interactions. In virtually every decision we make, every one of us is influenced to a remarkable extent by other people, mostly the people we spend time with in the "real world." Human beings are a fundamentally social species, and virtually all of our decision making, including consumer decisions, are based on the influence of the people around us—and most powerfully, the influence of those who are physically near and emotionally close to us. The discovery of how we influence each other in the offline world is the true breakthrough unfolding today. Scientists are finding the most important action is happening not online, but in our hearts, in our minds, and in our neural systems—in other words, in the real world.

The Burgeoning Science of "Social"

While face-to-face conversation may be as old as time, our understanding of the importance of social interaction is new and still emerging. Scientists today—anthropologists, evolutionary biologists, social psychologists, neuroscientists, epidemiologists, network theorists, and more—are uncovering powerful new evidence of just how connected we are to each other and the degree to which our decisions, large and small, are influenced by people around us. They are challenging the central conceit of marketing: that messages created by marketers can be transmitted to individuals, who become aware and ultimately persuaded, leading to a change in behavior. Instead we are discovering that messages are usually received in a supremely social context, in which people share with each other what they see and hear in advertising, compare experiences and opinions, and then make collective choices. Good marketing starts conversations, and chiefly because of those conversations people make decisions that ultimately determine which brands are successful and which fail.

This analysis of how marketing works received a strong endorsement in late 2011 from a well-regarded company that doesn't have a stake in the word-of-mouth industry. MarketShare is a leader in market mix modeling, serving half of the fifty largest companies in America. MarketShare undertook a broad analysis of how marketing really works on behalf of a half dozen of their clients. They used a wide array of data—from advertising and marketing expenditures, product sales, economic factors, and, critically for our purposes here, word-of-mouth data relating to their clients' brands and competitors (provided by our firm, the Keller Fay Group) as well as data about brands that are discussed via social media. MarketShare then ran sophisticated statistical analyses that came to the following conclusion: "Social voice represents a critical pathway through which more than half the impact of paid advertising and media passes in generating consumer purchases." In other words, advertising works most of the time because of social influence.

MarketShare is not the first to conclude that social influence is critical to the success of advertising and marketing. In fact the idea has its origins in the 1950s, when two Columbia University professors, Paul Lazarsfeld and Elihu Katz, published the results of a major research project in their seminal book, *Personal Influence*. They found that advertising was ineffective at directly changing consumer preferences and prompting purchase. Rather, they said, advertising is effective because it prompts conversations between "opinion leaders" and other people, who are persuaded to purchase based on personal influence. Though largely ignored for another five decades, the idea that social influence makes mass communications effective means that virtually every marketing campaign should strive to generate consumer conversations, engagement, and social interaction; otherwise the campaign is much more likely to fail.

How do marketers encourage conversations, sharing, and engagement? That's a key topic of this book, and it is a subject of great interest to many researchers and scientists today. One leading thinker in the field is Dr. Carl Marci, currently a member of the faculty of Harvard's Department of Psychiatry and the cofounder of a market research company, Innerscope, that uses biometric data, including heartbeat and blood pressure, to measure consumer responses. In an interview in his Boston offices in 2011, he discussed the importance of emotions and social influence. The function of emotions is to help us navigate our socially complex world—to make decisions that consider the needs and wants of others close to us. Our survival as a species has depended not merely on our being the strongest or most aggressive, but on our being collaborative. Because human brains take longer to develop than the brains of any other species—more than twenty years following birth—our survival has always depended on our ability to obtain care and support from others. The survival of our offspring—and, through them, that of our own DNA—depends on our willingness to provide support and to obtain the assistance of others to help raise those children. As a result, our evolutionary history has given us highly effective tools for reading the emotions and opinions of other people and for adapting to them. This means we have developed exceptional skills for empathy, morality, and affection—qualities that are essential to living and thriving in a highly social world.

These conclusions are achieving consensus across a wide variety of fields, spawning a growing literature, including, in ascending chronological order, *Social Intelligence* by Daniel Goleman (2006), *Herd* by Mark Earls (2007), *Connected* by Nicholas Christakis and James Fowler (2010), *Join the Club* by Tina Rosenberg (2011), and *The Social Animal* by David Brooks (2011). These books focus on implications of social interactions for human relations, education, sociology, medicine, social movements, and even politics.

The purpose of our book is to show how businesses and brands can benefit significantly from a new understanding of our highly social species and our social style of decision making, and to highlight the many paths that businesses and other organizations can, and should, take to engage on a more social basis with consumers, and in a way that produces concrete results.

Christakis and Fowler have done original research that offers compelling evidence for the power of social influence. Between them, Christakis of Harvard and Fowler of UC–San Diego have expertise in medicine, public health, politics, sociology, and genetics. In their 2010 book they argue that human beings are effectively part of a larger, interconnected human "super-organism." They find that emotions are transmitted rapidly from person to person, and so are behaviors and preferences of all kinds. Everything about us is contagious.

According to Daniel Goleman, one way to understand this behavior is to pay attention to the way emotions pass from person to person. We instinctively mimic people we are with. When we are with happy people, we are happier. When we spend time with sad people, we become sadder. What is surprising is the mechanism through which emotions are transferred. In a process called "affective afference" we mimic the facial expressions of the people we are with. Writes Goleman, "Whenever we gaze at a photograph of someone whose face displays a strong emotion, like sadness, disgust, or joy, our facial muscles automatically start to mirror the other's facial expression." In other words, expressions precede feelings, not the other way around. It is easy to imagine the power of such nonverbal communication to influence human evolution: even before language, early humans could quickly communicate messages such as "Run, fast!" upon realizing they were in the path of an oncoming predator.

Indeed the primitive human example is hinted at in the title of Mark Earls's book, *Herd*. Earls puts it this way: "Most of our behavior is . . . the result of the influence of other people because we are a super-social species. A herd animal, if you like." We agree with his advice to communicators, that "we will find it much easier to change mass behavior if we develop a better conception of humankind; if we abandon our existing ways of thinking and accept that we are not a species of independent, self-determining individuals."

The transfer of emotions and opinions seems to be strongest among people with close ties: family, friends, and loved ones, the people we are most apt to encounter face-to-face. In 2011 the Proceedings of the National Academy of Sciences of the United States published the results of a novel experiment that was conducted in the Spanish village of San Pedro Manrique, on the occasion of an annual ceremony commemorating the summer solstice. A group of scientists led by Ivana Konvalinka, a bioengineering doctoral student in Denmark, monitored the heart rates of twelve "fire-walkers" as they crossed a twenty-three-foot-long carpet of burning embers. In addition, the heart rates of spectators were measured, including nine family members of the fire-walkers and seventeen unrelated persons who were visiting the event. The study found that the heart rates of the related persons beat at almost the same rate and pattern as the fire-walkers before, during, and after the crossing of the burning embers, while the heart rates of unrelated visitors did not increase nearly as much.

Social contagion is not limited to emotions. Christakis and Fowler write about their analysis of a thirty-two-year longitudinal medical study, known as the Framingham (Massachusetts) Heart Study. Christakis and Fowler discovered that the original Framingham researchers had collected a large amount of personal relationship data for each of the 12,000 study participants solely for the purpose of being able to use friends and family to locate study participants who had changed addresses. For the study to be successful, it would be essential for the researchers to be able to reinterview their subjects at regular intervals over decades, and they had good reason to worry that their subjects would move without remembering to leave a forwarding address for the researchers. For each participant in the study, they knew the names and addresses of close friends and family members, many of whom were also participants in the study.

Christakis and Fowler realized that this information about personal contacts made it possible to map the social networks of study participants. They were able to identify the people who were located more centrally in the network, or who connected multiple groups, versus those who were more isolated. Most important, they had firm connections between participants that could allow them to monitor changes in lifestyles, behaviors, and health outcomes as they spread through networks. Their hypothesis was that changes for one participant would often be mimicked by those connected to them closely, and then by other people connected via mutual friends.

That is exactly what they found. Behaviors and health outcomes radiated across social networks in a way that Christakis and Fowler could dramatically illustrate with computerized diagrams. What happened to one person often also happened to his friends and to his friends' friends. The trends started centrally and rippled toward the periphery. Christakis and Fowler discovered that when a person's friend becomes obese, his own chance of becoming obese tripled—a startling finding that led to a considerable amount of media attention for their research. They also found that positive behaviors were contagious. For example, one of the strongest social effects they found was for smoking cessation: when one person stopped smoking there was a large increase in the chance that her friends also stopped smoking. While there has been some debate about whether true social influence alone can account for the enormity of effects measured by Christakis and Fowler, academics in the field believe social influence accounts for at least some of the observed behavior changes in the Framingham study.

As a species we have long realized that social factors are important to us and to changing behavior; this is why Weight Watchers and Alcoholics Anonymous (AA) have been so successful. Both organizations are focused on regular meetings of participants to discuss issues and share experiences with each other. With this kind of in-person social support, positive life changes become much easier to achieve. In her book *Join the Club: How Peer Pressure Can Transform the World*, Tina Rosenberg writes about the "social cure," which has been used to overthrow the dictator Slobodan Milosevic of Serbia, to improve health and raise living standards in impoverished areas of India, and to teach calculus to minority students. In these cases, programs are designed to deepen connections between people, to form mutually supportive organizations, and they produce results not otherwise possible.

The "social cure" can work when people consciously and voluntarily choose to participate, as in the cases of Weight Watchers and AA. The resulting changes in our lifestyles occur because we have made a conscious decision to make the change, and in our minds the supportive community merely helps us to achieve what is a highly personal goal. What's so startling about the literature on social influence is that most of the time this effect is unconscious. The Christakis and Fowler analysis of the Framingham Heart Study measured social effects that are unknown to the study participants: our friends can make us fat even when we aren't aware of it! It happens because our friends change our sense of what is a reasonable weight; we tend to copy their food choices and portion sizes, and we may also mimic their exercise routines.

Similarly with respect to smoking, regulatory bans against smoking in public places have reduced the prevalence of seeing people smoking. There's less smoking on TV and in movies due to pressure from advocacy groups. When people smoke, they often appear to have been ostracized to a company's loading dock or to a cold sidewalk on a winter day. As smoking becomes less prevalent and less glamorous, fewer people decide to smoke, or they smoke less, or they stop altogether.

Another example of the potential power of social influence can be seen in a state-funded "social norm" pilot program to reduce problem behaviors among local teens. The high school in Montgomery

Township, New Jersey, is one institution that participates in the program, run by the Rowan University Center for Addiction Studies and Awareness and locally managed by the school's substance abuse counselor. The program's premise is that young people often make poor decisions because they want to behave in ways that are "in keeping with the norms or beliefs of their social group, not in ways that are necessarily consistent with their belief system." Because many young people inaccurately overestimate the prevalence of behaviors among their peers, they may adopt destructive behavior, such as use of alcohol, drugs, or tobacco, subscribing to the fallacy that "everyone is doing it."

The program combats false assumptions by conducting an anonymous survey of students to determine the actual prevalence of "at-risk" behaviors, and then publicizing those results throughout the school on posters and through events and games linked to the survey results. Posters that have appeared in Montgomery High include such messages as "2 out of 3 of us have not used alcohol" and "More than 4 out of 5 of us think our friends would disapprove of us smoking cigarettes." By repeatedly emphasizing that most students aren't engaged in or supportive of alcohol or drug use, Montgomery officials—and those statewide—believe they can further reduce the prevalence of certain negative behaviors among teenagers.

Montgomery High happens to be the school that coauthor Brad Fay's two teenagers, Brendan and Allison, attend. The teens both participated in a very different social experiment with their father while driving home from Boston during a spring break vacation. The three were talking about the Framingham Heart Study and the power of social influence, Brad having interviewed Nicholas Christakis the day before and their route passing, as it did, through the town of Framingham. As the discussion progressed, Brad observed that they were being passed on the left by cars that seemed to be traveling in groups. There would be rather long stretches when no cars passed the family vehicle, followed by a series of cars passing in rapid succession. He suggested that they might be witnessing a form of social influence, according to which drivers were adjusting their speed to match that of others on the road, and thus traveling in groups.

So the Fays decided to try to test this hypothesis, based on the premise that if people were influencing each other's driving speeds, they would tend to travel in groups rather than pass by at random intervals. Driving west on the Massachusetts Turnpike, in the middle of three driving lanes, Brad set the cruise control of the family car at a speed only slightly above the posted speed limit. During the next thirty-eight minutes, seventy cars passed by. Brendan wrote down the number of cars that passed during each full minute as indicated on the dashboard clock. Upon reaching the Route 84 interchange, the experiment was ended and the analysis began.

It turned out that thirty-six of the seventy cars passed during only thirteen of the thirty-eight minutes. In other words, half of the cars passed during just a third of the minutes indicated on the clock. If drivers were making decisions independently of each other, one might expect roughly a third of the cars to pass in a third of the minutes. Thus it appeared that many of the drivers were adopting speeds based on the influence of other drivers—a rather vivid example of human "herd" behavior.

Undoubtedly there are a number of potential problems with this small experiment: some cars may have been blocked by cars immediately in front of them, forcing the second to travel close behind; also, the experiment was of short duration and it was limited to a single morning on a single road. Still, the finding is highly suggestive of a social effect.

Upon arriving home, Brad was intrigued to discover that there is an emerging literature on social influence and driving speeds. A Google search quickly yielded a 1993 article in the *Journal of Accident Analysis and Prevention* titled "Some Contagion Models of Speeding" by Terry Connolly of the University of Arizona and Lars Aberg of Uppsala University in Sweden. They conclude, in part, "We propose that a significant role may be played by drivers' comparisons of their own speed with that of other, nearby drivers." They based their conclusions, in part, on an observational study of 249 vehicle "pairs" and 843 "free-flowing" vehicles driving under several types of traffic conditions.

What is convenient about the example of social influence in the context of highway driving is that it is possible for almost any of us to run the same test that Brad and his children did. Most of us have had, at one time or another, the realization that we also are driving faster than we intended, likely due to the speed of traffic around us. It is not uncommon to catch ourselves unconsciously "driving under the influence" of other people.

We have many other opportunities to notice how people influence each other unconsciously in the real, offline world. For example, when one person in a room yawns or coughs, other people often do so as well; when one seated person crosses his legs, others often do the same; and when one person in a conversation leans forward, the other often does too. Now we also have evidence that people are eating and smoking (or not) based on the influence of other people. Can there be much doubt that we often shop, eat, drink, and watch TV "under the influence" as well?

Social influence, whether conscious or not, happens because we are the most social of creatures on Earth. In *The Social Animal*, David Brooks points to research by Michael Tomasello of the University of Leipzig, Germany, comparing infant humans to chimpanzees to test the degree to which being social is fundamental to our humanity. Brooks writes, "An infant of 12 months will inform others about something by pointing. Chimpanzees and other apes do not helpfully inform each other about things." Thus we see that even before language, humans instinctively give advice and recommendations. Brooks goes on to develop his thesis that emotional and social skills are much more important to success in life than intellect and rational decision making.

As we get older, social influence can happen both consciously and unconsciously, as discussed earlier. In prehistoric times, there was a great need to share information about where to find the best food and water and how to construct a shelter. These basic needs are still present, only the advice we share concerns the best brand of food or restaurant chain, the best tasting soft drink, or the best real estate agency to use. Nowadays a great many of the decisions we make, and the advice we share, concerns brands and companies.

Indeed the volume of daily consumer conversations about brands is staggeringly high, giving clear and compelling evidence that we are all under the influence and are active participants in today's social marketplace. According to our firm's research, about half of all Americans talk daily about food, beverages, and entertainment brands. More than a third of people talk each day about sports and hobbies, telecommunications, technology, health, and automobiles.

Because we are hard-wired to be social in all that we do, it is no wonder that social factors are important to the effectiveness of marketing and media.

Why (and How) We Study Word of Mouth

Of late it has become fashionable to study word of mouth in the consumer arena, but not because researchers and marketers recognize that social influence is deeply embedded in our DNA and critical to purchase decisions. Rather the primary factor has been the explosion of interest in online social media.

Huge sums of money are being shifted from traditional to digital media, with the greatest growth recently in the social arena, often called "Web 2.0." According to e-Marketer, a publisher of data, analysis, and insights on digital marketing, media, and commerce, social media spending in 2011 was expected to be $3.1 billion, up 55 percent from the year before. Marketing researchers have followed advertisers into social media as well, in part because research naturally follows marketing dollars, but also because social media offer the promise of a vast supply of consumer opinion that is unprompted and unmediated by survey researchers asking questions and preselecting study participants.

Hundreds of companies are now engaged in measuring "online buzz," or consumer opinions that are available publicly on social networking sites, forums, blogs, consumer review sites, and more. For further reading on this subject, an entire book, *Listen First!* by Steve Rappaport of the Advertising Research Foundation, describes the many companies and techniques involved in "social media research."

But "social" is not about technology, and as we have said, only a very small percentage of word-of-mouth conversation takes place via social networking sites. For this reason, our company measures all forms of word of mouth—face-to-face, over the phone, and online—and is the only company that does this on a regular basis.

We founded the company in late 2005 after about two decades at the market research company Roper Starch Worldwide and several successor organizations. Many of those years were spent working closely with Burns W. "Bud" Roper, the son of the company's founder and marketing research pioneer, Elmo Roper. Having helped to start the commercial survey research industry in 1933 when both Roper and the Gallup Organization were founded, Roper was early to word-of-mouth research in one specific way. Beginning in the 1940s he worked with the Standard Oil Company of New Jersey (now ExxonMobil) to devise a methodology for identifying everyday "opinion leaders" who were likely to share their views with others. The segment they identified represented the 10 percent most politically and socially active people who read influential media like the *Wall Street Journal* and *New York Times*, and they could be expected to spread their opinions to others.

In the late 1980s and 1990s we worked with our Roper colleagues to tell the story of this segment, ultimately dubbed "the influential Americans," leading to a 2003 book by Ed and colleague Jon Berry called *The Influentials: One American in Ten Tells the Other Nine How to Vote, Where to Eat and What to Buy. The Influentials* led to an invitation for Roper to become a founding member of the Word of Mouth Marketing Association (WOMMA), and Ed later became the trade group's first and longest-serving board president. From the beginning the need for research to help marketers understand the role of word of mouth and its impact was a cornerstone of the association and a key theme of WOMMA conferences. Upon leaving Roper in 2005 we began to think of how best to fill the need for research in word of mouth.

Already there was an enormous focus on buzz monitoring using blogs and chat rooms, which later was supplemented by social networking sites, all of which would eventually be known collectively as "social media." Research that relies on the data that can be mined by monitoring social media sites has become known as social media research (SMR). But our experience in consumer research told us that online buzz was only providing a partial picture—indeed quite often a distorted picture.

By the fall of 2005 we had the idea to launch a continuous survey among a representative sample of Americans to collect data on *all* their conversations, offline as well as online. The idea was that consumers would keep track of all the conversations they had "yesterday" about brands and companies, and we would probe for specific characteristics of the conversations. Studying "yesterday's" behaviors is a common approach among researchers to ensure the selection of a random time period for which people have fairly good recollection. We wanted to know how many conversations they had, and about what categories and brands. Were those conversations positive or negative? Did they happen at home, at work, or someplace else? Did those conversations happen face-to-face, over the phone, or online? How credible was the advice that people received, and did they plan to make a purchase because of the conversation? By doing this day in and day out, 365 days per year, we could have a continuous read on America's word-of-mouth conversations, including what gets talked about, where those conversations take place, and the forces that drive them.

We believed marketers would find the data valuable in several ways: it would be possible to determine which brands were truly engaging consumers, that is, which were winning and which were losing the battle for word of mouth; brands would also be able to develop better strategies for increasing word of mouth; media companies and agencies could be smarter about planning for word of mouth and for tracking their success in generating it. All of this was grounded in the belief that social influence is extremely important to the decision-making process for consumers—in the "real world," where most word of mouth happens—and that marketers were going to need a true and complete picture of consumer conversations about brands.

TalkTrack launched officially in June 2006 and has been conducted every week since, with each week's research being conducted among a new sample of 700 American consumers age thirteen to sixty-nine.[2] We work with some of the big online research panel companies to invite representative samples of people to participate in a survey about "conversations." If they agree, they receive an email link to the two-page diary, which they download and print for taking notes during the next twenty-four hours. The next day, with their conversation diary as a memory aide, they are asked to complete an online survey about those conversations.

The 700 weekly interviews add up quickly; about 3,000 people are surveyed per month, 36,000 each year—a very large sample for market research purposes. In 2011 we launched a continuous survey in the United Kingdom, and over the years we have conducted similar one-time studies in countries around the world, including Australia, Japan, Korea, Russia, Greece, Argentina, and Mexico. Through our research we have learned an enormous amount about word of mouth and have helped marketers make marketing and advertising much more effective: better insights to develop a "talkworthy" message that will be shared with others; better targeting of "influencers" to drive

---

2. We chose age thirteen as the youngest to interview in our TalkTrack surveys based on industry ethics guidelines. We chose sixty-nine as the maximum since online usage is not sufficiently widespread at seventy and older for this method to measure a true cross-section of behavior.

word of mouth; and better selection of media and marketing channels to facilitate conversation. These are all topics that we discuss in subsequent chapters.

The first results of TalkTrack taught us many things that were previously unknown about word of mouth. The study showed that the average American talks each day about roughly ten brands, and that the typical brand conversation lasts between three and five minutes. More than two-thirds of these conversations involve a recommendation to buy, consider, or avoid the brand. In other words, there are a lot of conversations each day, which are not just quick and passing references to brands, and which are about helping others decide which brands to buy and which to avoid. Results in most other countries are quite similar to those seen in the United States.

The 36,000 people interviewed every year in the United States are surrogates for the entire U.S. population of about 250 million people age thirteen to sixty-nine. Because the sample has been carefully designed to be representative of the U.S. population, it is possible to make estimates, or projections, from our survey sample to everyone, as if everyone had been able to take the survey. These calculations reveal that people are exposed to conversations about brands 15 billion times per week. With so many conversations about brands, there is no doubt in our mind that the marketplace is truly social. To succeed, marketers need to know how many of these conversations are about their brands versus the competition, what drives those conversations, what impact they have on people's behavior in the marketplace, and how their brand can improve its word-of-mouth performance.

TalkTrack also provided an answer to a critical question on the minds of many marketers: How much word of mouth (WOM) happens online versus offline? The answer almost always provokes surprise: 90 percent of word-of-mouth conversations are offline, while 8 percent are online.

Chart 1.1

Chart 1.1

HOW MUCH WOM HAPPENS ONLINE VS. OFFLINE?

Mode of Conversations

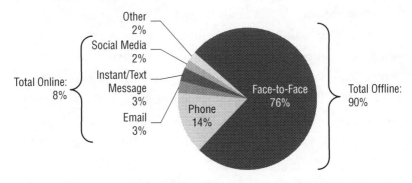

Weekly Volume of WOM Impressions (in billions): Offline vs. Online

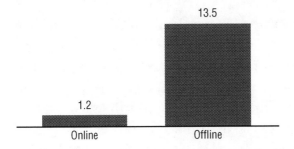

Source: Keller Fay Group's TalkTrack®, July 2010–June 2011.

The first reaction from many people is that 8 percent sounds very small in this Internet age, given all the excitement about social media. But if you remember that 15 billion word-of-mouth impressions are made on consumers every week, 8 percent actually translates into quite a few exposures to blog posts, tweets, status updates, emails, and instant messages: about 1.2 billion per week.

It's not so much that online is small, but rather that offline is enormous. We social creatures just can't stop talking and sharing. We live to share our experiences and opinions with each other. We rely on the kindness of others to help us make smarter decisions. We are born to share.

Two Different Conversations

In addition to knowing how many conversations take place offline versus online, an equally important question about social media is this: How well does the online conversation about brands represent the offline conversation? How closely aligned are conversations on Facebook, Twitter, Blogspot, and Gmail to the conversations that are happening at the water cooler, over the dinner table, at the neighborhood bar and grille? And how do those conversations translate into business success? If all conversations were fundamentally the same, it would obviously be most convenient for everyone to rely on readily available commentary posted on blogs and chat rooms as a proxy for "all word of mouth." But that's not the way it turns out.

In 2009 two Israeli marketing professors decided they wanted to better understand the relationship between online and offline word of mouth and how it relates to important brand characteristics, such as brand equity and imagery. The professors were Renana Peres of the Hebrew University of Jerusalem, who was then a visiting professor of marketing at the Wharton School of the University of Pennsylvania, and Ron Shachar from the Interdisciplinary Center in Herzliya, visiting at the Fuqua School of Business at Duke. As part of their project, they assembled a very large set of data, including online word of mouth, offline word of mouth, brand equity, and their own custom research on brands. Roughly 700 U.S. brands in total were analyzed, spanning sixteen product categories, covering the period 2007–2010. This was by far the most comprehensive and robust research effort ever undertaken to compare and contrast online and offline word of mouth.

Although a forthcoming series of papers by Peres and Shachar were still in progress as this book went to press, the authors released initial highlights of their findings at a December 2010 conference co-sponsored by Wharton and the Marketing Sciences Institute (MSI), and a working paper in late 2011. The results are quite startling. While the offline conversations were distributed somewhat evenly across sixteen product and service categories—none with more than 13 percent of all word of mouth—the social media conversations were found to be concentrated heavily in three categories. Thirty-two percent of all online WOM was about entertainment brands, defined as TV shows and channels, movies, and so on, versus 9 percent of all offline conversations. An almost equal percentage—thirty-four percent—of online conversations were about automobile and technology brands (17 percent each); these two categories comprise 10 and 13 percent, respectively, of offline conversation.

Chart 1.2

ONLINE WOM DOMINATED BY THREE BRAND CATEGORIES; OFFLINE WOM MORE WIDELY DISTRIBUTED

Distribution of WOM that takes place offline vs. online, by brand category

INDUSTRY (RANKED BY ONLINE)	% OF ONLINE	% OF OFFLINE
Media & Entertainment	32	9
Cars	17	10
Technology Products & Stores	17	13
Sports & Hobbies	8	3
Telecommunications	7	9
Food & Dining	4	12
Department Stores	4	5
Beverages	3	13
Clothing Products	3	7
Financial Services	2	4
Health Products & Services	1	3
Travel Services	1	3
Home Design & Decoration	1	1
Beauty Products	1	5
Household Products	-	2
Children's Products	-	2

Source: Renana Peres and Ron Shachar, "Multichannel Word of Mouth: The Effect of Brand Characteristics," presentation at the WIMI Multichannel conference, December 2010.

Meanwhile just 1 percent or less of online buzz was represented in important consumer categories such as household, beauty, and children's products, home decor, travel, and health. This is a far cry from the distribution of conversation that takes place offline, via real-world conversations. It shows just how different online conversations are from those happening offline, and challenges the idea that what gets said online is a mirror of what's being talked about offline. There are several reasons why this is the case, including the following:

- DIFFERENT PEOPLE. The people who talk about brands online are different from the people who talk about brands offline. Age is the most important factor. While the demographics of people who belong to social networks is well represented across age groups, young people are far more likely to post their opinions with regularity, and therefore their voices are far more prevalent. Within TalkTrack, we find that close to half of all social media conversations about brands come from consumers under the age of twenty-five, even though they are less than a quarter of the people interviewed in the survey. Young people participate in online social media with much greater frequency than older people, although face-to-face is still the most prevalent mode of communication for all ages, including teens and young adults.

- DIFFERENT BRANDS. Peres and Shachar found that the brands that get the most conversations online skew toward those that offer uniqueness, and thus encourage people to express opinions as a way of signaling their own uniqueness and social status. They also found that offline sharing had more to do with expressing emotions like satisfaction and excitement.

- DIFFERENT CATEGORIES. We believe there are category factors that are related to where word of mouth happens.

Food and beverages tend to get discussed over meals, where they are most relevant to the occasion and people tend to be sitting together face-to-face, but they are infrequently talked about online—a factor, no doubt, in the disappointing results from the Pepsi Refresh social media campaign. Retail brands, household products, children's products, apparel, and beauty brands may be talked about in stores or at a book club or PTA meeting. By comparison, brands that are dependent on the Internet for e-commerce or for comparison shopping (brands of cars, electronics) are better positioned to be discussed online (as well as offline).

In delivering a paper of her results at the Wharton/MSI conference, Peres reminded the audience of the old joke about an economist, although it could as easily apply to a marketer or market researcher. It goes something like this:

A man walks along a dark street, and finds an economist searching on the ground in the light of a lamppost. "What are you looking for?" the passerby asks. "My car keys," says the economist. They look together for a few minutes, but they find nothing. "Are you sure you lost your keys here?" asks the passerby. "Oh no, I didn't," says the economist. "But this is where the light is."

The point, of course, is that social media is "where the light is," given its accessibility to everyone. But that doesn't mean social media provides the solutions that marketers need most. The problem, say Peres and Shachar, is that "online data do not reflect well on offline behavior." In conducting research and writing this book, it has been our goal to begin shining a light on the vast size and essential importance of real-world conversations, so that marketers can make smarter, more intelligent decisions about how best to engage with today's social consumers.

This phenomenon of looking for answers only where the light is shining has been called "the digital dilemma" by Artie Bulgrin, who heads research for ESPN. Digital media provides an extraordinary ability to monitor and track things, but just because the analog world is harder to measure doesn't mean it is not important and real. Under Bulgrin's leadership, ESPN is a leading proponent of getting research measurements "right" so that decisions can be made on the basis of what is true and accurate, and not just what is easy to measure and observe.

Toward a "People Strategy"

Facebook understands that "social" is more than what happens on-line in social media. At a 2011 conference sponsored by the Word of Mouth Marketing Association, Paul Adams, an executive in product development at Facebook, told the audience, "You need to reorient your business around people, not technology. Don't have a 'Facebook strategy,' or a 'Twitter strategy,' or 'Foursquare strategy.' Map to human behavior and not to technology."

Adams talked about how the human brain has evolved over thousands of years. "Social," he said, "is like electricity. It is a given. It powers the [human] device." He went on to describe the Facebook user base using the terms of an anthropologist. Facebook statisticians have found that most users communicate directly with only four friends per week and five to six per month, a figure he says is consistent with other research that indicates people tend to have only four to six "strong ties" in their lives. Facebook has also found that people have "weak ties" to as many as 100 to 150 people, which is consistent with the size of villages in Neolithic times. Typically these are split into about four groupings, around such things as life stage, shared experiences, hobbies, and family. By this way of thinking, people are not adapting to Facebook; rather Facebook is adapting to people. It is a tool that increases the speed and efficiency with which we can connect with each other, but it is an accessory or a tool, not the main event.

Consider this in light of a study of Twitter tweets by Sysomos, one of the leading social media analytics providers. They studied 1.2 billion tweets and found that 71 percent produced no response, suggesting they fall on "deaf ears," according to the researchers. Of the remainder, 23 percent got a reply (generally just one), while tweets are retweeted only 6 percent of the time. Twitter has great potential to be viral, but most of the time it just doesn't work that way.

While the viral power of social media often is overestimated, face-to-face communications have some distinct advantages that are underappreciated. The nonverbal communication that is made possible through emotions, facial expressions, and tone of voice helps to strengthen the power of face-to-face communications. It was put thus in a classic 1966 sociology book by Peter Berger and Thomas Luckmann, academics from Boston University and the University of Konstanz, Germany: "The most important experience of others takes place in the face-to-face situation, which is the prototypical case of social interaction. All other cases are derivatives of it. . . . No other form of social relating can reproduce . . . the face-to-face situation."

Forty-five years later, despite generations of new technologies, this fundamental truth still pertains. According to a 2010 report on word of mouth by consultants at McKinsey & Company, "The environment where word of mouth circulates is crucial to the power of messages. Typically, messages passed within tight, trusted networks have less reach but greater impact than those circulated through dispersed communities. . . . That's why old-fashioned kitchen table recommendations and their online equivalents remain so important. After all, a person with 300 friends on Facebook may happily ignore the advice of 290 of them. It's the small, close-knit network of trusted friends that has the real influence." This has been observed as well in our TalkTrack surveys, which consistently show that people are more apt to view advice they get face-to-face as being even more credible than advice obtained from an online conversation.

Marketers haven't yet recognized the difference between the opportunity to connect online and making genuine, real-world connections. The problem is much broader than PepsiCo's failed Refresh campaign. Many brands are touting their huge numbers of "Facebook fans" online as evidence of social marketing success, but usually these are hollow statistics. In 2011 a social media marketing agency, Fan-Gager, published a list of the "100 most engaging brands on Facebook." The report showed that some brands have staggering numbers of Facebook fans: Coca Cola (34 million), Disney (28 million), and Starbucks (25 million). But how many of these people were "active fans," meaning they did anything beyond initially signing up? In nearly every case the number of active fans was fewer than 100,000, and usually less than 1 percent of their enrolled fans. Which brands had the most engaged fans? Sony Ericsson, Walmart, Red Bull, Disney, and Pepsi all had close to 100,000 active fans.

Yes, Pepsi's 79,000 active fans in 2011 represented 1.3 percent of its total 5.9 million Facebook fans. Despite the enormous reach of Facebook and other social media, the ability to truly engage brand advocates online is still rather limited, and certainly not adequate to the task of substantially influencing consumer purchases of the 14 billion gallons of soft drinks consumed in the U.S. market every year.

The tragedy of Pepsi's decision to shift marketing resources out of traditional media in 2010 and into social media is that Pepsi has been a perennial top-ten most talked-about brand in the real world since the first TalkTrack survey in 2006. What's more, Pepsi had been highly successful at driving offline conversations with its advertising and marketing. About half of all Pepsi conversations in 2009 and 2010 involved a reference to something consumers had seen in media or marketing (e.g., advertising, in-store activity, or promotional events).

The fact is, Pepsi is a very social brand in the real world. Adding social media to a media mix that was already working might have made good sense and helped it to be even more successful, and this is what Pepsi returned to in 2011. But going "all in" to chase a social media gold rush was a big bet that was neither necessary nor wise.

There are many pathways to tap the power of people's social connections and their desire to share and learn from each other. Some marketers recognize this and are responding appropriately. We applaud and celebrate them. But those marketers who are chasing one vein of opportunity—namely, social networking tools and technologies—are not seeing the full scope of an enormous social opportunity. And if history and research prove true, they will ultimately lose business because of it. The social marketing opportunity is too big for any business to ignore, and it's mostly happening face-to-face.

2

Conversation Starters:
What Makes a Brand Talkworthy?

Whene Steve Hershberger, a social marketing consultant, became a partner in a craft beer startup in Indianapolis, he
quite naturally began to spend a lot of time in bars. Trying
to understand his future customers, he didn't drink much during these
trips. Mainly he just observed. "I watched who came and went, and I
watched who attracted others like bees in flowers," he told us. "And
then in some cases I would just make composite sketches of who I
thought these people were. In some cases I'd strike up a conversation
and I'd talk to them about themselves."

One scene in particular stuck with Hershberger. While on one
of his tavern trips, he watched a customer order a Killian's, a widely
available Coors-brewed ale that's the bane of a craft beer fan's existence. Someone at the table intervened and insisted that he try out
a new beer from the craft brewer New Belgium, a recommendation
based on another beer he knew his friend liked. "It was a very polite
conniption fit," Hershberger said. Then a broader conversation about
beer ensued. "This guy gave him a thirty-second lesson on craft beer,
just simple stuff and really well thought-out. I'm just sitting there
watching, going 'Okay, that's it.' This guy was unremarkable. If you
put him in a mall with twenty other people you'd never pick him out.

Probably thirty-three years old, likely had a kid, probably played ultimate Frisbee or golf, somebody you'd want to hang out with."

Suddenly Hershberger understood not only his target consumers but also the role good beer played in their lives. They were people who certainly liked their craft beer, but it wasn't the be-all and end-all of their existence. Good beer was table stakes. It was an important part of the story but not the entire proposition, "something that is very important to the customer that I wanted, but it didn't define who they were, and that was an important distinction for us."

The moment informed the creation of what would be named Flat12 Bierwerks, whose name is a nod to the city's racing history and the Flathead 12-cylinder engine. Today Hershberger touts Flat12 as one of the Midwest's fastest growing beers. With a tiny marketing budget—calling it five figures is "aggressive," he says—Flat12 has achieved early success with very little help from traditional marketing. Instead it has ridden a wave of word of mouth that comes through associations with themes and events that are important to its consumers, including music and arts festivals and triathlons, and by tying up with a food truck that makes grilled pizza. Hershberger and his partners also rely on encouraging the brand's fans to talk up not just Flat12, but the craft beer experience more generally. More than a beer, Flat12 is a community that delivers the good life to its members. When its fans advocate the brand to friends, they are not saying "Drink this" so much as "Join our community that values what's good."

Hershberger's central insight, the idea that craft beer is "social glue," is a very important notion if you're interested in how brands can harness the power of word of mouth. It goes well beyond the fermenting of malted barley and wheat. It's an understanding that, contrary to many assumptions we all make about how people view marketing, social experiences aren't interrupted by brands or products but rather improved by them. As such, marketers can take advantage of the inherently social qualities of life without fear that consumers will balk, provided they tread carefully.

Brands aren't born social. They don't get talkworthy on their own or because an agency signs them up for Facebook and Twitter accounts. Not unlike the making of a TV commercial, word-of-mouth success takes planning and execution to make products worth talking about, to make a humble can of soda or a hot new cell phone into products that become that social glue between people. In this chapter we look at a broad range of strategies and tactics that provide customers with the fodder they need and even want to incorporate brands into their conversations: product features, packaging designs, messaging strategies, and even tchotchkes. Throughout all of these examples, you'll see a major theme emerge: any brand, regardless of its age, sexiness, or budget, can become talkworthy if it follows some key practices.

The Most Talkworthy Brands

What are the brands that Americans talk about most often?

If you said Apple you would be right. If you said Facebook or Google, you would be wrong. Blinded by the marketing community's obsession with these companies, you'd be overlooking some rather familiar contenders that do a great job of keeping top of mind among consumers. Few expect Coca-Cola, Walmart, and Verizon to be the three most talked-about brands. Indeed for every one of the first sixty months of our word-of-mouth tracking study, TalkTrack, Coke has been the most talked-about brand, earning approximately 212 million weekly brand impressions from consumer conversations. The average top ten brand gets 151 million weekly impressions.

The most talked-about brands share a few important characteristics. It certainly helps to have a ubiquitous product, like the omnipresent can of Coke, or a Verizon phone, or a huge retail footprint; these naturally generate conversation. ("Have you always preferred Coke to Pepsi?" "Have you heard about the white sale at Walmart?") Products consumed socially, like McDonald's, also have a leg up. And a big advertising budget definitely helps. Companies that have both tend to be among the most talked-about companies around, a fact that often surprises people. Half of the ten biggest WOM brands also are among *Advertising Age*'s top ten "mega brands" in terms of their annual measured media expenditures: Verizon, AT&T, Walmart, Ford, and McDonald's. The simple fact is, the more a brand advertises, the more visible it is, and that visibility, in turn, makes it more likely it will be talked about—and ultimately purchased. Every advertisement has the opportunity to stimulate a conversation between consumers, as we discuss in more detail in chapter 4.

Chart 2.1

THE MOST TALKED-ABOUT BRANDS IN AMERICA

RANK	TOP WOM BRANDS	WEEKLY WOM IMPRESSIONS (in millions)
1	Coca-Cola	212
2	Walmart	190
3	Verizon	185
4	AT&T	167
5	Pepsi	150
6	Apple Computer	147
7	Ford	145
8	Sony	108
9	McDonald's	106
10	Dell	99

Source: Keller Fay Group's TalkTrack®, July 2010–June 2011.

But what do you do if you can't afford a national ad campaign, or your brand isn't a household name?

Successful marketing isn't just about cuing more conversations; it's also about driving strongly positive conversations that lead to recommendations and purchases. The best marketers, we've found, use a variety of messaging techniques that lead to sharing and recommending. While not all of these techniques require big budgets, success will be more likely if you have a strong product.

The Steak *Is* the Sizzle

Many people assume that it takes high-tech, innovative products to get people buzzing. (Think iPad, for example.) We get asked this question quite frequently: Isn't it just cool, new, breakthrough products that get talked about? What about everyday brands or products that have been around for a long time? Isn't it harder for them to be "talkworthy"?

People are not wrong to ask this question. After all, they might have read Seth Godin's 2003 best-selling book, *The Purple Cow*, which gets its name from a trip that the Godin family took to France. As they traveled the country, they passed by pastures filled with cows. At first they were fascinated, but soon all of the cows began to look the same and failed to hold, or even get their attention. The Godins began to ignore them. A purple cow, however, would really stand out, says Godin. It would be unique, different, and thus it would be remarkable.

Godin believes that too many products are "me too's," just one more brown cow that begins to blend into the scenery after a while, becoming invisible. He says that for a brand to stand out and be noticed, it needs to be remarkable. "Something remarkable is worth talking about, worth paying attention to." And, says Godin, this means more than just well-crafted advertising or marketing; the offering itself needs to be truly unique, different, remarkable. It needs to be a Purple Cow, an iPad, or the newest Audi.

Our research, however, shows that Godin's Purple Cow thesis represents just one of the many ways to generate conversation.

As we've said, everyday brands with unexceptional products such as Coke, Walmart, and Verizon are also the most talked about. If we were to expand our analysis to the top forty word-of-mouth brands, we would find brands such as Bank of America, Dodge, JCPenney, and Dove. These are not brands that are normally expected to deliver on the "wow" factor, and yet they are frequent topics of conversation.

Even Apple, a brand that seems to effortlessly evoke word of mouth, takes pains to cultivate the seemingly endless conversations that go on about its products. If Apple's computers, phones, and music players were simply sleek for the sake of being sleek, they'd be museum pieces, not runaway hits. To a significant degree, Apple has taken over the consumer electronics world because it specifically designed its products and advertising to encourage conversation. Those distinctive white iPod earbuds were designed to be noticeable in crowds, to hit consumers with a bit of peer pressure. The iconic glowing Apple logo on the lid of a MacBook is upside down if you are the user who is preparing to open your computer. Why? The logo is designed for other people nearby to see once the laptop is open: the logo is a conversation prompt, a cue for social influence. The Apple stores themselves make it easy for people to try Apple products, and as soon as you walk into an Apple store you hear people talking—with those they came in with and with strangers, striking up conversations while trying out Apple devices or peripheral equipment. This is part of a deliberate strategy on Apple's part: the stores are designed to be a place for people to visit, meet friends, learn, and have an enjoyable time—a variation on the neighborhood bar or cafe. They are not designed solely to generate a transaction. Apple believes that whether a store visitor buys something or not, a payoff will come as visitors tell their family, friends, and colleagues about their positive experience at the Apple store.

One of the first things we did when we started Keller Fay in 2006 was undertake research among people who are very active in spreading word of mouth. We teamed with the word-of-mouth agency

BzzAgent (see chapter 7 for more detail) to better understand what the volunteer agents that they recruit like to talk about when they talk about brands.

The study yielded two key product-related insights. Both, we believe, dispel commonly held myths about word of mouth. The first myth the research rebuts is that word is mouth is only for "the latest thing": products that are new, revolutionary, and innovative, or inherently entertaining. In fact we found that word-of-mouth success is about communicating *solutions*: providing answers that consumers want to pass along to others, find easy to talk about, and feel good about sharing. In contrast, the factors that marketers often talk about as being attention-getting, like being "innovative," "entirely new and unique," or "entertaining," did not score very high.

A second insight from the study counters another myth: that the way to get word of mouth is through stunts and gimmicks, such as outrageous TV ads, websites, or public relations events. Instead we found the leading motivations for engaging in word of mouth are product-related—specifically, to learn about products and share those insights with others. In further evidence of their engagement with products, large numbers of respondents see their involvement as a way to voice their opinions to the products' manufacturers.

Here are the top reasons that people join an organized opinion-sharing network such as BzzAgent, which we can view as a sort of proxy to explain why an average consumer would willingly talk about brands:

- "*To learn* about the latest products."

- Because they "like being *one of the first* people to know about a new product."

- Because they "*enjoy sharing* new products and ideas with friends and family."

- "For the opportunity to *give feedback* to the manufacturers of the products."

All are more important than the ostensibly more tangible benefits of being word-of-mouth agents, such as getting products for free and earning points to redeem for rewards. The importance placed on learning about products, being able to share those insights with others, and giving feedback to manufacturers is even more pronounced among the most active agents.

Whether you are a marketer who uses a word-of-mouth network or are finding ways to get people engaged with your Facebook page or other forms of social engagement, the lessons here are important. Taken together, the insights from this study turn the old marketing mantra to "sell the sizzle, not the steak" on its head. In word of mouth, the steak—the product—is the sizzle. And that steak need not come from a purple cow. Success in word of mouth, in turn, is not for an exclusive club. It is available to marketers across categories and across the marketing cycle. The most important requirement is to have a strong product story—a solution that people will want to share with others.

In this study we reached two key conclusions. The first is that word-of-mouth basics—being recommendable, easy to talk about, worth talking about, and something people feel proud to share with others—are far more important drivers of word of mouth than being new, unique, innovative, or entertaining. The second is that products—learning about them, sharing them with others, and giving feedback about them to companies—are central to engaging in word of mouth.

Cue the Conversation

From the time we conducted our 2006 research with BzzAgent to the present, the word-of-mouth industry has not focused very much on what motivates word of mouth. Instead it has sought to understand the channels available for encouraging conversations, particularly online buzz. There has been little attention given to what truly motivates people to speak (offline) or share information (online). One person helping to fill that void is Jonah Berger, an assistant professor of marketing at the University of Pennsylvania's Wharton School.

Berger's research projects shed light on the psychological and emotional drivers of word of mouth, which, in turn, can be harnessed by marketers to focus on the content that is most likely to get talked about. To our way of thinking this is where word-of-mouth strategy needs to begin: What is a brand's story, and why should someone want to talk about it? Only then does it make sense to focus on who will tell the story, and "the how" (the channels through which the word will spread).

One of Berger's major studies, published in 2011, relied on a collaboration with BzzAgent. Unlike our research, which involved conducting a survey among BzzAgents, Berger's research involved sifting through the reports that BzzAgents submit to the company about their conversations with family, friends, colleagues, and others after being sent products to try. Using content analysis techniques, Berger and his team investigated thousands of conversations about hundreds of brands across multiple product categories (including both fast-moving consumer goods such as food, as well as more considered purchases such as automobiles). The research also looked at WOM levels over time, to see if there are differences between products that generate short-term and immediate word of mouth and those that generate sustained word of mouth over a longer period of time.

Berger's research found that average consumers think they talk about interesting things more than mundane ones, consistent with the view of many experts and marketers. But when it comes to what consumers actually do, a different picture emerges: "We find no evidence that more interesting products are talked about more frequently over the multi-month period of a marketing campaign." While products that are deemed more interesting might receive more immediate, short-term conversation, this bump is short-lived and tends not to translate into more ongoing word of mouth over a period of time, nor do these products receive more discussion overall. And without sustained word of mouth, it's much harder to have a sales impact.

So if it's not interesting products that get talked about over a sustained period of time, what are the key triggers of long-term WOM? It turns out, according to Berger's research, that visual cues, often prompted by product usage or marketing activity, are very important drivers of word of mouth; as a result, products that are used more frequently are talked about more frequently. In other words, according to Berger, "products that are cued more by the environment receive both more immediate and more ongoing WOM (though the relationship is significantly stronger for the latter). Products that are cued more frequently by the environment are also talked about more overall." In contrast, "more interesting products receive more immediate WOM, but . . . they do not receive more ongoing WOM."

The role of cuing in word of mouth is consistent with the results of Keller Fay's TalkTrack, which finds the most talked-about categories are ones that indeed get used the most frequently, especially food/dining, media/entertainment, and beverages. None are consistently driven by breakthrough technology or products that are "new and cool." But they are ubiquitous in people's lives.

Berger's research is an important reminder that word of mouth is not just for new or surprising products or outrageous stunt-based marketing. Indeed stunts probably are not the best way to drive sustained word of mouth. Everyday products can get lots of word of mouth if they are cued frequently by the environment, which suggests the importance of a holistic approach to WOM, one that takes advantage of all aspects of the consumer's engagement, from product labels to coupons and from point-of-sale displays to advertising of all kinds. The goal is to cue conversation and drive word of mouth whenever possible. (We discuss ways to trigger word of mouth further in chapter 5.)

All this needs to come, of course, on top of a product or service experience that fully meets (and ideally exceeds) consumer expectations so that people speak highly of the product when asked or otherwise prompted.

Orange and Blue: How MillerCoors Cues Conversations

To understand how this comes together, let's look at another beer brand, this one from the beer giant MillerCoors. Alcohol is perhaps the greatest social lubricant, but that doesn't mean marketers can't do their own conversation greasing to motivate engagement and sales. Encouraging bartenders, wait staff, journalists, and, of course, customers to talk about brands of liquor, beer, and wine is vital to building success. Much of this work is done on the premises, in the bar, where a fair amount of the drinking gets done. So it should come as no surprise that MillerCoors puts a lot of weight behind its face-to-face marketing. For Andy England, the company's executive vice president and chief marketing officer, getting talk value, no matter how big or small, for all of his brands is important.

"Bar staff are important," England says, "and bar staff, particularly when you teach them about crafts or imports, will tell you that if they can tell a story it's worth a bigger tip. So if you can give them something that they're capable of repeating that's interesting about your brand, and makes a punter"—British slang for a paying customer—"feel that they're smarter for having learned about it, it's certainly a valuable thing."

England, who's been in the marketing business for over twenty years, working with the likes of the Hershey Company, Nabisco, Dr Pepper/Seven-Up, and OpenTable Inc., is one of those marketers who talks a lot about word of mouth even though he's not using those precise words. To him, conversation is everything—and he doesn't mean conversation as defined by Twitter and Facebook. In fact England is skeptical of social media, though he experiments with it; he is much more bullish on the one-two punch of product innovation and strong advertising to get consumers talking, a recipe we happen to agree with.

One of the MillerCoors brands is Blue Moon, launched in 1995. Blue Moon positions itself as a craft beer, and craft beers typically talk about themselves as being discovery brands to be found in a bar. But that doesn't mean leaving the discovery totally to chance; there are ways of triggering that.

As England elaborates, "One of the things that really helped Blue Moon is its presentation in a tall Blue Moon glass with a garnish of orange. So it's not that people say 'Hey, check out my Blue Moon,' but it's that people see it and ask the bartender or drinker, 'Hey, what is that?' Which is a version of WOM strategy, creating an interesting retail theater, which helps drive discovery and conversation." England explains that there is a rationale for the orange: the product contains orange and coriander, and the slice of orange brings out the flavor. But it is also true that the brewer who invented the beer, Keith Villa, has said the garnish was intended mostly to grab attention (and spark conversation) when served at a bar. The orange helps provide the cue that gets people talking about Blue Moon.

It's easy for many marketers to see how word of mouth can help a brand on a relatively small budget, like Blue Moon's. But it works for big brands with big budgets too, according to England. Brands like Coors Light. "We already have 100 percent awareness in our target market, but you're not necessarily going to have a conversation about Coors Light until there's something to have a conversation about," England says. Coors is one of those brands that, like Walmart and Verizon, have that ubiquity we discussed earlier. He went on to explain how two recent innovations, "wide-mouth venting" in 2008 and "cold activation" in 2009, became important conversation starters for the brand.

With wide-mouth venting, package designers enlarged the opening on the can to improve the pouring and reduce "gurgling." Miller-Coors and its agencies came up with a campaign that played on the word "venting," in the sense of verbally letting off steam. One ad features a guy who escapes from his girlfriend to go to his buddy's place because he has "got to vent." England believes that one way to achieve success is when you have an idea that becomes part of the vernacular. He saw how the Coors "vent" trickled into the culture. "I remember playing tennis with this twenty-four-year-old, and we were playing doubles, and one of the other older guys said to me, 'So what's new in the beer business?' And I said, 'Well, there's the new wide-mouth Coors.' And the twenty-four-year-old instantly said 'Let's vent!' I thought, I love that!"

Cold-activated cans have been another hit for Coors. "If you want people to talk about your product, you've got to give them something to talk about," says England, "and at the end of the day I'd far rather that they were talking about my product than my commercial." This innovation allows the temperature of the can to determine its color. When the cans reach 48 degrees they start to turn blue, and when they drop to 44 degrees they turn fully blue. This reinforces and dramatizes the idea of "Rocky Mountain cold refreshment." When England refers to the copy line on the package ("When these mountains turn blue, your beer is as cold as the Rockies"), he says, "You know you've achieved something when guys start talking about whether their mountains are blue, when they literally use that copy off the package or the ads. That's just a beautiful thing. As vernacular for 'My beer is cold,' you've got 'My mountains are blue.'"

In both of these cases, the product was the underlying factor (remember, "the steak is the sizzle"), while marketing played an important role in the word of mouth that followed, by providing a vernacular for people to use and allowing for more cuing. This combination of product innovation and talkworthy advertising is working for MillerCoors. According to TalkTrack research, Coors and its sister brand, Miller, have both seen large gains in the role of marketing sparking word of mouth; in fact they are each among the biggest gainers in recent years. Thus MillerCoors is using the combination of product innovation and advertising to drive conversation and sales.

The Role of Emotion

Our TalkTrack surveys ask consumers to summarize, in their own words, the things that are said about a brand or company in their conversations. We also ask consumers how likely they are to tell others what they've heard in their recent conversations. This allows us to compare the words, phrases, and ideas that pop up in conversations, and which are very likely to be passed along to other people, compared to all other conversations.

One of the most interesting findings is that, overall, positive word of mouth is more viral than negative word of mouth. People are more than a third more likely to say they will pass along to other people a positive word-of-mouth conversation than a negative one. (See chapter 8 for a more detailed discussion of the power of positive versus negative word of mouth.) We also find that positive *emotions* are especially viral. In the technology category, people who say they will pass along what they've heard are twice as likely as other people to use strongly emotive words such as "love it" and "great" in describing electronics brands. For example, participants in our surveys said "We love our iTouch," "I love playing the Xbox," "incredible" about the iPad, and "The game is amazing" about Call of Duty.

These findings are consistent with the scientific literature that says emotions are contagious. In his 2011 keynote to a conference of the Advertising Research Foundation, the *New York Times* columnist David Brooks stated that he believes the primacy of emotions is one of the three most important "foundations" coming out of scientific inquiry in the fields of neuroscience and psychology. Referring to research discussed in his book *The Social Animal*, Brooks said, "Emotions are central to how we think and to the wiring of the fibers of the brain." He echoed the comments of another ARF speaker in 2011, Jonah Lehrer, who wrote in his book *How We Decide*, "Whenever we make a decision, the brain is awash in feeling, driven by its inexplicable passions. Even when we try to be reasonable and restrained, these emotional impulses secretly influence our judgment."

Wharton's Jonah Berger reached a similar conclusion when he undertook a study with his colleague, Katherine Milkman, of "most shared" articles appearing in Brooks's own newspaper, the *New York Times*. In addition to positive stories getting shared online via email and social media more than negative ones, the Wharton research found that articles that get shared fall into two categories: (1) those that provide practical utility, such as articles about how to save money or live healthier; and (2) emotion-laden stories, in particular ones that inspire awe. In describing to us what is meant by "awe" in this instance, Berger said, "Stories about curing diseases, discovering new planets, or people overcoming odds can all evoke a sense that the world is an amazing place and inspire senses of awe in the reader. It makes the reader feel that the world is an amazing place and that anything is possible."

The latest research is quite contrary to the conventional wisdom that says bad news travels farther than good news, and that funny or quirky or clever content is the key to helping something go viral. Instead marketers should focus on selling true and unique product benefits, ideally with a story that disrupts consumer expectations (though not necessarily in a quirky way). Give people things of value (e.g., utilitarian items such as coupons or tips for healthy living) and they will share them. Give them something that will drive strong emotions (what psychologists call "activation") and they feel inspired to share it with others. Says Berger, "When marketers are thinking about how to make their messages viral, evoking emotion is one key lever to pull."

Take the example of TOMS Shoes, a brand that, despite not advertising in any traditional sense and spending only a bit on search-engine marketing, has managed to create huge talk value. Its success is in its very simple proposition. TOMS' main product is a line of espadrilles for men, women, and children that typically retail for about

$54. For each pair of shoes the company sells, it donates a pair to a child in need. It's an elegant proposition, simple and brilliant. Writing on his blog, Emanuel Rosen, the author of *The Anatomy of Buzz*, identified seven factors that have led to this success; among them were the brand's success in getting customers to participate in the giving and in encouraging people to spread the word both in social media and in the real world.

"Last year," wrote Rosen, "I participated in one of their 'shoe drops' in Booneville, Kentucky and I've been talking about it ever since. . . . It was an unforgettable experience—measuring the kids' feet, fitting the shoes, helping the kids decorate their TOMS. Last Friday I met people who participated in shoe drops in places like Argentina and South Africa, and their stories were moving and memorable. Since most people cannot go on a 'shoe drop,' the company encourages participation through Facebook, by buying the shoes and by spreading the word."

TOMS also gives people ways to remember its brands, physical reminders like a TOMS Shoes flag that people fly. A bigger version of the flag that's for sale on the company website has inspired people to leave online comments on the site, like this one from "Leo": "I keep my flag up in my office at a church I work for. Students always come in and ask about it and it's an awesome way to spread the word of TOMS!! Love it." Or this one: "always keep a fresh TOMS sticker on my car and one on my skateboard and one on my macbook pro and anywhere else i can keep it! i been hanging up the small flags that come with the shoes but am so excited to see that a larger one is being sold!!! I Can't wait for this flag to come in the mail!!!!"

When TOMS donated its millionth pair in September 2010, the company sent its supporters a letter of thanks, a CD, and a bracelet, a classic talk trigger.

From the business strategy, which by the beginning of 2009 had yielded over $4.6 million in revenue, to the product to the marketing, TOMS Shoes is built for word of mouth. Even the name merits conversation. You might assume that the founder is some guy named Tom. Nope. It was Blake Mycoskie who launched the company back in 2006 after a trip to Argentina, where he saw a large number of children with no shoes. TOMS comes from an abbreviation of "tomorrow," as in "Shoes for Tomorrow." Beneath all of this is an appeal to the emotions of consumers and giving them a good, positive story that they're certain to pass along.

Chick-fil-A Breaks the "Schema"

Schemas are one of the primary ways the brain helps people sort out what's important to pay special attention to, and what's not. Things that are part of our normal, everyday routine fit our schema and generally don't require much thought. Things that disrupt our schemas cause us to focus our attention to figure out what's going on and what it means. This is the same theory put forth by Chip and Dan Heath in their best-selling book, *Made to Stick*. According to the Heaths, "Schemas are like guessing machines. Schemas help us to predict what will happen and, consequently, how we should make decisions." When schemas are broken or challenged, we become surprised. "Surprise," they write, "acts as a kind of emergency override when we confront something unexpected and our guessing machines fail. Things come to a halt, ongoing activities are interrupted, our attention focuses involuntarily on the event that surprised us." Unexpected events that cause us surprise are more likely to stick in our minds, they claim, because they cause us to stop and think.

For brands that can disrupt schemas, the payoff can be huge.

One that has been successful in doing so is Chick-fil-A, which, in many respects, is just like other fast-food restaurants in America. Its mission is certainly not distinct: "Be America's Best Quick-Service Restaurant." Yes, it eschews selling hamburgers in favor of chicken only, claiming to have invented the chicken sandwich, but you can find chicken sandwiches at most fast-food places. It also has memorable advertisements, featuring cows that carry handwritten signs saying "Eat Mor Chikin." But again, McDonald's, Burger King, KFC, and others in the category all have large and creative campaigns too. In other words, Chick-fil-A has the same basic business model, fulfills the same needs, and does so in a similar manner. And yet according to our surveys, Chick-fil-A has the most positive conversations, as a percentage of all its word of mouth, in the quick-service restaurant business. Why?

Chick-fil-A is a relatively large chain (the second largest chicken-only chain in the country), but is still privately held and family owned. Truett Cathy, who started his first restaurant in 1946 and founded Chick-fil-A in the early 1960s, remains the chairman and CEO, while his son, Dan Cathy, is president and COO. Its restaurants have never been opened on Sunday. While Truett Cathy is known to be devoutly Christian, the company says the decision to remain closed on Sundays is "as much practical as spiritual." Truett Cathy, the company says, "believes that all franchised Chick-fil-A Operators and their Restaurant employees should have an opportunity to rest, spend time with family and friends, and worship if they choose to do so. That's why all Chick-fil-A Restaurants are closed on Sundays. It's part of our recipe for success." And success has come Chick-fil-A's way: the company has enjoyed forty-three consecutive years of positive sales growth, and in 2010 saw overall sales grow more than 11 percent and same store sales growth of nearly 6 percent. And, according to our research, more than 80 percent of conversations about the brand are positive, well above the category average of 66 percent, and number one in its category with respect to the quality of its word of mouth.

To give you a flavor of the things people talk about when they have conversations about Chick-fil-A, Chart 2.2 lists some examples from our TalkTrack database.

Chart 2.2

SUMMARY OF SELECTED CHICK-FIL-A CONVERSATION TOPICS

CONVERSATION TOPIC	GENDER	AGE
"Best tasting chicken of all the stores."	Male	35
"Best chicken."	Female	42
"Wonderful food. Love Chick-fil-A."	Female	27
"How we like their chicken products better than their competition."	Male	49
"Love Chick-fil-A. Talking about what makes them great and wish that they would sell their sauces."	Male	23
"Best sandwich ever invented. Less is more."	Male	47
"How much Chick-fil-A does for its customer and the community."	Male	37
"The conversation was about how CFA is closed on Sundays and how that's a positive idea."	Male	31
"That place my friend and I love to go, as well as with the family. They have great humor and so pleasant to the customers. The food is always hot and fresh when you get it."	Female	48
"I was saying that Chick-fil-A is my favorite fast food restaurant and my wife and I have eaten there over the weekend."	Male	47

Source: Keller Fay Group's TalkTrack®.

Steve Knox, a senior advisor with Boston Consulting Group in the firm's advocacy marketing practice and the former CEO of Tremor, a word-of-mouth marketing agency within Procter & Gamble (see chapter 7 for more about Tremor), has some ideas about what gets people talking, and in such a positive way, about Chick-fil-A. Knox is a strong proponent of a view that for word of mouth to be effective, it must "disrupt schemas."

When our schemas are disrupted, people feel compelled to talk about it in order to help them sort it out and regain their equilibrium.

In Knox's experience, "significant disruption calls for significant conversation." He counsels that the surest way to get people talking about a product is to have a message that runs counter to a mental model, that is, a "common expectation" or "rule of thumb."As an example, we have a set of expectations about fast-food restaurants: that they are cheap, convenient, and nothing more than an everyday transaction. For companies that want to disrupt a schema, Knox offers these "must dos": make sure the disruptive message remains tied to the brand's core identity, and avoid shock for the sake of shock, lest people remember the funny message but forget the brand it promotes. "The objective," Knox asserts, "is to surprise people while remaining true to the brand."

So how did Chick-fil-A break away from the pack? Knox drew our attention to a program that the company runs in local markets called "Daddy-Daughter Date Night." Different Chick-fil-A operators hold these "date nights" on different evenings throughout the year. As the name implies, this is a special opportunity for fathers and daughters to go out together and share quality time. The local restaurant usually closes to everyone else except those who have signed up to attend. While each restaurant executes the program in a slightly different way, it is common for restaurants to offer memorable amenities such as a red carpet arrival, table service, dancing, live music, photographers, limo rides, and so forth. Each daddy-daughter pair also receives a tray liner with questions and topics for conversation—a conversation starter. And they receive a take-home booklet called *Continuing the Conversation* with ideas for future activities dads and daughters can do together and topics of conversation.

L. J. Yankosky, the senior manager of sponsorships and event marketing at Chick-fil-A, said that the program, which was started in 2009, was originally the idea of a single operator, Jeff Rouse, in Kansas City, Missouri. Yankosky identifies one of his roles as learning about good ideas that start at the local level, and then sharing them across all the operators nationally. "They are independent entrepreneurs," Yankosky says. "We learn from them and then push out the ideas to other operators." In fact in 2011 feedback from customers led to the first "Mother-Son Date Night" in Triad, North Carolina.

Yankosky says the payoff is not in the form of immediate sales, but rather in "emotional connections made with customers." Those benefits are two-sided, affecting both employees and customers. Yankosky sees a benefit in the form of a "morale boost to team members in restaurants." The customer benefits come in the form of short-term goodwill and advocacy, as well as long-term connections. Participating "daughters may grow up and remember that special night every time they pass a Chick-fil-A as adults," he said.

All this is a far cry from your typical quick-service restaurant experience. And that's the part that Steve Knox said really resonates: it disrupts your schema, while still remaining true to the brand promise of Chick-fil-A as a family-oriented food service brand with a commitment to the local communities in which they operate. "We don't expect this from a [quick-service restaurant]," Knox said. "We don't expect this level of caring, give back, authenticity. These are all schema disruptions. Because this causes a cognitive disruption, our brain needs to get back to equilibrium. It does not like being in a disrupted state. One of the ways our brains get back to the state of equilibrium is by talking about it with others. We want to make sure that others see the disruption the same way. Essentially we are asking 'Are we normal by seeing this variance from expectation?'"

Knox has used this example hundreds of times in talks about word-of-mouth marketing. "It is powerful because no one expects it. It is powerful because it disrupts on many different levels. Specifically, functional: they shut the restaurant down and put [out] white table cloths et cetera.—totally unexpected. And emotional: the connection between dad and daughter, the creation of special moments out of an everyday experience. The best word of mouth works on both of these levels."

Knox encouraged us to check our TalkTrack data on Chick-fil-A, saying that he thought we'd see a spike in conversation. And sure enough, we did. Not only do we see very high levels of positive word of mouth about the brand; as mentioned above, it is the number one brand in the quick-service restaurant category. We also saw a very pronounced increase in word of mouth about Chick-fil-A among two important groups of consumers who are not typically the most vocal advocates for quick-serve restaurants: teen girls and moms. One might think dads would also see a rise, along with teen girls. And there is indeed a modest-size bump for dads. But clearly this program is most meaningful for the teen girls, causing them to talk more about it, and it would appear that their moms appreciate the restaurant for helping to facilitate the father-daughter conversation (or giving them a night off!). Either way, the program is a conversation starter not only within families, but in the marketplace as well.

Domino's: When Honesty Surprises

If Chick-fil-A has had the most positive word of mouth among its competitors in the fast-food category, in 2009 Domino's was suffering mightily in that regard. When compared to its main competitors, Pizza Hut and Papa John's, our research showed that Domino's had far lower levels of positive word of mouth and higher levels of negative or mixed (both positive and negative).

This is consistent with what Domino's own research showed: people didn't like its pizzas. (And it didn't help that, in the spring of 2009, the pizza chain suffered a major PR disaster when a video of its employees shoving cheese up their nose and doing other gross things surfaced on YouTube.) In a dramatic response to the taste issue, Domino's decided to completely overhaul its recipe. The traditional way a brand would tell the world it changed would be to say something like "The Domino's you love is now new and improved." But that approach didn't sit well with its advertising agency, Crispin Porter + Bogusky, which also favors disruptive message strategies. (See chapter 4 for more about CP+B and how it designs advertising to drive word of mouth.)

CP+B believed the traditional "new and improved" approach

wouldn't work because customers didn't actually love Domino's pizza. Instead the agency advised that Domino's be transparent and honest about their problems, letting people know they understood that their pizza was not very good, and informing them that they had listened and fixed the problems.

An ad campaign dubbed "Pizza Turnaround" launched in December 2009. It started with a stark white screen and bold red letters that proclaimed, "Listening to our harshest critics inspired us to make a completely new Domino's pizza. But what would these critics have to say about the new pizza they inspired? In December 2009 we brought it to their front door to find out." Then the head chef from Domino's, Brandon Solano, makes surprise visits to the homes of real people who had been part of focus group research during which they were critical of Domino's. The ads flash back to their videotaped comments in these focus groups, in which the same customers say such things as "The crust is too rubbery," "Domino's pizza is low quality and forgettable," and "It doesn't feel like there's much love in Domino's pizza." The chef introduces himself outside the front door, announces that the people at Domino's have listened and have created a completely new pizza recipe ("We changed everything—the crust, the sauce, the cheese"), and asks each of the critical customers to try the new recipe. Each loves the new taste ("This is what pizza should taste like," says one) and thanks Domino's for listening.

Additional ads rolled out in late 2010 and 2011, each of which acknowledged some aspect of Domino's that was not good and that needed improving, followed by an explanation of how the problem had been fixed. Many featured Solano or other Domino's chefs; some featured Patrick Doyle, Domino's CEO; and some featured other "real people" who had communicated with Domino's about their problems. All conveyed honesty and asked customers to give Domino's another try.

CP+B's chairman, Chuck Porter, says the agency's advice to Domino's was, "If you are transparent and honest, it will work better." This is another prime example of breaking schemas—an ad that admits,

"We were bad, we listened, and now we are back with an improved product." It's not what people are used to seeing in a commercial. Because of this, people are compelled to tune in and then talk about it.

The results for Domino's, from a word-of-mouth perspective, have been much higher talk levels since this new campaign started, improved "WOM quality" (more positive word of mouth, less negative—although it still has a way to go before it catches up to Pizza Hut or Papa John's), and a sharp rise in the number of people who talk about their TV ads when they talk about Domino's. This is all leading to impressive results for Domino's in the marketplace. A 2011 article in the *Financial Times*, under the headline "Domino's Eats Slice of Humble Pie in Push to Boost Sales," reported that the impact of the campaign "was immediate. First quarter same store sales in the U.S. were up 14.3 percent year-on-year in the first quarter of 2010, the highest ever jump in the fast-food industry." That momentum continued, as Domino's saw double-digit same-store growth (excluding growth due to the addition of new stores), far outpacing Papa John's and Pizza Hut over a two-year period. The *Financial Times* also noted that its stock rose more than 150 percent from the time the campaign launched to May 2011.

The key here is transparency and honesty, traits that consumers don't expect from marketing campaigns from big brands. But, of course, adopting that as a central component of a marketing approach requires a certain amount of courage. "Clients don't get enough credit," said Rob Reilly, chief creative officer at Domino's agency, CP+B. "When that video came out and was all over social media, it took a lot of courage for Domino's to say we have to change our pizza and use that in the marketing. It takes talent and foresight and guts."

For Domino's to stand out it had to subvert our expectations of the company. No one expected a company to come out and admit that its product was bad, just as no one expects a shoe seller to give away shoes with every sale, just as no one expects a fast-food chain to try to enhance family relationships. The underlying values in play in all of these marketing programs—honesty, transparency, compassion, concern—aren't things we usually associate with brands. In breaking down these expectations, enterprises as diverse as TOMS Shoes and Domino's were able to successfully turn word of mouth in their favor.

The bottom line: All marketers, not just the managers of the hippest brands or the ones that spend the most, have the opportunity to tell their unique stories, offer surprises, and connect emotionally with consumers—and to be talkworthy.

3

Influencers: The People at the Center of the Conversation

Since the publication of Malcolm Gladwell's *The Tipping Point* in 2000 and Ed's book *The Influentials* in 2003, great changes have washed over the media and marketing world. While there is still general agreement that a relatively small number of individuals can often hold disproportionate sway over the actions of the masses, the growth of social media networks has led people to think anew about the art and science of determining who these influencers are and how best to reach them. Indeed the very definition of influence is in flux, clouded by the idea that influence now takes place primarily online via social networks. To those who advocate this position, the crucial question of who is influencing whom can be determined solely by looking at people's online activity and the people with whom they engage online.

In this chapter we explain why it remains important to focus on influencers because of their central role in word of mouth. But we also explain why it's wrong to look just at online influence and why it's important to define and understand influencers based on people's real-life friends and connections. Finally, we profile several brands, both small and large, and national political campaigns that have succeeded with influencer marketing of the type we advocate.

"Klout Is Not Clout"

As we write, there is a fast-emerging field of social media influence measurement that, like so many things related to social media, is gaining prominent attention. The goal, broadly speaking, is to identify the top people and content sources in social media. Venture capital–backed startup companies like Klout and PeerIndex have launched in recent years with the mission of identifying the top users of Twitter, Facebook, and other online social networks. Because of social media's rapid adoption by consumers and its appeal to marketers, these new systems are having an impact on how marketers define and target influencers. But the jury is still out on whether services like these actually provide a true measure of influence. We expect that people ultimately will conclude online influence is one piece of the puzzle, but wholly insufficient on its own. It's equally possible they will discover that when it comes to influence, it's the quality of each interaction that matters far more than the total quantity of people reached by any one influencer.

To understand what these companies are trying to do, let's look more closely at Klout, which at the time of writing was grabbing the most attention in marketing circles. Like many Silicon Valley startups, Klout has an interesting backstory. It was founded in 2008 after the entrepreneur Joe Fernandez underwent surgery that required him to spend three months with his jaw wired shut. During that time, social media became his primary communications outlet, and he came to believe there could be a significant business opportunity in identifying who has the most influence in social media. Thus emerged Klout.

At Klout's core is a score assigned to everyone with a Twitter login, though the service also measures activity on Facebook, LinkedIn, and YouTube and is continually adding channels. The score, based on a scale of 0 to 100, is determined by algorithms that weigh more than thirty-five variables grouped into three subscores that measure the size of your following, the likelihood your messages will effect some action, and how influential your network is. So, if you have an army of Twitter followers who are eager to retweet you (or recommend your

Facebook or LinkedIn posts), and those followers also have large followings, your score is likely to soar toward the 100 mark, where you'd be in the company of celebrities like the pop star Justin Bieber.

By the middle of 2011 Klout was gaining notoriety. In addition to raising over $10 million in funding and a growing volume of press coverage, the service had buy-in from brands such as Starbucks and Virgin America, both early participants in its Klout Perks program, which Klout describes as "exclusive offers or experiences, given as a result of [their] Klout." In other words, brands offer goodies to those with high Klout scores in the hope they will share that experience with others who follow them in social media.

The growing popularity of Klout elicited some skepticism, even from social media experts typically bullish on the integration of Twitter and Facebook into marketing culture. The central issue is that the Klout score hinges most of all on the size of social media followings and how likely you are to be retweeted or recommended. What a retweet is worth, however, is an open question. It's a pass-along of your message, often with no (or little) added commentary. Klout gives no indication of what a person is saying, and no interpretation of whether any given message is positive, negative, or neutral commentary. And there's no indication of whether it motivates purchasing or any other behavior. The reality of Klout—and of any system based solely on online social network statistics—is that it doesn't tell you much about a given person beyond the size of his network and his ability to post messages that get further shared. It reveals nothing about how credible his messages are, nor how they drive any type of online buying, much less offline behavior of any kind. By the end of 2011 Klout was clouded in controversy. A change to the algorithm that determines scores sparked an outcry among users, especially some folks who considered their Klout score to be a "badge" and had been spending significant periods of time working to get closer to that 100 mark, only to see their scores fall.

To understand the shortcomings of Klout, consider the case of Kenneth Cole. In early 2011, as pro-democratic Arab uprisings were raging, the fashion designer issued this tweet: "Millions are in uproar in #Cairo. Rumor is they heard our new spring collection is now available online." Instant backlash cropped up all over Twitter and elsewhere on the Web, causing a PR crisis for the company. But you wouldn't know it based on Cole's Klout score, which rose by 30 points after the misstep. In short, Klout rewarded the network growth and the mostly damning retweets, while its system failed to recognize that all this action was coming to the detriment of the brand.

Not long after this, the well-regarded social media analyst and advocate Jeremiah Owyang of Altimeter Group concluded, "I must warn against blind enthusiasm to note that a single metric is not sufficient. In fact, a single metric, like Klout's 100 point scoring system applies well for [a]bsolute influence (global influence) [but] it's unable to provide [r]elative influence, [that is] influence related to a specific market, like baby diapers." Rishad Tobaccowala is the chief strategy and innovation officer at VivaKi, a unit of Publicis Groupe. He is a highly regarded and thoughtful observer of the media and marketing landscape, and he too has concerns about Klout, which he expressed as follows (via a tweet, hence the shorthand): "Klout is not Clout. Little to no offline influence. Easy to game. Bias to Frequency vs Quality." We wonder if Klout is listening. After all, Tobaccowala has a Klout score of 79.

A service like Klout measures online influence primarily based on a person's status updates on Twitter, Facebook, and LinkedIn. The people who are the most active via this channel are what Forrester's Josh Bernoff and Ted Schadler, authors of *Empowered*, call "mass connectors." A very small group (6 percent of all online consumers) account for the vast majority (80 percent) of what gets written via these channels. It is a group, they say, that "lives in the moment" and communicates frequently with a large group of online "friends." Although they post frequently, the impressions they create for brands are "fleeting," say Bernoff and Schadler. There is another group of online influencers, whom they call the "mass mavens," who create "more lasting influence." They are the people who contribute to blogs, discussion forums, and online reviews at levels that are nearly ten times the average. Their posts tend to be longer and more thoughtful than the more frequent but shorter posts that define the mass connectors. This group is not quite as concentrated, with 14 percent of online consumers creating 80 percent of the content via these channels. While many companies tend to lump together all forms of online social influence, the Forrester analysis is a helpful reminder that it is important to look differentially at what gets said, who is saying it, and in which online venues. And, of course, the influence of online conversation—and the people who have influence online—may be quite different from the influence that happens offline, in the real world.

Nowhere is this point made more clearly than in two of the most important marketing campaigns of our time: the presidential elections of 2004 and 2008.

The Road to the White House Is Lined with Influencers

Ask your typical political junkie how Barack Obama was able to come from nowhere to become the first African American U.S. president and you'll probably be told that it had a lot to do with his campaign's deft use of the Internet in general, and online social networks in particular. This is a mistaken conclusion, albeit an understandable one given what the press was reporting. The mainstream media loved the story of the one-time community organizer taking advantage of the newest organizing tools that had played smaller roles in earlier campaigns, most notably Howard Dean's unsuccessful run for the Democratic nod in 2004. Obama's millions of Facebook and MySpace friends were often given credit for pushing the election in his favor.

But campaign insiders have a different view. Jon Carson, Obama's 2008 national field director, says that the focus on the campaign's use of social media tools "was misinterpreted by the press a lot," adding, "Our online efforts were a net, they weren't the engine." Said Carson, "At the end of the day, voter contact happened because trained field organizers got their volunteers into a system that was getting doors knocked and phone calls made. . . . To win these Republican states, you have to persuade a lot of people who had never voted for a Democrat before. A lot of that is peer pressure, frankly. And so we put a top premium on local volunteers talking to their neighbors."

Mary Joyce, who was the new media operations manager for the Obama campaign in 2008, also believes that "offline engagement was most of what was going on" and that house parties in the homes of everyday supporters were a "crucial organizing strategy." She said, "It was all about leveraging people's personal networks."

Social media grabbed many headlines in the election of 2008, but the heavy lifting and "the sale" was made through the human network, person-to-person word of mouth. Identifying influencers and activating them offline, in local communities, was critical to the strategy. According to David Plouffe, the head of Obama's 2008 campaign, "We studied the Bush [2004] campaign pretty carefully. They did a great job."

To understand better what Plouffe and the other campaign aides were referring to, let's go a little further back in time, to May 2004, when the incumbent George W. Bush and John Kerry were locked in a battle for the White House. The *Washington Post* ran an article that month titled "In Ohio, Building a Political Echo: Campaigns Rely on Word of Mouth to Spread Message."

The story began with a profile of a voter, Christa Criddle, noting she "is not the sort of person who springs to mind when political operatives talk about 'opinion leaders.' She does not have a column, or talk show, or website. But if someone wants to influence opinion in her patch of Ohio suburbia, this 35-year-old mother of three is a good place to start." The writer then went on to say that Criddle is an example of what Bush's campaign manager Ken Mehlman calls an "influential," with specific reference to Ed's book. "You have a world where a wealth of information creates a poverty of attention," said Mehlman in the *Post* article. "The way people get through is by turning to people they trust."

The campaign's chief strategist, Matthew Dowd, laid out for us the inside story about how the Bush campaign harnessed the power of word of mouth and empowered local influencers like Christa Criddle to help get out the campaign's essential message in key battleground states such as Ohio. The campaign encouraged everyday Bush supporters to spread the word to their friends, family, and neighbors. They were encouraged to invite the people they knew, including the undecided voters, to coffee get-togethers, talk to them at community gatherings, write letters to the editor, and call local talk radio. The idea, which they dubbed "echo politics," was that Christa's talking about Bush's plans for the economy or education or his take on the war in Iraq would create more credibility when the campaign's talking heads went on Sunday morning talk shows or were featured on the evening news talking about the same issues. Similarly campaign ads would be more effective if they "echoed" what people had already heard from their friends. They wanted people to say to themselves, "Oh yeah, that's what Christa was talking about. That makes a lot of sense to me."

The motivating factor for the campaign's influencer strategy was an insight Dowd made in advance of the 2004 campaign. He observed that the percentage of true independents who could be courted by either party to swing an election was dropping fast, and by 2002 stood at less than 7 percent of the electorate. To Dowd, this meant that it no longer made sense to spend upward of 75 percent of a campaign's resources on finding, targeting, and communicating with a smaller and smaller group of swing voters, as was the norm in politics. Instead, thought Dowd, the bulk of time and money should be spent on targeting passive and inactive Republican voters and getting them to vote. And the best way to do that, he realized, was no longer via the mass media, but through word of mouth, with a particular focus on influencers (or people the campaign referred to as "navigators"). According to Dowd, "The information flow has become a flood, a torrent of messages coming at a confused, cynical public from all angles. People are turning to one another once again. As they did a century ago, today's opinion leaders work on the grassroots level rather than from the high perches of media, politics, or business. The twenty-first century opinion leaders are average Americans who know lots of other average Americans, trusted souls with large social networks. These Navigators are influencing public opinion one casual conversation at a time."

The campaign recruited the local influencers, like Christa, in a methodical and large-scale way, and offered them tools that made it easy for them to get access to information and spread the word to their friends, family, colleagues at work, and others in their social network. The campaign knew the indicators that separate influencers from average folk, and they used sophisticated data mining and other statistical techniques to ferret out those who would qualify as influencers. From an email list of 7 million people who volunteered to be Bush supporters, Bush's team built a database of 2 million navigators. Each received regular emails from the campaign with talking points that they might consider discussing with their friends and neighbors. They were also provided with information about numbers to call to reach local talk radio shows and tips for how to get past the producers' screening questions and onto the air.

In the final days of the campaign, the real value of people-to-people connections kicked in. While the Democrats relied on a "traditional" get-out-the-vote organization (including volunteers brought in to key battleground states from out of state), the Republicans mobilized the navigators, the local volunteers who promoted Bush to others in their personal network. "The Bush team realized that the best media for influencing people are the oldest: everyday conversations," said Dowd. "This is where Bush had a huge advantage over Kerry."

In 2008 the Obama team studied the Bush influencer playbook and borrowed heavily from it. An influencer strategy was also critical to the Republican takeover of the House of Representatives in 2010, in which the GOP had a net gain of sixty-three seats. At its core, the "Tea Party" is a vast social network of generally like-minded and influential people who connect with each other at numerous events.

Frequent personal contacts, reinforced by messages in the mainstream and online media, help to reinforce commitment to the movement and to turn out supporters on Election Day.

The 2010 congressional and the 2004 and 2008 presidential elections were decided in no small part by the candidates' success in identifying and mobilizing the right set of influencers. Think about what you did not hear in the words of Mehlman and Dowd: nothing about online activity or any type of social media algorithms. How does the influencer Christa Criddle perform on Klout? With a score of 13, not well. But that doesn't mean she's any less influential if your focus is Ohio politics. Should she be disregarded because she doesn't spend much time on Twitter? Klout's Fernandez typically describes this as the Warren Buffett problem. The legendary investor is enormously influential, but because he doesn't have a Twitter account he's invisible to a service like Klout. That raises an interesting dilemma for a service that bills itself as "the standard for influence" and one that hasn't been addressed.

Means, Motive, and Opportunity: The Cornerstones of Influence

When our firm launched our continuous study of consumers' word-of-mouth conversations in the United States in 2006, we felt it was important to identify influencers in each of our studies in order to compare and contrast findings for them with those of other consumers. Through discussions with other members of the Word of Mouth Marketing Association, we have come to define the influencer as "a person who has a greater than average reach or impact through word of mouth in a relevant marketplace." This means that an influencer does not have to be a celebrity, or even a blogger with a huge platform, though those two types of people certainly have influence. What it means is that everyday people are often influencers. People like Christa Criddle, whom you might think of as "the influencer next door."

To find such people, we don't ask survey respondents if they are influencers. Nor do we ask how many followers they have on Twitter or other social networks. Based on a careful review of the academic literature and our experience as market researchers who have engaged deeply in the study of influence and influencers, we determined that there are three fundamentally important criteria that determine whether or not a person is an influencer: Does the individual have the *means*, the *motive*, and the *opportunity* to influence other people?

In order to have the means to influence others, a person needs to be in touch regularly with other people. You can be the most knowledgeable person in the world about a particular topic, but if you are a loner and don't interact with others very often it is hard for your ideas to spread. So the size and breadth of your real-world social network is central to your influence. A large network of people you interact with in your everyday life gives you the means to engage actively in conversation.

Motive plays an important role as well. Do you have a built-in "need-to-know" about things that are new, different, better? People who are inquisitive in this way will invest their time and energy using multiple channels to keep up, whether through their own media usage, going to stores or expos to see the latest and greatest innovations, or engaging in conversation with other people to learn what they are doing. Influencers are information hounds, motivated to keep up.

Finally, influencers must have the opportunity to share what they have learned with others. Do people seek them out because their opinion is valued? Do their opinions have sway over what others think and ultimately do?

We identify influencers in our research based on a series of questions that relate to the key dimensions we just discussed: means, motive, and opportunity. Take, for example, the size of your social network. The average American keeps in close personal contact—meaning real-world offline communications—with approximately sixteen friends, family, and acquaintances. Influencers, meanwhile, have a social network that is twice as large: thirty-three friends, family, and acquaintances with whom they communicate often.

Through the use of our firm's Conversation Catalysts™ influencer segmentation system—that's the trade name we use to describe our type of influencers—we have determined that about one in ten Americans, or about 20 million people, qualify as influencers. While relatively small on a percentage basis, this is still a large number of "everyday" people who have disproportionate impact in the marketplace.

Chart 3.1

SIZE OF SOCIAL NETWORK: TOTAL PUBLIC VS. CONVERSATION CATALYSTS

Average number of people one communicates with fairly often

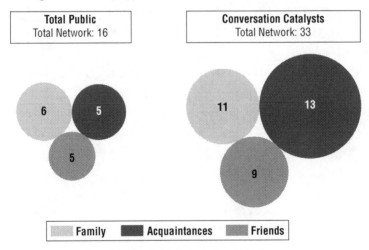

Total Public	Conversation Catalysts
Total Network: 16	Total Network: 33

Family   Acquaintances   Friends

Source: Keller Fay Group's TalkTrack®, July 2010–June 2011.

Conversation Catalysts also keep up with what is new. They are twice as likely as the general public to keep up across a whole host of categories that we at Keller Fay track on a regular basis, from fast-moving consumer goods categories such as food, beverages, and personal care products, to travel and financial services, to big-ticket items such as automotive and technology products.

And the opportunity to share their views is abundant for influencers. Conversation Catalysts are sought out by others for their advice and recommendations at levels that are also twice the average, across a spectrum of category areas.

Chart 3.2

CONVERSATION CATALYSTS GIVE TWICE AS MUCH ADVICE ON AVERAGE

Percentage of people giving category advice and recommendations

	CONVERSATION CATALYSTS	TOTAL PUBLIC
Food/Dining	77%	36%
Retail/Apparel	61	25
Media/Entertainment	59	26
Beverages	56	24
Technology	55	26
Sports/Hobbies	52	21
Personal Care/Beauty	50	21
Health/Health Care	48	22
Household Products	46	19
Automotive	41	19
Public Affairs/Politics	41	18
The Home	40	16
Telecommunications	40	15
Children's Products	37	18
Financial Services	37	17
Travel Services	31	12

CONVERSATION CATALYSTS: MORE LIKELY TO KEEP UP WITH
"WHAT'S NEW"

Percentage of people following category closely

	CONVERSATION CATALYST	TOTAL PUBLIC
Food/Dining	68%	41%
Media/Entertainment	66	36
Retail/Apparel	66	33
Technology	63	37
Sports/Hobbies	55	29
Beverages	55	30
Personal Care/Beauty	51	28
Health/Health Care	48	27
Household Products	48	26
Public Affairs/Politics	48	24
Automotive	44	25
The Home	44	22
Telecommunications	42	20
Children's Products	37	21
Financial Services	36	20
Travel Services	31	15

Source: Keller Fay Group's TalkTrack®, July 2010–June 2011.

Clearly, the Conversation Catalysts pass the "means, motive, and opportunity" test. The result is that this group drives a disproportionate share of the nation's word-of-mouth conversations. Whereas the average American has about 65 conversations per week about brands, Conversation Catalysts have nearly two and half times as many: 150 conversations per week. When we project this out to the total U.S. population, we see that of the 15 billion conversational brand impressions that are created every single week in the American marketplace, 3 billion involve these Catalysts. This is a group of people who, if they can be engaged and activated on your behalf, can certainly drive the conversations that drive results.

Chart 3.3

CONVERSATION CATALYSTS: NEARLY 2.5 TIMES AS MANY
BRAND CONVERSATIONS

Average number of brand conversations per week

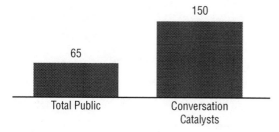

Source: Keller Fay Group's TalkTrack®, July 2010–June 2011.

Some people in marketing circles are skeptical that it's possible for a single individual to be a credible source of advice and recommendations across a wide variety of subject matters, such as cars, travel, financial services, and technology. Indeed we find it is possible to identify category specialists who are particularly active recommenders in a single category. But there is quite a lot of overlap among categories; people who recommend in one area are much more likely to do so in others too.

"People come to me and ask about everything," said Teresa Graham, one of the people profiled in *The Influentials*. "They think that if I don't know the information, I can get it. And nine times out of ten, I think I can." In other words, she is knowledgeable about a number of areas, and in areas where she isn't, she is sufficiently networked to know who to ask. Influencers like Graham are a combination of Malcolm Gladwell's mavens, connectors, and salesmen all rolled into one. So when influencers are not playing the role of maven, they can still play the role of connector because of the size of their real-world networks.

How Big Is the Payoff from Influencer Marketing?

We have seen that influencers talk more than the average American. But do these conversations make a difference, or is it just more talk? Can we calculate exactly what the return on investment is for a recommendation from a Conversation Catalyst versus one from an average Joe or Jane?

We were given the opportunity to address these issues head-on in a 2009 research study we conducted on behalf of Condé Nast Publications, publishers of *Vogue, Vanity Fair,* and *The New Yorker,* to name just a few. Many of Condé Nast's magazines have a heavy concentration of influencers as readers, and the publisher wanted to let advertisers know whether the economic multiplier is greater when those influencers spread the word about products and services versus noninfluencers. In other words, to what extent do recommendations from influencers lead to higher monetary value for the brand being discussed when compared with recommendations from other people? (We talk more in chapter 5 about media planning for word of mouth, including ways to identify media outlets that have a large concentration of influencers.)

Our research for Condé Nast involved interviews with a large sample of female magazine readers about their recent word-of-mouth conversations in a number of product categories, such as apparel and accessories, personal care and beauty, and consumer technology. We asked the necessary questions that are required for us to determine which of the people in the study were Conversation Catalysts, so that we could compare them to the rest of the sample. In this regard, the study was fairly comparable to our ongoing word-of-mouth research that we share throughout this book. Then we went an important step further: we asked each person we interviewed if she would put us in touch with the people with whom she had given recent advice and recommendations so we could interview them as well. This enabled us to close the conversational loop and talk to people on both sides of the same conversation. From those conversational partners we were able to find out how valuable the advice they received was, and what actions they took as a result of it.

We saw a big difference in the persuasiveness of conversations when a Conversation Catalyst gave the advice compared to when the advice came from others in our sample, so-called average Janes. (Note that the conversational partners were blind to whether or not we had classified the advice giver as an influencer.) For the first time, we had hard evidence that influencers are not only more prolific in giving advice, but also more persuasive than others.

This was an extremely important finding. But our research went even further. Armed with the information we received from both the senders and the receivers of word-of-mouth recommendations, we had the required building blocks to calculate the economic value of these conversations. For this part of the research we collaborated with Professor Barak Libai, a leading expert in the economic value of word-of-mouth conversations. We built an economic model that factored in four potential sources that can drive the economic impact of word of mouth:

- The volume of conversations about products.

- The credibility and persuasiveness of the word of mouth.

- Expected profitability of their friends, based on volume of purchase and price points purchased.

- Probability that a person's word of mouth is driven by media/ marketing (in this case, with Condé Nast as the sponsor, we focused on ads and editorial content in magazines).

The result: word of mouth from influencers produced a dramatic 3.8 times as much economic impact as word of mouth from the average magazine reader in our sample. In other words, if a recommendation from an average woman produces $100 in economic value for the brand, a conversation led by an influencer will produce nearly $400 in impact.

About a year later consultants at McKinsey & Company also reported on word-of-mouth research they had undertaken. Using a different research approach, they reached the same conclusion: not only do influencers generate far more word of mouth than noninfluencers do, but "each message has four times more impact on a recipient's purchasing decisions." That makes two different sources reporting that the impact of influencer word of mouth is four times that of noninfluencers. That's quite a substantial difference and offers hard data that influencer marketing can produce substantial returns for marketers.

How Influencers Can Help Brands of All Sizes

Now that we've defined the influencer and described her economic impact, we arrive at the multimillion-dollar question: How do businesses go about creating an influencer marketing program to help their brands? The first thing you need to know is that it doesn't matter what size your business is. Smart influencer marketing can help. While building and activating a community of ambassadors isn't always cheap, it is cost-effective relative to other types of marketing and thus is popular with brands with small or even nonexistent budgets. Even for those with large budgets, influencer marketing programs can be efficient and effective, making it appealing to them as well. To illustrate these points, we'll look quickly at three very different business: a new, small, regional company; a much older company with a low marketing profile; and a global giant with a massive marketing budget. What all three have in common is recognition that offline influence is crucial in sparking word of mouth for their brands and that it leads to positive business outcomes. Then we'll take a deeper look at a campaign that masterfully used a surprising influencer group to help market a product we all take for granted.

Remember Steve Hershberger and his craft beer that we discussed in chapter 2? Flat12 Bierwerks has a small but growing brand community of about 400 people at the time of this writing. The brand's fans are known as Hopstars; they register on the company's site and receive points for various activities, from the whimsical (having a dream about craft beer) to the practical (making sure a quarter of the beer in the refrigerator is Flat12). But Hopstardom isn't all about playing games. The advocates help the brewery get feedback on its product and spread the word about its virtues to their friends, ultimately growing the small beer company's sales.

To illustrate how Flat12 uses this community, Hershberger tells an interesting story about a time when a Hopstar recommended Flat12 to a friend. When the friend tried it in a bar, he was deeply disappointed and told the advocate as much. To try to sway him, the Hopstar brought his friend into the taproom at the brewery so he could drink right from the source. He ended up loving it, of course, but that's not the end of the story. A taproom associate heard what was going on and decided there was probably a problem with the bar where the friend originally tried Flat12. Further investigation determined that there was a problem with the bar's plastic tubes (or "lines") that deliver beer from keg to tap. This knowledge allowed the brewery to address what could have been a much bigger and longer lasting problem yielding a negative brand experience for many local consumers.

Flat12 Bierworks' experience with influencer marketing shows that there can be more than one advantage to cultivating a network of influencers and advocates for the brand. Not only does it spread the word and grow the business, but having a dialogue with your advocates can uncover problems that the business needs to address.

About a half a dozen years before Flat12 was founded, a very different kind of company realized the power of influencers. The

Finland-based Fiskars, the world's second oldest corporation, makes a lot of things, including boats, navigational equipment, gardening tools, knives, and orange-handled scissors that you've probably seen or even used. Back in 2005 Fiskars realized it had a problem: there was basically no conversation about its scissors. No loyalty. No emotional attachment. The crafts enthusiasts who should be paying attention to the tools of their trade didn't know or care about the common practice of counterfeiting its scissors, inferior knockoffs from China. Deciding it had to do something to cultivate both brand awareness and loyalty, Fiskars's U.S. executives approached Brains on Fire, a South Carolina–based brand identity and word-of-mouth agency, for help.

Working together with Brains on Fire, the brand devised what turned out to be a classic case study of the power of influencers. It taught the word-of-mouth community that influencers could be deployed for ongoing, sustained efforts, not just short-term publicity blasts for product launches. Let's look at how the program came together.

After a deep dive into the online conversations—or lack thereof—around Fiskars, and learning more about the crafting community, Brains on Fire got down to building out the branded community. The agency held a series of auditions for brand "ambassadors" in four markets: Los Angeles, Chicago, Charlotte, and Baltimore. The idea was that the ambassadors would be paid by the company to be evangelists for the brand, doing craft demonstrations around the country using Fiskars scissors and recruiting other customers of the brand to be influencers and advocates for the brand. Rather than keep the program a secret until it was ready for launch, it quickly became well-known that Fiskars was looking to build a community of scrapbookers. And the word-of-mouth benefits began accruing immediately. For instance, Brains on Fire reached out to influential bloggers to get their opinion on what Fiskars's community presence should look and feel like, and that got them talking in general terms about Fiskars being up to something cool. To source possible candidates for the job of lead ambassadors Brains on Fire asked the owners of craft stores in the launch cities for recommendations. Remember that the Fiskars brand had a low profile, so any bit of chatter helped. "Looking for ambassadors became a conversation in itself," said Robbin Phillips, president of Brains on Fire, in an interview. "We were transparent from the beginning, and that helped to ignite word of mouth."

After about 120 auditions, four lead ambassadors were chosen for these paid, part-time positions. The selection criteria didn't have to do with their fame within scrapbooking circles or having a single-minded focus on crafting. In fact the leads had careers and other interests. One was a Los Angeles police officer, another was a special education teacher in Chicago. Another owned a scrapbooking store, and the fourth, a stay-at-home mom, was the most technically proficient. What they had in common was they were passionate about crafting, good storytellers, and avid networkers. As such, they were classic Conversation Catalysts, everyday people who, with the help of Fiskars, could achieve disproportionate influence.

"These lead ambassadors were aspirational but not unattainable," said Phillips. "We didn't look for the most technical scrapbookers or the most influential scrapbookers. We believed that the ones that did have big followings already were only interested in creating their 'personal brand' and less interested in the community."

The Fiskateers, as they were named after a training session in Madison, Wisconsin, where Fiskars's U.S. operation is based, were given a host of tools to help grow their ranks. The website, with its message board, chat room, gallery, and blogs run by the lead Fiskateers, is the hub of the community. But getting online interaction was only part of the mission. Offline word of mouth was also very important. To ignite it, Brains on Fire used some classic word-of-mouth tactics that gave Fiskars-chosen influencers a way to get the conversation flowing. Brains on Fire equipped new Fiskateers with a pair of scissors available only to Fiskateers, each pair engraved with a unique number. Said Phillips, "If you're out with your friends and you take out these scissors that look different, that's a tool that ignites conversation."

In 2008 the lead Fiskateers planned and conducted regional events dubbed "Fiskafrenzies," large gatherings of craft enthusiasts. The programs were all about giving people an outlet for their passions.

Many of the Fiskateers are out-and-out fanatics, proudly wearing the orange and green colors of the company. Their enthusiasm, Phillips said, "scares some people. But people still love to belong to things. It's not just a 'like' on a Facebook page. We want to see ourselves in a story bigger than our own life."

Community growth has been easy for Fiskars, despite the fact that it has set a relatively high bar for membership. In order to join, people have to reach out to one of the leads, who will then ask the applicant to explain why she's interested. At that point, 60 percent drop out. This works to keep the quality of the community high; credentialing is very important to the program. When the original Fiskateer leads began blogging, they hoped to get 200 new Fiskateers over a few months. They hit that number in twenty-four hours. Now the community is over 9,000 strong and providing real sales benefits. Fiskars has noticed that stores visited by a lead Fiskateer enjoy three times the average sales success, and the company attributes stability and market share growth during the recession to Fiskateers' loyalty. Moreover the Fiskateers have developed their own marketing tools and are often used in the company's product development processes. They also act as a feedback channel, telling the company whether or not its products are working.

The Hopstars are helping Flat12 extend its brew, and the Fiskateers community is spreading the word about the value of Fiskars scissors to the crafting community. But can offline influencer marketing work for big brands with really ambitious objectives? The answer is yes.

One of the biggest brands to put influencer marketing at the center of its efforts is Nintendo, whose Wii video game console was a breakout hit a few years back. Prior to the Wii, the gaming category was dominated largely by young males. Nintendo's strategy was to expand the market considerably with a product that would bring gaming to the masses. To achieve this goal, they determined that they needed to market the product to moms, given their influence over household purchasing decisions, especially those related to kids. But research showed that moms were not generally interested in video games. So Nintendo and its agency, A Squared Group, recruited a group of "Wii Ambassadors," local influencers (or "Alpha Moms," as they dubbed them) to try the product prior to the official marketing launch, and then to host Wii parties where thirty or so of their friends would also get a chance to experience the Wii, talk about it with each other, and then tell their other friends.

The word-of-mouth strategy was then coupled with PR outreach, where these Alpha Moms were featured on television and in newspapers and magazines, playing with the Wii and sharing their experience. Further, the Wii Ambassadors and friends who attended the Wii parties also were encouraged to spread the word digitally. This initial word-of-mouth effort targeted to influential moms was then followed with game placements on cruise ships, in senior citizens homes, on college campuses, and in malls. In each case, the core idea was to give people a chance to have a personal experience with the product, alongside other like-minded people to share the fun (and perhaps overcome some initial hesitation to use a product that was not traditionally one they would use). The expectation was that they would then share their stories with others.

With marketplace interest primed by the word-of-mouth campaign and the PR that came along with it, a $200 million TV and print advertising campaign followed. Nintendo, whose sales had been flat, rose from number three in the market (behind Xbox and PlayStation) to number one. And the Wii grew the entire category by driving first-time game console sales among women and people over thirty.

In naming Nintendo marketer of the year in 2007, *Ad Age* observed, "For all the discussion and hype and strategizing, no one else has been able to expand the global $30 billion video-gaming market into a social experience that includes everyone from grandparents to babies." Word of mouth led the way, and TalkTrack research showed that Nintendo enjoyed more positive word of mouth than any other player in the market for several years after the launch. Additionally it retains its considerable WOM advantage among the new, expanded market of females, earning about half of all video console word of mouth among moms, an advantage that has peaked during the critical holiday shopping season ever since launch.

Would You Like a Little Chocolate in Your Milk Mustache?

In 2005, after noting that per capita milk sales in the United States were on a steady decline for a twenty-year period, the dairy industry began investing in several acclaimed ad campaigns to spur sales, including the milk mustache campaign and "Got Milk?" ads. Efforts didn't end there, however. A campaign dubbed "Refuel" was launched in 2009, anchored by word of mouth and influencer marketing. It was conceived by a word-of-mouth agency, Fizz, whose founder, Ted Wright, gained notoriety in the marketing world for his contributions that helped to revitalize Pabst Blue Ribbon beer in 2000. After decades of decline, Pabst had become one of the fastest growing beer brands in America in only a few years. Under the headline "Marketing with a Whisper"— a nod to its word-of-mouth marketing strategy—*Fast Company* named Pabst one of its "Fast 50 Winners" in 2004 and declared, "Its 'no-marketing' marketing approach is the buzz on Madison Avenue."

To begin to address the milk challenge, Fizz and its client, the American Dairy Association, determined that it would be best to focus its efforts at a population of consumers already drinking milk and try to get them to drink more, rather than trying to bring new milk drinkers into the fold. But for word of mouth to work, Fizz knew that it needed to uncover a "talkable idea." It found one in an Indiana University research study that found chocolate milk is the best drink for the body to consume after strenuous activity. The word-of-mouth campaign Fizz proposed to launch would focus on the idea that milk—specifically chocolate milk—is "the perfect beverage to drink after strenuous activity, a better for you, high tech sports drink."

Next they addressed the question of who would spread the message. The answer turned out to be high school football coaches, who are the de facto source for nutritional and performance information across Ohio, where it would be test-marketing its program. "Coaches," Wright says, "are one of the few groups addressed according to their honorifics by even the most skeptical high school teenagers. These men are Influencers across Ohio from small towns to large metro communities. As such, the strategy became obvious: Win over the support of the high school football coaches and the rest will follow."

Fizz decided to have conversations with coaches where they naturally convene: football clinics. Every year high school football coaches attend intensive training clinics, and the Fizz team positioned itself at these clinics to facilitate conversations about chocolate milk. They mailed information about chocolate milk, as well as an invitation to discuss it and to find out more, to high school football coaches throughout Ohio. How does direct mail relate to word-of-mouth marketing? "Coaches are accustomed to receiving poorly executed and cheaply printed marketing material," Wright explained, "so we designed interesting luxurious high-end mailers. They were not only cool, but they were packed with information about chocolate milk's benefits. It worked. The mailers were so successful at generating conversation among coaches that they brought these mailers with them to the clinics with yellow Post-it note questions attached."

To drive the message home, Fizz recruited NFL and MLB alumni and state championship athletes (whom they called the "We Won a Ring" gang) to attend the football clinics and interact with the coaches. "They sent a strong nonverbal message," Wright said. "The bright gold rings these former athletes wear needed no explanation; they tacitly convey that the wearer knows what it takes to win the championships. Their presence supported the verbal message that chocolate milk is the drink to drink after strenuous physical activity." After the clinics the athletes were also engaged to visit some high schools to pass out chocolate milk and reinforce the message.

The program started a word-of-mouth cascade as the high school coaches began recommending chocolate milk to their players. Players started asking for it at home. Word also got out to nonathletes. Booster clubs started providing chocolate milk at games and at schools. And not too long thereafter, the media started picking up the story, including a four-minute feature about chocolate milk that ran on ESPN during a College Gameday program. At the end of the feature, Lou Holtz, the legendary college coach and ESPN commentator, turned to camera and said, "Had I known this, my kids would have drank chocolate milk."

The impact on sales of chocolate milk was clear. In Cincinnati, for example, Kroger reported increased sales of 475 percent; in markets across Ohio, milk consumption increased 12 to 28 percent in the first year, which was ten times the rate of the rest of the country. Within a couple of years, consumption of chocolate milk across the United States increased by nearly 50 percent.

Igniting Real-World Influence, with Scale

At this point, even if you're convinced of the power of influencer marketing, you may be skeptical that most marketing organizations have the resources or ability to identify a significant amount of influencers in an efficient way. Flat12 beer is a regional company with 400 influencers. The Fiskateer program numbers 6,000. But if you are a large brand, you might well feel that such programs would be too small to really have an impact for you. For brands that wish to undertake influencer marketing on a large scale—finding lots of people, perhaps 10 or 20 percent of a potential market, who have the largest social networks and a motivation to share and recommend—it sounds like a daunting challenge to do this via offline programs of the type we have been discussing. Yes, the presidential campaigns of George Bush in 2004 and Barack Obama in 2008 did it, but not everyone has the funds that a presidential campaign is able to raise to organize such an effort. Many people assume it's either impossible for them to do, or simply easier to activate influencers through ready-made social channels like Twitter and Facebook and applications built on them, like Klout. This, however, is something of a myth. We saw how Nintendo did it, with a smart, well-integrated approach that deployed influencers in advance of a PR rollout, which then led into national advertising. There are companies out there that have created scalable methods for recognizing real-life social networks, cracking the code on how influence really works, and allowing companies to identify and reach such people in large numbers.

One of them is Pursway Ltd., which uses the identification of "friends" to help companies in industries such as telecommunications, retail, travel, and financial services identify the influencers in their vast customer databases. They, like we, believe that real influence comes from real-world friendships rather than social media "friends." Pursway was founded in 2005 and today operates in markets around the world. Two of its founders, Elery Pfeffer and Guy Gildor, came from a background in math and computer sciences; they met while working together in the Israeli Defense Force. While at IDF, Guy worked on highly analytical data-mining assignments, including the development of ways to identify people's social networks based on the analysis of large, unstructured streams of data. Their third founding partner, Ran Shaul, came from a marketing background and was able to help them apply their analysis of social networks to marketing challenges.

Pursway applies the power of algorithms to allow marketers to identify influencers within their customer set and to prove the impact of their influence on those who follow their lead. They rely on the type of data that most consumer-facing organizations have invested considerable resources in collecting and analyzing. It is what customer relationship management systems are all about. Many companies use databases like this to identify their high-value customers (those that spend the most), and often market to them on this basis. Others use them to identify loyal customers. This same type of data is being leveraged differently by Pursway on their clients' behalf—namely, to understand the actual social relationships within the customer base, using what they call "shop together" analysis. Pursway's software can analyze and understand billions of transactions and uncover when people buy together, repeatedly and in different categories; through this, it can determine if they have connections with other people in the customer file, and how strong their connections are. In short, Pursway analyzes the pattern by which customers shop and consume together over time, in the real world.

Once their analysis reveals the social network among a firm's customer base, based on consumption and purchase data, this technology also reveals the hub and spoke of each customer within a certain product or service behavior. The hubs are those who the data suggest are the influencers who act first within a social network, and the spokes are those who follow the lead of the influencers with whom they shop. The influencers are therefore defined not by the size of their online social network or how much they tweet or are retweeted. Rather they are defined by their offline network and how much they impact the purchase behavior of those with whom they shop. Pursway's analysis finds that these influencers can generate ten times more sales within their social circle than an average consumer. Once they have identified the influencers in a company's database, special marketing activity can be targeted at the influencer segment, with results that demonstrate a 50 percent increase in their friends' spending in the relevant merchant categories.

We have shown many different approaches that companies big and small are taking to identify and activate influencers. Some are based on relatively modest numbers of influencers (hundreds or thousands), but with results that help to drive business success on behalf of a startup brewery, or reviving sales of products like scissors or chocolate milk, or launching a breakaway hit new product like the Nintendo Wii. Others use statistical methods to reveal millions of influencers who can help to elect a president or increase the use of a certain credit card in new venues. All agree that influence is about what happens on a person-to-person basis,

It's unfortunate that the term "social networking" has been virtually appropriated (pun intended) by online social networking applications, because these tools are most powerful when they reveal existing or latent social structures that originate in the real world. The word "friend" is a noun, not a verb: our friends are the people we live and work with, not the strangers who offer to "friend" us online. Among those real-world friends, there are some who sit near the center of a complex social system, and due to their positions and personalities, they play a bigger role than average in how we choose to live our real-world lives. These are valuable people, both to their friends and to the marketers of brands. And, as we've shown, their unique value can be measured and used to the benefit of a company or a cause.

4

Word of Mouth
Meets Madison Avenue

Consumers trust each other, and they don't trust advertising. And even if they find some ads to be funny, those ads don't really motivate them to buy. That's what surveys show consumers think, and it's the narrative that explains why word of mouth and social media is on the ascendancy. It's also what has led to a cottage industry forecasting the death of advertising.

The problem with this narrative, however, is that it's not quite true. Yes, it's what people say, but their behavior suggests something else. In 2011 we released the results of research conducted on behalf of NBC Universal that illustrates this quite vividly. In the study, conducted among a nationally representative sample of women, we looked in particular at their decision making at various stages of their purchase process, from the time they first entered the market for a product or service through the time they were researching and narrowing down their choices, to the final decision. One part of the study allowed us to track differences in what consumers *say* and what they actually *do* as they get closer to making a purchase decision.

Chart 4.1

ADVERTISING PLAYS A BIGGER ROLE THAN PEOPLE THINK (OR SAY)

What Consumers Say

Consumers say they rely on advertising to learn about products, but claim it plays a diminishing role as they approach an actual decision.

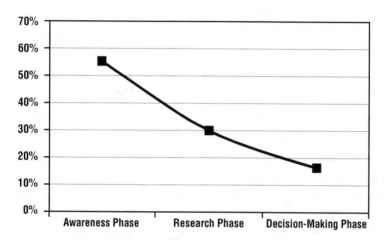

What Consumers Do

But in fact the closer they get to a decision, the more they talk about ads in their word-of-mouth conversations.

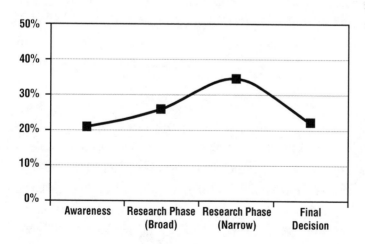

Source: Keller Fay Group for NBC Universal, March 2011.

Asked about the information sources that helped them along their purchase journey in a dozen categories, consumers readily gave advertising high marks for helping them become aware of brands early in the process. They gave advertising less credit for helping them at the research phase, and even less credit at the decision-making stage. But when we compare the word-of-mouth behavior of consumers along the various phases of making a purchase decision, we find a dramatic increase in the number of consumers who are actually talking about advertising as they get closer and closer to the purchase decision. In other words, exactly the opposite of what they say.

It's also the case that word of mouth itself is an increasingly popular behavior as people approach the time of a purchase decision. These two findings, taken together, make clear that advertising and word of mouth work together most often when consumers are getting serious about making a purchase, in contrast to what consumers say.

No, advertising is not dead or even dying. But for it to remain a vibrant force in the marketer's arsenal, it needs to change and adapt. That's where word of mouth comes in. Long after leading academics first described the relationship between advertising and word of mouth (as described in chapter 1), the idea that advertising and word of mouth need to work together is beginning to take hold. In this chapter we explain the role advertising plays in word of mouth and, more important, the strategic role that word of mouth should play in advertising.

How Baby Carrots Became the New Junk Food

In the spring of 2010 Jeff Dunn, the CEO of Bolthouse Farms, realized he had a problem. The hundred-year-old company still enjoyed a 40 percent share of the U.S. carrot market, but was seeing large declines in the sales of its popular and profitable baby carrots. Consumers were opting for cheaper and longer-lasting regular carrots. Dunn, who had spent most of his career at Coca-Cola before joining Bolthouse three years earlier, decided he needed to hire an ad agency and launch a new marketing campaign to spark the lagging sales. He undertook an extensive agency review, but none were giving him what he wanted: something edgy rather than a more conventional approach talking about the health benefits of carrots, which he felt was too obvious and wouldn't work.

In a rare moment of interagency generosity, one of the agencies in his review (after realizing they were not going to be the winning agency) suggested he might find that edge in an agency called Crispin Porter + Bogusky. During a visit to the agency's Boulder, Colorado, office, Dunn liked what he saw enough to put his business on a client roster that included blue-chip brands like Microsoft, American Express, Old Navy, Domino's, and Best Buy.

CP+B has risen to the heights of its business by understanding that for advertising to be successful it must get people talking, and by creating a disciplined approach to make sure that word of mouth is built into the very fabric of its creative process, something many creative ad agencies have historically struggled with. Bolthouse wanted the agency to work its magic once again, reviving its sagging sales by making baby carrots into a topic of conversation.

CP+B has always had big, bold ambitions for its client brands, as encapsulated in the mantra of Alex Bogusky, the former creative director and cochairman: "We want to make brands famous." A dozen years ago it was known as a regional ad agency doing standout work for small brands from its offices in the advertising backwater of Miami, Florida. With a prolonged burst of new business and creative success, it went from the industry's best kept secret to probably the most talked-about ad agency in the United States, having done breakout work for Burger King and Volkswagen, graced the cover of any number of national magazines, and won closets full of awards. It won Agency of the Year from the industry trades numerous times, and *Ad Age* named it the Agency of the Decade in 2010.

Though Bogusky left the agency in 2010 to work on social causes, Rob Reilly, his successor as creative executive, has carried on where Bogusky left off, with big expectations for the brands it handles and with the process that gets them there. "Talkworthiness" figures heavily in CP+B ideas. That means it's not enough to make a great TV spot that picks up awards. Greatness is achieved only when an ad infiltrates culture, earning press mentions, getting pickup in social media, and making it to the water cooler or locker room. That's quite different from the way that a lot of creative ad agencies work. Typically the creative process is more insular, with a focus on what the brand stands for and how that can be expressed in ways that are creative and will be persuasive. The notion that an idea can—and should—spark conversation, or even create culture, doesn't often enter the picture, at least not traditionally.

For Bolthouse Farms, CP+B knew a social media campaign pushing the health benefits of carrots would not work and was not what the client wanted, nor would a big "Got milk?" type of campaign designed to grow the entire category. Instead they determined that what was needed was to redefine baby carrots into something else so they could steal market share, and that something else was snack foods. Armed with the insight that carrots need to be seen less like veggies and more like snacks, and eager to parody over-the-top junk food marketing techniques, Reilly and his CP+B colleagues created flashy junk food–like packaging for the carrots, promoting them at point of sale. They installed baby carrots vending machines in high schools, right next to machines distributing Doritos, Skittles, and the like. Signage told consumers, "Eat 'em like junk food." All this effort caught on with the media and was featured (in color) on the front page of the *New York Times* and also in the *New York Times Magazine*. It yielded powerful results: the campaign got more than $10 million worth of "earned" media through public relations on less than $500,000 in actual spending. Stated differently, the agency paid for 38 million consumer impressions for its message and received 491 million.

The baby carrots campaign is a great example of how contemporary brands should view their communications strategies. Rather than tell consumers what to think, a contemporary brand should be giving them something to talk about. "Marketing by interrupting people isn't cost-effective anymore," wrote Seth Godin in his 2000 book *Unleashing the Ideavirus*. "You can't afford to seek out people and send them unwanted marketing messages, in large groups, and hope that some will send you money. Instead, the future belongs to marketers who establish a foundation and process where interested people can market to each other. Ignite consumer networks and then get out of the way and let them talk."

But how do you organize your company to create these kinds of ideas? While creative legend Alex Bogusky's leadership style and the cult of personality he inspired helped his agency win a reputation for edginess, its long-term success can be attributed to its structure and processes, which differentiates CP+B from many other creative ad agencies. First and foremost, CP+B benefits from a tight, integrated structure in which digital, PR, experiential marketing, and word of mouth are all built into the very crafting of the idea. Other agencies say they do that too, but those functions are often an afterthought, offering additional ways to translate the ad idea but not at the core of the idea itself. Alternatively representatives from all the different disciplines and functions are invited to the planning session, but the power still really resides with the creative team, and what they think will work is what ultimately gets made into advertising.

At CP+B the process also requires that the creative team comes up with WOM-friendly ideas. They do this by adding a twist to the typical creative department briefing process. As Rob Reilly explained, when a copywriter and an art director receive a creative assignment, they're asked to submit their ideas in the form of a press release, thus forcing them to think about whether an idea might get media pickup at its origin. In the process of doing this, they are also framing the idea in a way that consumers will likely talk about the ideas too. The elements of a story that make it "newsworthy" have much in common with what will also be "talkworthy." After all, press coverage and word of mouth are both "earned" forms of media, in which the story or idea has to earn an article or a conversation.

The CP+B approach offers a few lessons. First, it's important to note that there is a very media-agnostic approach in play. CP+B resists the temptation to put the medium—TV, digital, print—before the idea itself. This extends to social media. "If you've got a great idea people will talk about it, and that fact is just amplified by social media," Reilly says. "I don't think it's going to work if you go in there with the idea of blowing an idea up on Twitter."

Second, this process inverts the usual way that brands attempt to get their new marketing ideas to the public. In most cases, the writing of the press release comes not only after the idea has been crafted and approved but also after the ads have been produced and are set to air, rendering that all-important outreach not much more than an afterthought. This way of thinking can leave a PR team with the futile task of trying to publicize an inherently nonnewsworthy idea. The approach that Reilly describes heads off that problem. Press-friendliness is a hurdle cleared at the outset—a good way of ensuring that the ads don't die a quiet death with no one talking about them.

The CP+B agency is the modern master of the art and science of word-of-mouth advertising. It did not invent the practice, but it is the first to succeed in doing so, and over a significant span of time.

Before we move ahead to explore more fully how advertising can be used most effectively to create conversation, and why conversation creation should be the new goal of advertising, let's take a look back at the origins of the idea and see how (and why) it has come in and out of vogue over the years since.

Dichter's Dictates and the Rise of the Mad Men

As far as we have been able to determine, the phrase "word-of-mouth advertising" was coined by Ernest Dichter in a 1966 article published in the *Harvard Business Review*. Dichter is generally considered to be "the father of motivational research" and the first to coin the term "focus group," a technique that helped him understand why people are motivated to buy or do or think something. He counseled his advertising clients to shift their focus from straightforward product information and statistics to image and persuasion. His advice was a natural follow-up to the insight of Columbia University professors Paul Lazarsfeld and Elihu Katz in their classic 1955 book, *Personal Influence*, that described a "two-step flow" for marketing, in which advertising sparked conversations that in turn led to purchases.

Dichter brought this perspective to his *Harvard Business Review* article, which led with the observation that whenever his firm would ask consumers what made them buy a particular brand or product, the answer invariably was that a friend, expert, or relative had told them about it. To Dichter, this prompted the important question "Why in a time of increasing advertising volume does Word-of-Mouth recommendation loom so high?"

Dichter's research investigated the ways word-of-mouth recommendations affect advertising, and the flip side: the ways advertising affects word of mouth. His goal was to help advertisers refine their techniques so that they could embrace word of mouth and use it to their advantage, rather than see it as a force that was at odds with their ad messages. In many regards, his approach was a precursor to the desire many marketers have today to integrate three major communications assets: paid media (advertising, including search marketing and sponsorships), earned media (PR and word of mouth), and owned media (the brand's website, packaging, and anything else it owns and controls).

Rather than treating them as independent silos, or worse, forces that work in opposition to each other, Dichter sought to understand how these assets should work together. His underlying messages to the advertising community, given almost fifty years ago, are still incredibly relevant:

- "Advertising cannot sell against personal influence."

- Advertising must change from its traditional role of "a salesman who tries to get rid of merchandise," to a new role of "a friend who recommends a tried and trusted product."

- Advertisers should do so by understanding the steps that make person-to-person interaction powerful, and modify mass-media approaches accordingly. "There is a symbiotic relationship between the impersonal and the personal, or the formal and informal, avenues of communication."

• "There is a ready-made market of 'influencers, experts, or aficionados' who can be reached and, in turn, influenced by advertising in [the right media] and by the appropriate creative approach."

With forward-thinking ideas like these, advertisers and agencies were given a blueprint to maximize the impact of their marketing efforts by embracing, rather than ignoring, the power of personal influence and word of mouth in the buying process.

Sadly, this didn't happen. Instead marketing was overtaken by the era of the "Mad Men," as illustrated by the hit cable show on the AMC network. Advertising executives, enamored of their own brilliant creativity and their ability to persuade the mass market through the power of their ideas, delivered ads primarily through TV commercials and print ads in large-circulation publications. It was a top-down, "Father knows best" world, despite the reality that decisions then, as now, were being made "horizontally" and "socially."

Many call this period "the Golden Age of Advertising." And if you were in the ad business, undoubtedly it was. We call those decades a long, missed opportunity for Madison Avenue's clients. During those years the power of word-of-mouth advertising, influencer marketing, and the like not only failed to take hold; they receded from the marketer's consciousness. There was relatively little focus throughout the rest of the 1960s right up through the late 1990s. Marketers, for the most part, embraced other approaches instead, especially creative advertising, as well as promotions, PR, and direct marketing.

But during that time there were a few contrarians and trailblazers, exceptions that proved the rule. One was the ad agency Kirshenbaum & Bond.

The Snapple Lady Hits the Tarjay

When it launched in 1987, Kirshenbaum & Bond took on a provocative position for an ad agency. The upstart declared, "People don't trust advertising. . . . People trust other people," positioning itself as an agency that knows "how to create word-of-mouth advertising." A well-executed word-of-mouth campaign, KB touted, "expands your sales force" and makes a client's ad budget go further and work harder: "When you run advertising that has talk value, you literally add sales people to your staff by turning consumers into 'evangelists' for your brand. . . . Word-of-mouth advertising creates a 'multiplier effect' by making every dollar spent look like five or ten dollars."

But this wasn't a proposition many brands readily latched onto. Cofounder Jon Bond recalls that at the time most of his agency's "respectable clients didn't buy into the idea, preferring more traditional advertising approaches instead." A few clients took the plunge, including Target and Snapple. For these risk-taking brands, KB created notable and memorable campaigns driven by word-of-mouth objectives. It's worth looking back at these campaigns to see how the mold can be broken. Given the amount of advertising that still ignores word-of-mouth principles, these case studies are still relevant today.

For Target, KB was charged with helping the company open its first store in the New York area. The challenge was that many "fashion insiders" in New York had never set foot in a big box retailer, and many had never heard of Target. But the agency also had learned through its research that there was a sizable minority of New Yorkers who had previously lived in a market where Target had a significant presence. These became the target group for the ads.

There was an ad featuring the logo but not the identity of the sponsor that invited people to a pre-opening event. If you knew the logo, you knew what the ad meant; if you didn't, it was a bit of a mystery. As Bond recalls, "This made Target fans living in New York feel 'in the know,' and many came with their New York–born friends who had no idea what Target was and would never have been caught dead in a big box retailer. We were betting that these folks would get the 'secret code' of the ad that said in effect 'We know that you know.' We showed them that we had confidence in their sophistication to 'get it.' This, from a consumer base that was already using code to talk about the brand as 'tarjay'—Target with a French-sounding accent."

But not everyone had this level of confidence in the Target customer, not least Target executives. In fact, Bond said, Target executives were very nervous and didn't think the blind ad would work. So KB offered to pay for the ad if it was unsuccessful. The result? "The event sold out an hour after the newspaper [with the ad] hit the streets," Bond said, "and became standard operating procedure for all Target store openings in new markets from then on."

From a word-of-mouth perspective, what worked so well about the Target campaign was that it created mystery and allowed certain people—past customers or advocates of the brand—to be "in the know." Those people could then share with their family and friends who didn't know what the Target logo was, and therefore what the ad signified. Those people would feel compelled to seek out an explanation from the ones who might know. The event itself also stimulated conversation, as people who were brought along then shared what they had learned with others who didn't, thereby sparking a viral campaign, long before "viral" meant watching videos on YouTube.

For Snapple, Kirshenbaum and Bond deployed word-of-mouth principles in a different way. Snapple was founded in 1972 by three friends from Brooklyn—Hymie, Arnie, and Lennie—and grew organically for the next twenty years without a significant advertising investment. Originally it focused on selling fruit juices and natural sodas, primarily through health food stores on the East and West Coasts. Then in 1987 it launched its iced tea. Tied to a growing health consciousness in America, Snapple was the only ready-to-drink iced tea with natural ingredients. Sales soared in part because of consumers who switched from carbonated soft drinks.

Snapple was bought in 1991 by investors from Thomas H. Lee Partners, who saw a need for the brand to grow faster, on a national scale, in order to fend off competitive threats that were emerging from established players in the beverage market with much larger budgets. Coke's partnership with Nestea and Pepsi's with Lipton loomed as large, deep-pocketed challengers.

Enter Kirshenbaum and Bond, who created what would become one of the iconic ad campaigns of its era, starring "Wendy, the Snapple Lady." KB understood that Snapple was perceived as being honest and trustworthy, while marketing (and especially advertising) was seen as being dishonest and untrustworthy. So to launch a national ad campaign that wouldn't instigate any ill feelings, KB took a completely new approach. According to Bond, "Since the brand was built on word of mouth (and research showed that 42 percent of Snapple drinkers said they first tried it due to WOM), and we couldn't compete with Coke or Pepsi on flash, we decided to only do marketing that was itself 'real.' Our strategy was to create '100 percent Natural Marketing,' which, in fact, is the essence of WOM." This meant that all the communications needed to make the consumer feel as though he or she was hearing about Snapple from a friend. This is precisely what Ernest Dichter had encouraged twenty-five years earlier, but few had followed his advice before now.

At the heart of that strategy was Wendy Kaufman, an employee at Snapple's Long Island headquarters who had taken it upon herself to answer Snapple fan mail. She did this in her free time because nobody else in the office wanted to do it. She was not the typical commercial star of the time, so it took some convincing to get Snapple on board with KB's vision. "The Snapple founders—who still owned a sizable minority stake and continued to run the company—wanted celebs and hot babes," Bond said. "When we proposed Wendy they said quizzically, 'Our Wendy?!' Then we showed them pictures of the most popular women in America at the time: Oprah and Roseanne Barr, both overweight, and explained that most women would relate more to Wendy than a sexy celeb type. Plus Wendy was real, and the brand was all about real and natural."

The ad campaign sought to replicate Wendy's regular activity of writing letters in response to consumers, but scaled it via mass media by having her answer letters on TV. Most of the time the ads featured both the letter writer and Wendy. By featuring the letters, KB was giving a megaphone to Snapple customers who loved the brand, in effect spreading their word-of-mouth advocacy through mass media. Wendy's personal authenticity helped prove that the letters were genuine, not invented in some Madison Avenue brainstorming room.

As Bond explained, "We looked for interesting letters where even without a script we could get entertaining spots, much like reality TV of today. In one letter a lady said her dog, Shane, came running every time he heard a Snapple bottle open, so we dubbed him Shane the wonder dog. When we got there, though, the dog lay down and never got up despite opening dozens of bottles, so we just ran that! The idea isn't to be 'perfect,' it's to be authentic, something key to social media of today."

The campaign was wildly successful. Sales soared, and Thomas H. Lee Partners sold the company three years later for $1.7 billion to Quaker Oats, after having invested only $200 million. That is a return of 850 percent, attributable, in large part, to a WOM-based advertising campaign.

If the lesson from KB's Target advertising was to build WOM based on people with insider knowledge and let them share with others, the lesson from Snapple's success was that there can be tremendous value and impact with marketing that is natural and authentic. "The trick," Bond explained, "was to find people like Wendy, and situations that were inherently interesting and didn't need any special sauce or fancy production values to capture viewer attention."

Despite these successes, Bond and his colleagues couldn't sell word of mouth to top-tier clients in those days—and if they couldn't, no one could. Despite compelling evidence that word of mouth was crucial to persuasion campaigns, advertisers much preferred a simpler "one-step" communications model that cast their brands as stars on the television screen in their own family homes. Though word of mouth drove growth for KB, the agency abandoned it as a strategy. "It was too far ahead of its time," Bond said. "Large clients just wanted good TV spots."

But, says Bond, the word-of-mouth idea wouldn't go away completely, and KB kept coming back to it. When the digital revolution came along, he recounts, "it made it obvious that WOM was big business." Nearly a quarter-century after his ad agency first tried to convince its clients about consumer advocacy, Bond is now heavily invested (financially and personally) in word of mouth and social media. He left KB in 2010 and took the helm of a social media marketing firm called Big Fuel, joining as CEO in 2011. (Shortly thereafter the communications conglomerate Publicis Groupe acquired a 51 percent stake in Big Fuel.)

P&G to Madison Avenue: Fix It!

Though the marketing world wasn't prepared to listen to Kirshenbaum & Bond in the 1980s, it certainly took note in 2004 when Jim Stengel, the chief marketing officer of the world's largest advertiser, Procter and Gamble, told the country's largest advertising agencies at their 2004 Media Conference and Trade Show, "Today's marketing world is broken." In this highly publicized speech Stengel went on to say, "Consumers today are less responsive to traditional media. They are embracing new technologies that empower them with more control over how and when they are marketed to. They are making purchase decisions in environments where marketers have less direct influence (in store, word of mouth, professional recommendations, etc.) . . . . We need new channels to reach consumers. Brands that rely on mainstream media, or are not exploring new technologies and connections, will lose touch."

Even in a pre-Facebook world, the growth of the Internet as a mass medium where average Joes could form their own social networks, praise and pan products, and share content of all kinds had led to a tectonic shift in the marketing world. By the time Stengel took the podium, smart agencies like CP+B were already taking advantage of the new reality. A number of independent authorities had taken notice. The *Wall Street Journal* published a headline that asked, "As 30-Second Spot Fades, What Will Advertisers Do Next?" Marketing gurus like Sergio Zyman and Joseph Jaffe were publishing books with titles like *The End of Advertising as We Know It* and *Life after the 30-Second Spot*. Even the venerable industry publication *Advertising Age* declined to name an Agency of the Year for 2006, declaring it to be the "Year of the Consumer," testament to the power of consumer-generated content about brands circulating online. The magazine cover photo was drawn from the consumer-created viral YouTube video that documented, very humorously, the uncanny power of Mentos candies to create awesome plumes of liquid and gas when dropped in bottles of Diet Coke.

It was as if the advertising industry believed consumers themselves would make advertising agencies obsolete.

Of course, nothing really becomes obsolete; there's just change and confusion. Ad agencies, still alive and kicking, work with word-of-mouth shops, as well as their digital, PR, and direct marketing brethren. Yes, digital advertising is growing faster than more traditional media, especially print, but television was enjoying a major rebound by late 2010. Sponsors committed earlier than the year before, and at record prices, to participate in the 2011 Super Bowl. By the spring of 2011 the annual television industry upfront sales process produced rate increases in the range of 7 to 15 percent for the major broadcast networks, compared to the prior year. This impressive rebound was consistent with this December 2010 prediction by Deloitte: "Television will solidify its status as the current super media, defying some commentators' prophecies of imminent obsolescence." TV may offer fewer truly mass events than in its past, but it still offers more than other mediums. To paraphrase Mark Twain, rumors of TV advertising's death have been greatly exaggerated.

What has remained true throughout history is that advertising and word of mouth must work together. For the remainder of this chapter we discuss how.

3.8 Billion Times per Week

What would you characterize as an experience worth talking about? An unexpected upgrade to first class? A cleaning product that really does remove the red wine stain from the sofa? A calm insurance adjuster who makes everything all right after an accident? All those great customer experiences will get you talking about a brand, right? Now what about a commercial that's funny or insightful or informative aired during your favorite show? You may be less certain of the answer.

Our research shows that all of the above examples turn up in consumers' conversations. Yes, great experiences get people talking. Innovative products do too. But to a surprising extent, ads are a tremendous source of conversational fodder. TalkTrack finds that about 25 percent of all consumer conversations about brands involve one consumer telling another about an advertisement he or she has seen. By our estimate, that translates into more than 3.8 billion instances every week in America when consumers are exposed to brands through word-of-mouth conversations that are sparked by or include references to ads. Other forms of marketing besides advertising—retail displays, coupons, direct mail, and public relations—also play important roles. Combined, they are the source of content in another 30 percent of conversations. This brings the percentage of conversations related to marketing and advertising to about half. In other words, advertising and marketing are fundamental to word of mouth. We also believe the opposite to be true: word of mouth is fundamental to how advertising itself works, as described by Katz, Lazarsfeld, and Dichter so many years ago.

What is interesting to us is that although there is variation in this finding by category, it largely holds true across categories. Ads are talked about most frequently in conversations about entertainment and movies, followed by telecom, beauty, technology, and automotive. But even for the categories where ads are least likely to be part of brand-related conversations (health and financial services) we still find that in almost one in five conversations advertising plays a role. So the right ad at the right time with the right message can spark word of mouth, regardless of category.

Chart 4.2

ONE-QUARTER OF BRAND WOM REFERENCES ADS

Industries ranked by the percentage of WOM influenced by advertising

INDUSTRY	% OF WOM INFLUENCED BY ADVERTISING
Media/Entertainment	31
Telecommunications	29
Personal Care/Beauty	28
Technology	27
Automotive	27
The Home	27
Household Products	26
Retail/Apparel	25
All Category Average	25
Travel Services	25
Food/Dining	24
Children's Products	23
Beverages	22
Sports/Hobbies	21
Financial Services	19
Health/Health Care	18

Source: Keller Fay Group's TalkTrack®, July 2010–June 2011.

For many of us, the dominant image of a word-of-mouth recommendation begins with a moment of surprise and delight, when a company goes above and beyond all expectations, delivering much more than mere satisfaction. These experiences provide the model for how word of mouth works—and advertising seemingly has no role to play. It is for this reason that some people imagine that word of mouth and advertising are in an either/or relationship for building brands. They believe that the best way to grow a brand is to keep on delivering experiences that surprise and delight customers, and word of mouth will follow. You'll know you are doing things right, this theory says, when your business is thriving without the need to invest in advertising. Never mind that some of the greatest word-of-mouth brands, like Apple, actually do a lot of advertising.

Unfortunately, in the marketplace as in life, moments of surprise and delight are rare. While companies should absolutely strive to generate those moments, many will have difficulty doing so affordably, consistently, and on sufficient scale to achieve their growth objectives. Indeed advertising can play a critical role in shining a light on great experiences and in reminding consumers to tell the brand's stories. That's why advertising is so important—especially advertising that is designed to generate, amplify, or nurture word of mouth. That's what Wendy the Snapple Lady did when she read those letters of appreciation from Snapple customers.

In our research we have found that word of mouth generated by advertising is *at least* as valuable as word of mouth generated in other ways, in the sense that all of these avenues lead to equally strong purchase intention. Advertising-inspired conversations are not just passing comments about how "cool" or "stupid" a particular commercial might be. Indeed the typical conversation about a brand stimulated by advertising is between three and five minutes in length—plenty of time to talk about features and benefits and personal experiences and to make a recommendation.

There are a number of mechanisms by which advertising can generate word of mouth. An important one is that it can remind people of a highly positive experience and stimulate them to share it. In other words, a strong ad can amplify word of mouth related to an authentic experience.

But serving as a reminder is not the only way advertising can generate productive word of mouth. Entertainment or information value in an advertisement can also trigger conversation, often prompting one person to discuss with another (concurrently or later) whether the new car with better gas mileage is really all it's cracked up to be, or the new travel website really does a better job of revealing travel bargains, or the new zero-calorie soft drink being advertised really tastes as good as the original. At other times advertising can serve to fill "conversational white spaces," an industry term that could also be called "awkward silence marketing." Many of us experience those times when we lack something to talk about. At these moments a marketer can do us a service by delivering a well-timed and engaging advertising message that fills a conversational void. The value of doing so can be considerable to the marketer.

Of the brand conversations in which consumers talk about advertising, television ads are the most prevalent, which is consistent with the fact that more money is spent on television advertising than in any other medium. But on a collective basis, other forms of advertising (the Internet, newspapers, magazines, radio, and outdoor) are about on par with TV. So all media should be considered eligible for driving word of mouth; the key for marketers is to find the right type of message that will reach the right type of consumer, at the right time, via the right channel.

Chart 4.3

ADS THAT SPARK WOM, BY MEDIUM

Percentage of all WOM conversations driven by advertising

TYPE OF AD	% REFERENCED IN WOM
Television Ad	11.4
Internet Ad	4.5
Newspaper Ad	4.0
Magazine Ad	3.0
Radio Ad	2.0
Billboard Ad	1.7
Any Other Ad	2.8

Source: Keller Fay Group's TalkTrack®, July 2010–June 2011.

Whatever the medium, the name of the game is engagement—advertising that provokes a conversation, a sharing of advice, experiences, and opinions. Schoolteachers know this secret. Lecturing at students is not as effective as teaching that invites participation. This, we believe, should be the new measure of success for all advertising and marketing: Does it provoke and support productive conversations? If so, it's likely to help propel brand growth; if not, it is probably not worth paying for.

At no time is this question more important than during the Super Bowl, whose ad breaks are the costliest marketing opportunity around. Advertisers spend in excess of $3 million for thirty seconds of commercial time, not only because of the large audience but also because of the possibility of generating word of mouth. Viewers tend to watch the game with other people, so there is ample opportunity to talk about the brands and the ads are widely acknowledged to be part of the entertainment. Many of the marketers justify the exorbitant cost because of the value of word of mouth, or "buzz." "Close to 50% of viewers tune in to actually watch the commercials, more than they watch the game," Stephen Master, vice president of Nielsen Sports media research, told CNN in 2011. "The level of engagement for those people who choose to advertise is obviously very high."

Chart 4.4

TOP PERFORMING SUPER BOWL ADS GENERATE LARGE INCREASES IN WOM

Brands with the largest increase in weekly WOM impressions following the 2011 Super Bowl (vs. the prior month's WOM)

RANK	TOP ADVERTISERS	INCREASE (IN MILLIONS)
1	iPhone	24
2	Bud Light	23
3	Doritos	17
4	Verizon	14
5	BMW	13
6	Chevrolet	10
7	Pepsi MAX	9
8	Budweiser	8
9	Audi	7
10	Motorola	6
Average across All Super Bowl Advertisers		4

Source: Keller Fay Group's TalkTrack®, December 2010–February 2011.

One would expect therefore ads appearing during the Super Bowl to be cleverly designed to generate word of mouth. In fact the 2011 broadcast produced the largest "lift" in word-of-mouth levels, across all advertisers, of any of the five Super Bowl games that we've studied, dating back to 2007. Collectively the 2011 Super Bowl advertisers gained 170 million conversational brand impressions about the advertised brand the week following the game, compared to the average weekly levels for the full month before.

But the benefit was largely concentrated among half of the advertisers—twenty-one of forty-two measured—who gained at least 2 million or more weekly conversational impressions after the Super Bowl. The leaders in 2011 were iPhone, Bud Light, Doritos, Verizon, and BMW, all of whom gained over 10 million incremental additional exposures through conversation. Pepsi returned to the game as a top-ten performer in driving word of mouth in 2011, after leaving in 2010 to focus on social media marketing; it gained more than 9 million conversational impressions, the overwhelming majority of which took place offline. Indeed the online buzz generated by Super Bowl commercials overall pales in comparison to that which happens face-to-face.

Advertisers that didn't do well suffered from a variety of problems, but the most common may have been a lack of strong branding. Sometimes a memorable and talkworthy advertisement produces conversation for the ad more than for the brand itself. This was true for a memorable 2010 ad that featured the veteran actress Betty White being tackled in a backyard game of football. Lots of people talked about Betty White and how her career had been revived, but very few talked about the advertiser: Snickers candy bars.

Now compare the Snickers approach to Audi's during the same Super Bowl. Chief Marketing Officer Scott Keogh told us that relevance is important in creating conversations. "You could run a Super Bowl spot where someone throws a football at my private parts and it hits me and I fall down in pain. You could start a conversation like that, but the trick is to start a conversation that's topical, is relevant, means something to the brand, and is not just 'I'm in pain, on the ground, because someone threw a football at me.'"

But that's not as simple as just bludgeoning consumers with messages about price or product attributes. "If you look at our creative work, we fundamentally recognized that we'd refuse to do anything that I'd call dead-end advertising," said Keogh. "There's no advertising that was like 'This is our product, this is what it does, it goes fast, it costs this much.' It's impossible to get a conversation off of that because no one is going to go to a cocktail party, or go online, and go 'There's a new A4, it costs $38,000, and it goes fast.' No one's ever going to repeat that. So we plunged in and said, What can we get conversations around and where can we get them started?"

Wary of funny for funny's sake, Audi's 2011 Super Bowl ad was a well-thought-out, creative idea that poked fun, gently, at old luxury, specifically Mercedes, Keogh's old boss, which was an advertiser in the big game as well. The ad, titled "Release the Hounds," featured two gentlemen escaping from a mansion/prison, decorated with "old luxury" furnishings. One man jumps into a Mercedes, despite the other's warning that "it's a trap" and that he should get away in the Audi A8 instead. "Nonsense," the first man says, rejecting the advice, "my father owned one." He then drives away, only to end up following a path right back into the mansion/prison from which he had escaped, and declares, "I've been hoodwinked." The other man speeds away to freedom in his Audi A8. The commercial fades to black, and white letters appear saying, "Escape the confines of old luxury. The new Audi A8 is here. Luxury has progressed."

To Keogh, the investment in this new ad campaign is linked directly to its word-of-mouth potential. "Advertising is really a conversation starter," he told us. "If it's good, the conversation will keep moving online and move into the coffee shops and the golf clubs. If it is not any good, you'll know right away that it's a dead-end conversation." In the case of the 2011 Super Bowl, the investment paid off mightily. In Keller Fay's annual study of the word-of-mouth impact of

Super Bowl ads, we found that Audi generated about 7.2 million more exposures to the brand through conversations the week following the Super Bowl compared to what they had in the weeks prior to the game. This word-of-mouth increase meant Audi was an impressive ninth best among over forty Super Bowl advertisers.

Audi is hitting the right buttons that are helping it to become a more successful word-of-mouth brand. According to our research, Audi's word of mouth has improved dramatically of late. From 2009 to 2010 it had one of the strongest improvements of any brand in America (and was number one among auto brands) in terms of strong recommendations to buy the brand; it was also the number one automaker in 2010 and 2011 when it came to people talking about its advertising when they talk about the brand. Helping to prove that talk is not just nice to have but leads to business results, in 2010 Audi set a U.S. sales record and, for the first time, moved more than 100,000 vehicles in the United States.

Toward a Better Advertising Model

Advertising as we know it does need to change if it is going to deliver against marketers' expectations. The retailer John Wanamaker famously said, "Half the money I spend on advertising is wasted; the trouble is I don't know which half." Amazingly this is probably still true, and as the cost of advertising continues to rise, advertisers are demanding a better return on their investments.

Consumers are frustrated too. They are inundated by commercial messages: on TV screens at the checkout aisle and behind the deli counter, on their mobile devices, on posters on the walls of public restrooms, and even in doctors' offices. Much of the advertising they see is not relevant to them, or it interrupts them, or it offends them, or it bores them. For every award-winning ad, consumers see or hear scores that are dull, vapid, or offensive. There's no question that consumers would prefer to see and hear advertising that is more relevant to them—to their needs, their interests, their lives. Reducing the amount of irrelevant or uninteresting advertising would be welcomed by consumers and good for advertisers.

The importance of word of mouth to the success of advertising is starting to be more widely recognized in creative circles. One reason is that ad executives are very focused on online social media and want to see their campaigns uploaded, forwarded, tweeted, and shared. Although social media are just a small part of the opportunity, as this book demonstrates, it is helpful that "sharing" is becoming an objective for creative officers in advertising agencies.

We believe advertising works *primarily* by generating conversations among informed people who then spread the news—and their recommendations—to new customers. Advertising that is designed primarily to reach prospects, especially loyalists of competitive brands, is unlikely to have an impact because of inattention or preexisting opinions that are hard to sway. You need current customers to help with the persuasion process if converts are to be won. In other words, preach to the choir, providing them with a melody that can, in turn, help them persuade their friends and family to join your flock of customers.

Although this sounds like a fairly simple idea, it involves radical changes in advertising. For the most part, it means that advertisers should focus less on targeting prospective customers for the purpose of direct persuasion. While advertising aimed at creating awareness has an important role to play, the sale is not generally going to happen because of mere ad exposure. Instead advertisers should be targeting two key types of people: the consumer influencers we discussed in chapter 3, people who are interested in information and very engaged in spreading information through their social networks; and current customers and advocates of the brand who are ready to be rallied to the cause. A benefit of this change in targeting is that it will reduce the amount of irrelevant advertising consumers are being exposed to daily, generally without much negative effect. It's a win-win for both the advertiser and the consumer.

To be effective, the content of advertising messages should lend itself to word of mouth. As discussed in chapter 2, this means messages need to be simple, memorable, and worthy of sharing; ideally they should evoke emotion and disrupt people's schemas, both of which compel people to share what they have learned with others. There are many approaches to achieving this, and not all require a "breakthrough" or funny creative idea. Ad messages that focus on meeting people's needs, solving a problem, or providing "new news" are likely to be more effective than ads that are primarily funny for the sake of being funny or creative for creativity's sake.

Ernest Dichter provided concrete ideas to advertisers about ways to "earn" word of mouth and thereby earn a bigger return on their investment in paid media. Although his advice is almost fifty years old, many of his ideas are similar to the guiding principles that social media and word-of-mouth practitioners deploy today. Some of these include the following:

- Advertisers should provide "proof of friendship" to the consumer, in order to separate themselves from their role as "sales channel." Examples include providing small but thoughtful "gift packages" to say thanks; helping your customers to feel that they are being initiated into an "exclusive" group by using your product; and "establishing audience kinship" through the messages and style of your advertising to illustrate that you have things in common with your customers and truly understand them.

- "Trace [the] company myth"—that is, convey the backstory of the product's founding or the way early consumers used it—in order to personalize the product and create authenticity. This approach allows customers to see themselves as being connected to a long tradition, or perhaps to a very recent innovation with a story that consumers might want to tell when they talk about the product.

- Provide "customer testimonials" to simulate word of mouth, which if done properly will allow the viewers or readers to believe that the third-party endorser is truly speaking "spontaneously and disinterestedly," and not as a hired hand.

- Design the advertising itself to provoke, stimulate, or produce word of mouth.

Given the importance of word of mouth to the way consumers make decisions, the traditional advertising model needs to shift. It should be designed to connect with current customers and brand advocates. The goal should be to give them new information, effective language, and motivation to talk about the brand and recommend it. In survey after survey, we've found that people often have a visceral sense for why they like something, but often they can't put their preference into words. Advertising can help give people the words to use or an easy means to share information online. Through repetition, advertising can also give people cues that become conversation sparks as they watch TV with others, or talking points to help them the following day when they are discussing a show they have watched or something they have seen online or in a magazine.

The objective for marketers should be to create ads that spark conversation; the conversation then persuades the prospect, which leads to a purchase. That's the new model for Madison Avenue.

5

Rethinking Media:
Planning for Word of Mouth

We have made the case that the most effective advertising sparks conversations. Achieving this demands that the creative component of advertising, including its underlying message about the advertised brand, be "talkworthy." It's not enough to generate conversation about ads themselves because they are funny or clever; the advertising has to generate talk relating to the brand being advertised. Done right, ads spark curiosity and inspire people to ask others for their opinions about the brand, or cause a current customer to turn to a friend or colleague and endorse what is being said about the brand in the advertisement.

But beyond the content of any advertisement, it's also true that the chance of provoking conversations can be greatly improved by delivering the message at times, in places, and in contextual environments that are well suited to sparking conversations. This is often a job for media agencies, which plan and purchase the hundreds of billions of dollars spent on advertising every year worldwide, and for the media departments within brand marketing organizations that oversee the media planning-and-buying function. There is a big opportunity for media planners and buyers to improve the efficiency and effectiveness of their media investments by setting word of mouth as a key marketing priority, and executing against this objective. Our use of such terms as "planning" and "efficiency" may make it sound like these are activities only for the largest brands. But small businesses can also think about ways to plan and execute advertising and marketing programs that are more likely to prompt conversation. Critical marketing decisions made by small businesses should answer the question "Will it be easy for people to share this?" Decisions that can benefit from this way of thinking include whether to participate in a coupon mailer or free-standing insert, how much to spend on designing a website, whether or not to buy a local TV spot ad campaign, and whether to invest in search advertising so that their name pops up when someone searches for their category on the Internet. Local and small businesses are increasingly turning to tools like Yelp and Angie's List, Groupon and Living Social, because they provide a new "social" twist on older forms of marketing. Indeed one classic small business media opportunity—purchasing ads on paper place mats in local diners or on tables in the mall—could also be considered "social marketing" because of the opportunity to reach people who are eating together and looking for something to talk about.

Whether for a business that is big or small, media that can reach people while they are in a social environment or mind-set have special opportunities to prompt conversations. Planning media with social influence firmly in mind can yield significant dividends, and a growing number of companies are learning how to turn this from a matter of luck to a science.

Watching and Talking at the Same Time

Nowadays media planners worry a great deal about distractions that may cause target consumers to be inattentive to their messages. They worry about TV viewers leaving the room during a commercial message to go to the kitchen or bathroom, or channel surfing during breaks, or fast-forwarding through commercials if they have recorded the program on a DVR. Planners also worry about consumers turning their gaze from the main television screen to some other screen—a computer, a mobile device, an e-reader or tablet, or even a second television set in the same room.

Of course, this is not just a problem for television. Computer users can click "skip this ad" before seeing the intended message, magazine readers can just turn the page, and radio listeners can change frequencies during commercial breaks. But the fact is, television still commands the greatest share of media budgets, and therefore television has been the focus of the most research on ad effectiveness—and consumer distraction. Today there are television ratings not just for programs, as has traditionally been the case, but also for the average commercial that airs, what is known as "average commercial minutes." Soon there will be ratings for each individual commercial.

The push for commercial ratings is predicated on a belief that commercials have value only if people watch them, and the reality that as the tools to enable so-called commercial avoidance rise, we can no longer assume that program viewing is the same as commercial viewing. To help minimize commercial avoidance, commercials are being designed so they can deliver a message even when blurred by fast-forwarding. Transitions between programs and commercials and the number of commercials during each break, or "pod," are being modified to minimize disengagement, and efforts are under way to improve the matching of content and advertising in order to improve engagement. For example, Turner Broadcasting has coded many of the movies in its library based on thematically appropriate advertising, so that a car crash at the end of a chase scene in *The Bourne Supremacy* can be followed by an OnStar commercial demonstrating the value of roadside assistance following an accident. The goal for much of the media planning and buying business is to try to hold on to viewer attention in a world full of distractions.

Possibly the oldest form of distraction for TV audiences is simply other people in the same room. When people watch television together, there is a good chance that during commercial breaks people may decide to chat among themselves about something else—homework that needs to be done, meals that need to be prepared, or weekend plans to be made. A 2011 study called "How Co-viewing Reduces the Effectiveness of TV Advertising" by Steven Bellman of the Interactive Television Research Institute in Australia and three colleagues begins with a review of literature on the subject. The authors cite a 1965 study that found "co-viewing may have a detrimental effect even when co-viewers are apparently watching the screen with full attention, due to the 'mere presence of another' effect which interferes with the [mental] processing of the commercial."

Starting from the founding premise contained in the 1965 study, the Bellman paper is primarily devoted to a new experiment he and his coauthors conducted, involving hundreds of subjects who were recruited to a central location to watch a thirty-minute situation comedy, including twenty thirty-second commercials. The subjects watched the program, with commercials, either alone or paired with a person they brought with them to the facility, based on the criteria that they usually watched television together. The study design called for comparing the impact of advertising on those who watched alone versus those who watched with somebody else. Accordingly, all the participants were asked which of the advertised brands they remembered immediately after viewing, and then were asked to recall advertised brands in a follow-up interview conducted between twenty-four and thirty-six hours later.

The study found that immediate ad recall was unaffected by co-viewing, but that "delayed ad recall"—a day after exposure—was substantially affected. Solo viewers still recalled 63 percent of the commercials, compared to only 43 percent for co-viewers. Based on this drop, the study concluded "that commercials that were co-viewed were only 68% as effective as the same commercials solus viewed." The main explanation offered was a "loss of [mental] processing" of the commercial messages when viewed in a social context. In other words, the cognitive brain functions less effectively when others are present, particularly when conversations unrelated to the advertising occur. The authors ultimately recommend that "advertisers should adjust TV commercial audience ratings to allow for co-viewing," which may be accomplished by reducing the estimate of how many people viewed the programs based on the proportion of audience that is viewing with somebody else. The authors even proposed that advertisers "demand that they pay a lower price for co-viewed spots."

We believe these conclusions are incorrect, and we have considerable evidence to support our position. Indeed we would suggest the opposite to be true: that co-viewed commercials are more effective and, if anything, might warrant charging advertisers a premium. Even if cognitive brain activity were to be impaired during co-viewing, we believe that the social viewing context increases the strength of emotional response, which is far more important for influencing consumer purchasing and other behaviors. We are not alone in our view that emotion matters more than rational or cognitive response. Reports from the leading U.S. and U.K. advertising trade associations have come to the conclusion that rational response is overemphasized in advertising research and that there is a need for greater emphasis on emotion and audience engagement and participation in advertising. A 2007 report from the American Association of Advertising Agencies (now known as the 4A's) concludes, "Over reliance on verbal test measures and linear, rational models of how advertising works has probably contributed to a decline in advertising impact." These conclusions follow those of the Canadian neuroscientist and Parkinson's disease researcher Donald Calne, who in 1999 was among the first to write about the primacy of emotion, suggesting that decision making is chiefly emotional rather than rational.

What follows from this notion is that advertising viewed socially has the opportunity to benefit from a richer emotional context, as well as the opportunity for greater audience engagement and the kind of co-creation that occurs when advertising succeeds in sparking conversations about the advertised brands.

Sports programs attract some of the largest audiences of co-viewers because friends and family often make it a practice to watch live-action sports together, whether at each others' homes, at sports bars or offices, or in other venues. This is most dramatically illustrated by the parties people organize for watching big games, such as those involving their favorite college or professional teams, and especially for the Super Bowl every February. We've had an opportunity to study the impact of sports advertising on word of mouth for sponsor brands, and this has informed our thinking about the value of co-viewing.

Since 2008 ESPN and Keller Fay have been working together to understand the connection between advertising during broadcasts of professional and college football games and word of mouth for the advertised brands. In that first year we found that the fifteen major Monday Night Football advertisers for the NFL season collectively enjoyed 3 billion more word-of-mouth impressions about their brands during the football season among male ESPN viewers, compared to males who were nonviewers of ESPN, a gap that was not nearly as large before or after the football season. One sports apparel brand, for example, enjoyed a dramatic increase in WOM levels in late September one year, attributable to the concentrated ad dollars they dedicated to ESPN and football, leading to 93 million additional word-of-mouth impressions for the brand throughout the season when compared to the period before the season began and the advertising started. This illustrates to ESPN advertisers that advertising drives consumers to talk about brands. And those conversations, as we know, bring with them tremendous credibility and enhanced likelihood to purchase.

Chart 5.1

ESPN VIEWERS: 93 MILLION MORE IMPRESSIONS ABOUT
"ADVERTISER A" DURING FOOTBALL SEASON

Weekly brand impressions about sports apparel brand "A," among male ESPN
viewers and Nonviewers

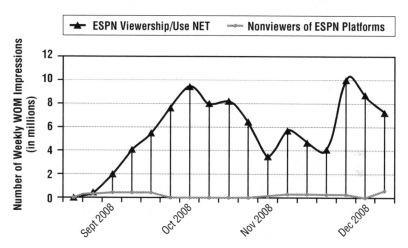

Source: Keller Fay Group's TalkTrack®, September–December 2008.

Although our initial work for ESPN did not make an explicit connection between co-viewing and word of mouth about advertisers, right away we suspected that co-viewing was probably a factor in the high levels of conversations we observed for ESPN's football advertisers. So in 2010 we took another step toward assessing the power of co-viewing in a study we did for ESPN regarding the other type of football—soccer. ESPN had the English-language rights in the United States to the 2010 World Cup soccer tournament, plus the ambition to provide coverage worthy of the "biggest sporting event on the planet." Despite America's historically modest enthusiasm for watching the sport on TV, ESPN clearly succeeded. Combined with the efforts of its sister network ABC, ESPN achieved an average audience size of 3.27 million, up 41 percent from the prior World Cup. The final game for the U.S. team, against Ghana, was seen by 15.2 million viewers, putting it in the same ballpark, so to speak, as the average audience for a World Series baseball game.

ESPN believed that in addition to large audiences, the World Cup offered advertisers an environment that was likely to generate word of mouth and hired Keller Fay to help test that theory. ESPN was particularly interested in assessing the value of large out-of-home audiences expected for the World Cup. Because the games were held in South Africa, the significant time zone difference would mean that many of the games would be broadcast live during weekday mornings and afternoons, and thus it was anticipated that fans would be inclined to watch at the office or in bars and restaurants before work, at lunch, or after work. Indeed some bars and restaurants in Los Angeles planned to open as early as 4:30 in the morning to accommodate patrons who wanted to watch the games.

Because out-of-home audiences are almost certain to be in the company of other people, they tend to be more social than at-home audiences. ESPN's World Cup research therefore contrasted the word-of-mouth behavior of those who watched the World Cup at home versus away from home, which provided us with an indication of the impact of social viewing on engagement with advertised brands. The results were startling overall, and especially for the out-of-home audiences. Among those who watched the World Cup at home, word-of-mouth levels about the seven main sponsors were, on average, *twice* as high as measured among nonviewers, providing evidence that viewership was helping to drive word of mouth for those brands. Among those who watched the game in a bar or restaurant, word-of-mouth levels were *three times* as high. It's easy to imagine why: bar and restaurant TV viewing often puts together people with weak or modestly strong social ties, such as coworkers, acquaintances, and even strangers. TV commercials can be helpful in providing a topic of conversation in social settings where there isn't a significant relationship history to draw upon. In this sense, advertising plays the role of "social currency," to the significant benefit of advertisers. Far from being a drain on attention, as Bellman and his colleagues suggested, this research provided evidence that co-viewing, and especially out-of-home viewing, probably led to more conversation about advertised brands.

Chart 5.2

WATCHING THE WORLD CUP 2010 IN SOCIAL ENVIRONMENTS
(ESPECIALLY BARS AND RESTAURANTS) LEADS TO HIGHER LEVELS
OF ADVERTISER WOM

Percentage engaging in WOM about World Cup advertisers in the
past day, indexed to Nonviewers

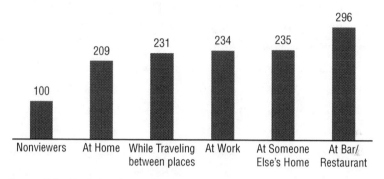

Nonviewers	At Home	While Traveling between places	At Work	At Someone Else's Home	At Bar/ Restaurant
100	209	231	234	235	296

Source: Keller Fay Group's TalkTrack®, June–July 2010.

LeBron James and America's Idols

The out-of-home findings for the World Cup were presented at a
marketing conference in the spring of 2011 by ESPN's top research
executive, Artie Bulgrin. One of the people in the audience was
Stacey Lynn Schulman, who at the time was an executive with Turner
Broadcasting. Schulman brought to our attention a study she had
done years earlier when she worked for the big ad agency Initiative
Media. Conducted with Alex Chisholm and his colleagues from
MIT's Comparative Media Studies Program, the Initiative project
investigated the audience of Fox's *American Idol*, then in its second
season. The team wanted to understand the dynamics that led to high
engagement levels with the then highly popular—and "talkworthy"—
program.

In a paper called "Walking the Path: Exploring the Drivers of
Expression," the Initiative/MIT team found that "group viewing"
was one of the key factors that promoted engagement with both the
American Idol show and the advertisers, some of whom had "product
placements" embedded in the show itself in addition to commercials.

AT&T provided text messaging to facilitate voting by the television audience, and red cups emblazoned with the Coca-Cola logo were prominently displayed on the judges' table. The study found that, "in almost all cases, the quantitative data suggests that the recognition of advertising and product placement is much higher among viewers in groups than those viewing alone." The paper acknowledged that the finding was contrary to some of the conventional wisdom of the time: "This may seem counter-intuitive, as multiple viewers may be perceived as distractions to understanding content. The presence of other individuals in a viewing environment, however, is much more dynamic, allowing for multiple viewer responses to content both within and outside the actual program."

With the results of the World Cup building on those of the 2003 Initiative/MIT paper, Turner Broadcasting wanted to extend the learning even further. The opportunity presented itself almost immediately, with the upcoming broadcast of the 2011 NBA Eastern Conference Finals on Turner's TNT network. The series, featuring LeBron James's Miami Heat versus Derrick Rose's Chicago Bulls, would ultimately involve six games over a two-week period. Turner commissioned a research study among males eighteen to fifty-four, the main target audience for NBA playoff games. The study found that the word-of-mouth levels for the top twelve advertisers during TNT's coverage were over 80 percent higher among those who frequently watched the playoffs with other people, compared to the levels among nonviewers. That was also more than double the size of the 39 percent boost in word of mouth that occurred among viewers who watched alone. The research team also considered the impact of out-of-home viewing. For those people in the study who watched both out of home *and* socially, conversation levels for the top twelve advertisers was 2.2 times higher than for nonviewers! Turner showed that the conversation in America's sports bars is not just about whether LeBron will ever win the big game; the study found that sports fans are also keen to talk about iPads, Verizon, and Ford, three of the best performing advertisers in the Turner NBA study.

Given these findings, media planners might very well decide they should be giving *priority* to ad environments that are more social, and media companies offering those environments might very well seek to charge a premium.

What about that 2011 paper, "How Co-Viewing Reduces the Effectiveness of TV Advertising," by Stephen Bellman and his colleagues? One flaw in this study, we believe, is that the authors overrelied on "delayed" advertising recall as the critical metric upon which to assess the effectiveness of the ads. While being memorable to a large number of viewers is a worthy goal, it's not the only thing—or even the main thing—that should matter to advertisers. The experiment did not measure either immediate emotional response, or word-of-mouth behavior following the broadcast. Nor did the published paper reveal insight into the impact of co-viewing on viewers' likelihood of ultimately purchasing the advertised brands. We think it is fair to assume that advertisers would be perfectly happy to suffer a few fuzzy memories from co-viewers if they obtained higher purchasing levels due to higher levels of word-of-mouth recommendations at the time the commercials appeared, or shortly thereafter.

The title of the Bellman paper bluntly describes co-viewing as detrimental to advertising, but the study actually provided important support to the alternative thesis. The authors acknowledge an exception to their overall conclusion related to instances when, during the viewing experience, "co-viewers talked about the ad playing on the screen." As part of the study, they noted that co-viewers engaged in conversations about the advertised brand between 8 percent of the time (for a Jell-O commercial) and 26 percent of the time (for an Oscar Mayer spot), and that such conversations increased the chance that the commercials were remembered a day later. They concluded, "It may be possible to fine-tune an ad's creative [execution], so that it deliberately generates talk about the ad by the co-viewers, and therefore increases processing of the ad's main message." With regard to this part of Bellman's paper, we couldn't agree more.

Few advertisers today think about generating word of mouth as a key goal for their advertising, and yet we have shown that advertising still generates a considerable volume of word of mouth, a key factor in the ultimate success of the advertising. Imagine the impact advertising might have if it were always developed with the goal of generating conversation—and especially sought out program environments likely to be watched socially. Which types of media would they select? Which days, and times of day, would be most productive? Tools to make such decisions are now available for those who wish to avail themselves of this new way of thinking about and planning media. The range of options to help spread a social message is far greater than many assume.

All Media Are Social

Television is not the only medium that drives word of mouth. In many categories the Internet has emerged as the communications channel that drives the most conversation—but not because of social media, as so many marketers assume. Our research has found that the main role of the Internet is providing fodder for conversations that mostly happen offline, and most of that effect comes from the more traditional "Web 1.0" sources such as brand websites, e-commerce sites, Internet publishing sites, and search portals.

TalkTrack surveys always ask consumers whether the brand conversations they had yesterday contained any "references" to information from a media or marketing source. This helps to determine which content sources are sparking or providing supporting information to conversations. In chapter 4 we reported that about 25 percent of conversations about brands contain a reference to paid advertising. But advertising where? And what about articles, programs, and product placements that might occur on TV or radio, in print, or online? When you include paid, owned, and earned communications, the Internet beats television, and all other media types, in nine of fifteen categories measured in our ongoing research. The Internet wins in product and service categories such as automotive, technology, retail, and travel, while television wins big for entertainment and sports, categories for which the television has the advantage of being the primary delivery vehicle. In three categories—household products, beverages, and beauty—it is neither TV nor the Internet that provides the content that drives the most conversation, but rather coupons, point-of-sale elements, and other promotional activity. The food and dining category, which is the most talked-about category, has a tie between television and coupons/promotions.

Chart 5.3

INTERNET IS MOST REFERENCED IN CONVERSATIONS ABOUT PRODUCTS AND SERVICE CATEGORIES, WHILE TV IS NUMBER ONE FOR MEDIA AND ENTERTAINMENT WOM

Percentage of media and marketing elements referenced in type of WOM

	PRODUCTS	SERVICES	MEDIA & ENTERTAINMENT*
Any Media/ Marketing Reference	<u>49%</u>	<u>49%</u>	<u>61%</u>
Internet	15	23	15
TV	13	13	35
Point of Sale	12	6	5
Coupons/Promotions	11	4	3
Newspaper	6	5	6
Magazines	5	4	5
Mailing	5	8	4
Radio	3	3	4

*Includes Media/Entertainment and Sports/Hobbies

Source: Keller Fay Group's TalkTrack®, July 2010–June 2011.

This means that all forms of media and marketing have the potential to drive conversations, provided the message is talkworthy, and especially when the medium reaches people in a social or conversational context. Indeed each medium offers different advantages when it comes to sparking or supporting conversation, and these are also important considerations for marketers and media planners.

The Internet Is a Powerful Reference Source for Conversation

The Internet is unique among media because it delivers messages that are paid for (Internet ads of all kinds and paid search), those that are owned by the brand (branded websites or Facebook pages), and those messages that are earned (news coverage, social media comments, consumer ratings, reviews, organic search, etc.). It will come as a shock to many marketers that social media provide content to the smallest share of word-of-mouth conversations. Across all categories, only 2.6 percent of all conversations involve a reference to social media, including blogs and social networking sites. Brand websites are talked about twice as often. Paid Internet advertising is also far more dominant than social media as a source of online content that ends up being discussed in conversations. These marketing channels should not be abandoned or ignored.

Chart 5.4

ONLINE SOURCES TALKED ABOUT IN WOM

Percentage of media and marketing elements referenced in all WOM

MEDIA/MARKETING ELEMENT	% REFERENCED IN WOM
Internet (any reference)	16.0
Company Website	5.2
Internet Ad	4.5
Other Website	3.1
Online Consumer Reviews	2.9
Social Media	2.6

Source: Keller Fay Group's TalkTrack®, July 2010–June 2011.

In late 2010 Keller Fay did a study for Google that investigated the role of the Internet in three phases of conversation: before, during, and after. The hypothesis was that the Internet may facilitate conversations, including the overwhelming majority that are offline, by providing content at any of these three points in the conversational process. A conversation can draw on content that somebody read or saw online *beforehand*, perhaps months ago, or the day before, or even just minutes before a conversation happens. The Internet is also rather uniquely suited to providing content *during* a conversation. Imagine you are at a cocktail party in Manhattan and you tell a friend about how much you loved the Woody Allen movie *Midnight in Paris*. She immediately gets out her smart phone and Googles the name of the movie and "NYC," which leads her to the Fandango website, which, in turn, points her to a convenient theater where the movie is playing at 9:15. Within an hour she may be meeting her sister at the theater. That's an example of providing content in the midst of a conversation, something that has become easier to do since the advent of the smart phone. Finally, the Internet also is by far the most powerful medium as a source of information *after* a conversation—a place to go to get additional information about prices, availability at nearby retail stores, consumer reviews, and so on minutes, hours, or days after learning of a brand or product in conversation, but before making a purchase.

The Google/Keller Fay study compared the role of the Internet to other media types, particularly TV and print. The study further learned that the Internet and TV play very large and roughly equal roles in "before" conversations, while the Internet takes a narrow lead in "during" conversations. But as a follow-up resource in "after" conversations the Internet is the clear leader. And the Internet is the only medium that is a leader—either in a tie or with a clear lead—at all three phases.

Chart 5.5

INTERNET IS MOST IMPORTANT SOURCE OF CONTENT BEFORE,
DURING, AND ESPECIALLY AFTER A CONVERSATION

Percentage of brand conversations involving references to TV and to
the Internet, before or during WOM conversations, or use of source after
conversations for seeking out more information

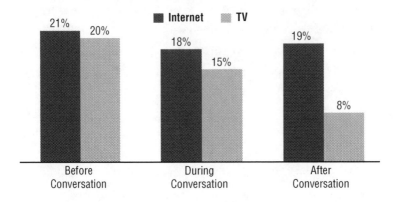

Source: Keller Fay Group for Google, June 2011.

What kinds of Internet sites are the most important in terms
of generating meaningful conversation in this context? Search
sites edge out e-commerce sites as the source of information, followed by brand websites and social media. When you add methods
for navigating to the ultimate information source, search engine
sites have a commanding lead as the first online stop for supporting conversations. While a skeptic may think Google's sponsorship
of the study made this a foregone conclusion, consider your own
methods for finding information quickly online; chances are it starts
with one of the major search engines. Why wouldn't the same hold
true when you are engaged in conversation and in need of related
information?

The source of the Internet's big advantage for supporting conversations is that it provides highly efficient self-service information at the moment it is required, which is crucial for conversational
purposes. Its advantage is not tied to social networking. When con-

versations about brands are mostly happening offline, the Internet provides a quick reference source. If you're in a conversation comparing prices of consumer electronics brands, you are probably going to visit Amazon or the Best Buy site, or some kind of price comparison website. If you're talking about the fat content in Subway's $5 foot-long sandwich, you are going to visit the Subway site, or perhaps do an online search in the hope of finding a nutrition-related website. If you are looking for a sushi place close to the train station, you are probably going to go to MapQuest, or Google Maps, or OpenTable. In none of these examples does Facebook or Twitter provide you the most efficient answer to a question that arose in a conversation.

Print Media: Connecting with Influencers

There is a false equivalency that has developed in the marketing world between the terms "social" and "social media websites," and between the terms "social networks" and "online networks." Sometimes it even seems that the word "friend" more often stands for an online connection on Facebook than a close relationship that's existed since you were in grade school. Just because the marketing jargon of the day has appropriated terms like "social" and "social network" doesn't mean that we must all surrender those terms to the Web 2.0, as the social web is called. Ironically the facts suggest that these terms are more aptly associated with the audiences for some of the most traditional media around: newspapers and magazines.

At a 2011 advertising conference, Brad spoke on the topic "How Social Are Social Media Audiences, Really?" His presentation started off by showing that the users of Facebook and Twitter exceed the national average when you look at measures associated with sociability, such as counting up the number of real-world friends the users have, the frequency with which they give product advice, and the number of brand conversations they have. These results didn't surprise anybody in the audience; influence and large social networks are fundamental to the promise of the social media websites.

But the first part of the presentation was merely a setup to the second part, which showed that the audiences of Facebook and Twitter actually fall well short of many other audiences on these social metrics. What are those other audiences? None other than readers of the print and online editions of the *Wall Street Journal*, *New York Times*, and *USA Today*; magazines such as *Vogue*, *Southern Living*, and *National Geographic*; and the content-rich websites of iVillage and the NBA, among many others. In fact Facebook and Twitter never ranked close to the top-ten audiences for social and influence-related criteria. The lesson: All media can be social, including those related to print and online publishing.

Chart 5.6

AUDIENCES WITH THE LARGEST NUMBER OF PEOPLE IN REAL-WORLD SOCIAL NETWORKS

Average number of people—friends, relatives, acquaintances—one communicates with "fairly often." Top 10 of 113 media audiences shown.

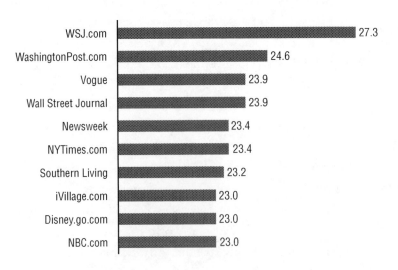

WSJ.com	27.3
WashingtonPost.com	24.6
Vogue	23.9
Wall Street Journal	23.9
Newsweek	23.4
NYTimes.com	23.4
Southern Living	23.2
iVillage.com	23.0
Disney.go.com	23.0
NBC.com	23.0

AUDIENCES WITH THE MOST WEEKLY BRAND-RELATED WOM CONVERSATIONS

Average number of brand conversations per week. Top 10 of 113 media audiences shown.

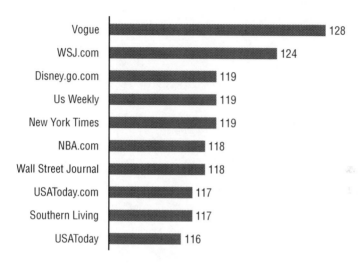

Vogue	128
WSJ.com	124
Disney.go.com	119
Us Weekly	119
New York Times	119
NBA.com	118
Wall Street Journal	118
USAToday.com	117
Southern Living	117
USAToday	116

Source: Keller Fay Group's TalkTrack®, July 2010–June 2011.

Most marketers today fail to appreciate the social and influential traits so strongly associated with print audiences, which is one reason print media are struggling. We believe that the print and Internet editions of publications excel in the delivery of influential audiences because they attract highly educated readers, and education is the demographic factor most associated with people who are influencers. And influencers tend to be information-hungry individuals who like to keep up with what's new and interesting. Print and the online editions of print publications provide a perfect vehicle for them to find the information they so crave. (This theme was also explored in our discussion of influencers in chapter 3.) Going forward, advertisers can take better advantage of these media by using them as a way to introduce "new news" that they want to spread, by making ads in online publishing environments easy to share with others, and by using messages that people will feel compelled to share with others. Indeed online publishing environments may be one of the best places to originate content that the marketer hopes will be shared via social media status updates and tweets, as well as by email and face-to-face conversation.

TV Commercials Lead in Sparking Conversation at Scale

We've mentioned that the Internet generally beats all other media, including TV, in providing content for conversations. But television has two advantages no other medium can touch: paid TV beats all other forms of *paid* media, including the Internet, in reaching the largest number of people having conversations about brands, and TV has a unique capability to spark a conversation with compelling video that can be served up at the behest of the advertiser.

"Scalability" is a frequently mentioned problem among advertisers seeking to generate word of mouth offline, for example via WOM sampling programs and influencer-driven programs. These methods often deliver quality but not always sufficient quantity when it comes to word of mouth. As a result many turn to social media, which they claim offers word of mouth "at scale." However, the medium that offers the largest scale when it comes to WOM potential is none other than television. When we ask people what media, if any, are referenced in their brand conversations, television commercials account for over 11 percent of all conversations, more than any other single touch point, and well ahead of the next highest paid advertising medium, the Internet, at 4.5 percent. While the Internet overall fares best in many categories due to the inclusion of owned media assets (such as brand websites) and earned media (such as news and social networking), TV does best when it comes to paid media investments.

Chart 5.7

TV ADS AND PROGRAMS ARE TOP-REFERENCED MEDIA SOURCES IN BRAND CONVERSATIONS

Percentage of media and marketing elements referenced in all WOM

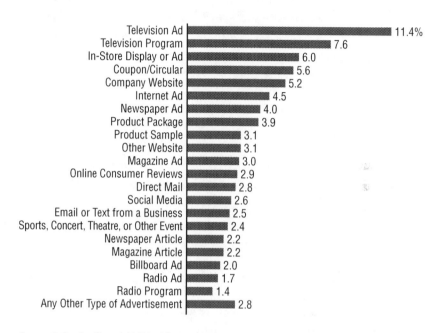

Television Ad	11.4%
Television Program	7.6
In-Store Display or Ad	6.0
Coupon/Circular	5.6
Company Website	5.2
Internet Ad	4.5
Newspaper Ad	4.0
Product Package	3.9
Product Sample	3.1
Other Website	3.1
Magazine Ad	3.0
Online Consumer Reviews	2.9
Direct Mail	2.8
Social Media	2.6
Email or Text from a Business	2.5
Sports, Concert, Theatre, or Other Event	2.4
Newspaper Article	2.2
Magazine Article	2.2
Billboard Ad	2.0
Radio Ad	1.7
Radio Program	1.4
Any Other Type of Advertisement	2.8

Source: Keller Fay Group's TalkTrack®, July 2010–June 2011.

The ubiquity of television in our lives is clearly a major reason why. A comparison between social media's audience leader, Facebook, and television's audience leader, CBS, makes the point dramatically. In presentations to the industry, CBS's top research executive, David Poltrack, compares the total reach offered by television to that delivered by Facebook. While Facebook reached 151 million unique Americans per month in late 2010, CBS reached 240 million. And while the total time Americans collectively spent using Facebook each month was 42 billion minutes, time spent with CBS was five times greater: 210 billion minutes.

People Love to Talk about Deals

Conventional advertising media such as TV, the Internet, and print are important, but they aren't the only form of media or marketing to consider when thinking about how to prompt or spark word of mouth. And whether your brand is large or small, there are other important points of contact that can be used to drive the conversations that will drive your business forward.

For a number of brands, especially in the areas of food, personal care, household products, and retail, promotional efforts are significant drivers of word of mouth. More specifically, coupons and circulars are major topics of conversation about retailers ("Did you see the great deals being offered this week by . . . ?"). Think about brands such as Rite Aid, CVS, Kroger, Bed Bath & Beyond, and Kohl's, all of which score well on this dimension, according to our research. Meanwhile product samples give the WOM spark for beauty brands such as Clinique, Avon, Mary Kay, and Nivea. Word of mouth for food brands such as General Mills, Kellogg's, and Pillsbury also benefit greatly from coupons. While these are the brands that stand out on a national basis, smaller brands can follow their lead. But don't just offer deals to bring new customers in the fold; it can be expensive to capture their attention. Instead let your best customers know when you are offering discounts or samples of new products, and encourage them to take advantage and to share the word with others.

Online sites also offer "promo codes" for online purchases, and of course, Groupon and Living Social have become popular ways of sharing deals between friends, neighbors, and strangers alike. All of this is attributable to the inherently social nature of the quest for a great deal. As revealed in a study by IBM (described in chapter 6), the opportunity to get discounts is the most popular reason why people "friend" or "like" a brand or company on social networking sites. This is a reflection of a real-world impulse to save money. They will like you just as much, if not more so, if you give them these same rewards at your store or in the mail.

Shop Talk: The In-Store Conversation

Marketing within retail stores also plays a big role in generating conversations about beverages, food, household products, and consumer electronics. Indeed 5 percent of all brand conversations actually occurs inside stores. Though not a very large percentage, this is a very large volume, as consumers are exposed to in-store conversations some 750 million times per week. One of the real benefits of a strategy that focuses on retail environments is that word-of-mouth conversations that take place in a store are by far the most likely to have active recommendations to buy or try the brand being discussed, and they have the highest levels of purchase intent.

Chart 5.8

BRAND WOM IN STORES IS MORE LIKELY TO LEAD TO
PURCHASE INTENT

Percentage rating WOM highly likely to inspire purchase intent
("9" or "10" on 0–10 scale)

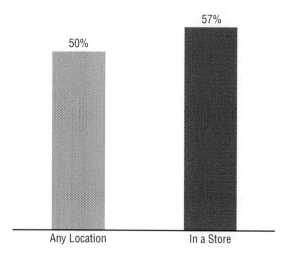

RECOMMENDATIONS TO "BUY OR TRY" A BRAND ARE HIGHEST WHEN WOM OCCURS IN STORE

Percentage of WOM containing specific recommendations to "buy or try it"

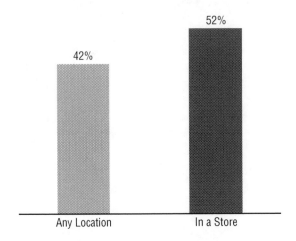

Any Location	In a Store

Source: Keller Fay Group's TalkTrack®, July 2010–June 2011.

What sparks in-store conversations? Some are driven by the product package itself, and some are a result of in-store displays or videos. Some are just a matter of people shopping together and talking about the relative merits of one brand versus another, or about which brands are offering deals that day and are therefore worth buying. But retail is also a place where people can see and sometimes sample products that excite them, and can share the excitement with friends or family in the store. This is the key to Apple's highly successful retail stores: they are places to shop and buy, but also places to experience Apple products and get caught up in the emotional energy that seems to compel visitors to talk to one another.

Around the time Steve Jobs passed away in 2011, his biographer Walter Isaacson wrote that retailing was one of seven industries he revolutionized (the other six being personal computers, animated movies, music, phones, tablet computing, and digital publishing). One of Jobs's great accomplishments was making Apple stores a center of consumer conversations—those that happened on premise, as well as the stories of a great shopping experience shared later, at the water cooler or over the kitchen table. This was not an accident. As Isaacson explains, Jobs realized in 2000 that for Apple to be successful, it needed to have a way to communicate directly with customers, and the best (and really only) way to do that was within retail stores. It was not just conversation between Apple's employees and customers that mattered, however. "In July 2011, a decade after the first ones opened, there were 326 Apple stores," recounts Isaacson. While they proved to be very successful from a sales perspective, "the stores did even more. They directly accounted for only 15 percent of Apple's revenues, but by creating buzz and brand awareness they indirectly helped boost everything the company did." As we mentioned in chapter 2, Apple is a company that has consistently prioritized offline conversation over social media. Retail was one part of that strategy.

Sony Plans Media to Maximize WOM Impact

An increasingly popular approach to measuring the effectiveness of media is a form of statistical analysis called "market mix modeling." There are a variety of approaches to doing this, but what they all have in common is an effort to estimate the contribution of each marketing activity on the ultimate objective of most marketing: sales. And if not sales, then at least some other important outcome, such as store visits, intentions to buy, brand imagery, or even word of mouth.

In chapter 1 we wrote about a market mix modeling initiative by the MarketShare company, which has found that advertising and marketing drive sales most of the time because of the impact that they have on conversations. MarketShare came to this conclusion after an extensive statistical analysis of data relating to advertising and marketing expenditures, word of mouth, and product sales for their clients in a half-dozen categories. The big media agency Universal McCann also has done some groundbreaking statistical analysis of the relationship between word of mouth and advertising. This work was sufficiently innovative that UM and its client, Sony, were honored in 2010 with a Gold WOMMY award from the Word of

Mouth Marketing Association. A top-five media agency, UM is part of the IPG Mediabrands group of Interpublic and is in the business of selecting and buying media that are most likely to drive business results for its clients, Sony being one of its largest. They won the WOMMY award for the best use of research to drive word of mouth because UM's Graeme Hutton was the first to publish a model that demonstrated the ability of advertising expenditures to drive word-of-mouth levels for a brand.

The purpose of the modeling was to explain how advertising by Sony and its competitors impacts word of mouth, and to do so both at the aggregate level and by media type. Such insights help UM optimize its media spending for many of its clients. Each time, the aim is to create a mechanism by which UM can predict word-of-mouth brand mentions from three separate perspectives: (1) to test the degree to which advertising expenditures can predict WOM; (2) to measure the impact of advertising expenditures by competitive brands; and (3) to compare the return on investment for media types (i.e., TV, online, print). Taken together, this helps UM recommend spending levels and media buys that will drive more positive advocacy, and with it greater sales for Sony, and to do so based on science and not serendipity.

UM's statistical analysis produced the following insights for Sony:

- Approximately two-thirds (63 percent) of Sony's potential WOM is unrelated to advertising, and instead involves people talking about their own personal experience or seasonal variation (e.g., more talk about consumer electronics around big gift-giving times such as the holidays) in WOM levels.

- Of the remainder, 14 percent of all Sony Electronics' WOM was driven by its own advertising.

- Sony's WOM is eroded by 23 percent due to the impact of competitors' advertising. In other words, in the same way that Sony's advertising can drive word of mouth, advertising by the competition can erode Sony's word of mouth as people talk about competitive brands instead.

Chart 5.9

SOURCES OF SONY WOM

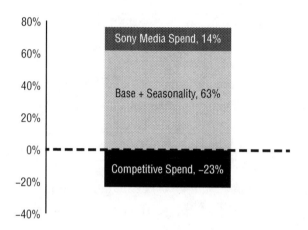

Source: UM regression analysis of Keller Fay Group's TalkTrack®, Kantar & AdRelevance.

UM's finding about the relative importance of Sony's advertising versus the impact of competitive spending is quite an important insight. UM has estimated that every $6 million that Sony invests in advertising (whether it be TV, digital, magazine, out of home, or radio), Sony's WOM will increase by 1 percent, or 58 million conversations. At the same time, for every $59 million spent by competitors, Sony's WOM decreases by 1 percent, or 58 million conversations. Looked at another way, that's about $0.10 of Sony spending and $1.02 of competitor spending associated with each Sony conversation.

While these results are Sony-specific, UM has created similar models for other clients in other categories. The results vary, but a similar set of dynamics is at play, with the lessons being (a) that an investment in advertising can drive positive word of mouth for brands, and (b) it's important not only to look at your own investment, but to do so in a competitive context. There is truly a competitive risk associated with *not* advertising sufficiently.

According to UM's Hutton, "The negative effect of competitive activity is a major feature we see in many of our WOM models. . . . Prior to our developing models such as these, we had hypothesized that advertising-generated WOM would be similar to ad awareness. It is generally accepted in the industry that a brand's own media advertising is the prime driver of its ad awareness and the effect of competitive activity is comparatively small. But these types of models imply competitive activity has a significant effect on WOM. This implies that ad-generated WOM models behave quite differently to ad awareness models. If anything, arguably, word of mouth models are closer to sales models."

Brands that decide to save money in the short term by reducing advertising expenditures may find their competition taking over the conversation about the category. The danger of *not* being talked about is at least as great as the opportunity to be a leading topic of conversation.

Advertising in a Social Context

We believe that any media, at any time of day, has the potential to influence consumer conversations and word-of-mouth recommendations. News, entertainment, and advertising can provide us with information and ideas that we will naturally want to share with each other. For a media planner or buyer, however, it makes sense to choose the media with the best chance to influence conversations, and a critical consideration is this: Which media are most apt to reach us when other people are available to talk? It's common sense that we are most likely to talk about ads that we see when we are with another person, and perhaps even looking for something to talk about.

In a study conducted for NBC Universal, described in chapter 4, it was determined that conversations inspired by TV commercials happen immediately (31 percent) or somewhat later (24 percent) relative to exposure on television. Those immediate conversations, in particular, are not likely to happen when a consumer is watching alone. In an era in which people have TVs in every room and on every device, it is harder to reach consumers who are co-viewing. Nevertheless some programming still pulls audiences that cross gender and generational lines, such as the Olympics, football and other live sports, children's programming that is often watched by parents and children together, and reality programs such as *American Idol,* itself the biggest word-of-mouth program on television as of the end of the 2010–2011 season, thanks to lots of conversations among family members.

But television is not the only medium that reaches people in a conversational context. The British trade association for advertising agencies is the Institute of Practitioners in Advertising, or IPA. Starting in 2006 they have undertaken three large-scale multimedia research studies called TouchPoints. (A fourth such study is under way as of the time of writing.) The third wave, which was conducted in 2010, was expanded to include WOM-related insights.

At the heart of TouchPoints is a diary administered via mobile device that reminds participants every thirty minutes to record what they were doing the previous half hour. Among other items, the diary includes the media they were using as well as whether respondents were having conversations of any kind. The new data provide the first window we've ever had into what specific types of media are most likely to reach consumers when they are conversing with others, and at what times of day they are talking. Throughout the entire day, 32 percent of people are having conversations during each half hour, on average, including at night. But during half-hour intervals when media are being consumed, an average of 45 percent of people also engage in conversation. In other words, people are more likely to be having conversations at or close to the time they are consuming media. This confirms an important theory: that media and conversation often go together. Based on the opportunity to measure both conversation and media exposure throughout the day, the study finds that there is wide variation in the "sociability" of some media versus others, and across different times of day.

Chart 5.10

CONVERSATIONS MORE LIKELY TO TAKE PLACE AT TIMES WHEN
MEDIA ARE BEING CONSUMED

Percentage of people having conversations during each half hour on an
average day

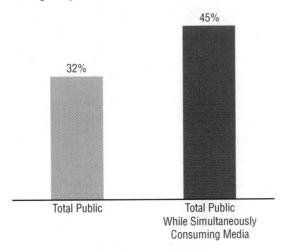

Total Public	Total Public While Simultaneously Consuming Media
32%	45%

Source: IPA TouchPoints3, United Kingdom.

It turns out that the Internet and radio are the most sociable media because people are most apt to be having conversations close to the time they are using the Internet and listening to the radio. In fact about half of all Internet and radio use occurs during half hours when people are also talking. Television also is above average in terms of sociability, although not quite at the same level. Magazines and newspapers are the least sociable, with usage happening only about one-third of those time periods when people are conversing. This latter finding will not surprise anybody who's been chided for the "antisocial" behavior of reading the morning paper at the breakfast table while in the presence of others.

Time of day matters a lot too. The sociability of the Internet peaks above 60 percent between the morning hours of 8:30 and 11, when people are generally starting their workday, turning on the computer, and saying hello to their coworkers. The sociability of television peaks in early morning and early evening, during breakfast and dinner hours, when people are preparing and eating meals together, often while the television is on. The early evening dinner hours seem to have an advantage over the later prime-time period, when family members are more apt to move into separate rooms to watch their own favorite TV programs.

Armed with insights such as these—the TouchPoints surveys are now ongoing in the United States and the United Kingdom—advertisers interested in encouraging word of mouth can better connect with consumers by making media buys according to when and where people are more likely to be in a social context. Doing so can achieve the benefit of more engagement and recommendations generated by their advertising.

The Medium Is Us

One of the most frequently quoted phrases in the media world is "The medium is the message," from the communications guru Marshall McLuhan in his 1964 book, *Understanding Media: The Extensions of Man*. The phrase is often taken to mean that the communications channels (television, Internet, magazine) are more *important* than content, a powerful idea in a world of rapid growth and constant change relating to the channels available to people and to marketers.

But McLuhan meant something else altogether. In his view, the message is based on human language, and human beings are part of the media process; media technologies are merely an extension of people. On the first page of *Understanding Media* he wrote, "The personal and social consequences of any medium—that is, of any extension of ourselves—result from the new scale that is introduced into our affairs by each extension of ourselves, or by any new technology." In his conception, communications tools such as the printing press, the telegraph, the radio, the telephone, and the television, as well as those that came after his book, such as the computer and the Internet—all have become extensions of ourselves, as hammers serve as extensions of our arms, to borrow another McLuhan analogy.

Thinking of people as media is fundamental to marketers seizing the word-of-mouth opportunity. Language was the medium that first enabled the efficient sharing of thoughts and ideas among people. Language and conversation are fundamental to all modern media tools—to the purpose they serve and to their impact on each of us individually, on our society, and on the marketplace.

In order to make media effective, we need to think of people first and of media as extensions of ourselves. Media strategies should have as their primary goal to stimulate further communication through conversation. The relationship between mass communication and human conversation and sharing ought to be seamless, and the most effective marketing campaigns will capitalize on this insight.

6

All Things in Moderation: Where Social Media Fits

In investing circles, social media has been the darling of the past few years, with companies like Facebook, Twitter, Zynga, and Groupon awash with money from Silicon Valley and Wall Street. Investors are betting that all the consumer eyeballs and engagement being captured by these companies will cause a massive shift in the marketing strategies for major brands that will direct spending from TV and other traditional media into social channels.

So far, however, social media's performance on behalf of advertisers has been more modest. Brands that have gone all-in on social, like the PepsiCo example in chapter 1, have gotten burned, while brands like Old Spice and Zappos that have taken more measured approaches to social media have fared better. Both Old Spice and Zappos are often heralded as masters of social media, and they may very well be, but they also understand that social media, while exciting and at times powerful, is but one channel among many and has to be considered as part of a holistic marketing approach that employs still very impactful traditional media, as demonstrated in chapters 4 and 5.

But let's face it: social media is the 800-pound gorilla in the room that dominates marketing discussions today. In this chapter we examine the pros and cons of social media marketing, looking at a few companies that have done it right and talk further about one that's done it wrong.

The biggest player in social media is Facebook, of course. We therefore begin our discussion of social media with Facebook's pitch to its marketing partners. One of the regular speakers on behalf of Facebook is Dan Rose, the company's vice president for partnerships and platform marketing. At a marketing event in April 2011, Rose took the stage to give an overview of the social network's impact on culture and business. He showed video of a wedding ceremony in which the bride and groom updated their Facebook relationship statuses before sealing their union in that more traditional way, with a kiss. And he told of the burglar who was arrested because he updated his location at a house he was robbing and didn't check out. Rose's broad point is that the message and the medium have become intertwined. Tools like Facebook aren't just about recording and communicating your activities; they *are* your activities.

"Have you noticed recently that your life online has started to mirror your life offline?" Rose asked the audience. "It didn't use to be that way. Today what we do online feels a lot like the way we live our lives."

After demonstrating Facebook's cultural reach, Rose turned to commerce, tallying up the small businesses for which Facebook has become a lifeline and the larger brands that have seen the needle move, thanks to installing "like" buttons and buying into Facebook's brand of social advertising. Rose quantified the impact in breathless terms. Citing the company's research, he said that when a friend's name pops up in a Facebook ad, the person looking at it is over 60 percent more likely to remember the ad and over four times more likely to purchase the product being promoted.

"This is word of mouth," he said. "This is word of mouth at scale. This is what, as marketers, we've always tried to bottle up. The social web is finally allowing us to do that." A little later he ramped up the rhetoric, saying, "This is word of mouth on steroids."

The fact that an executive from Facebook, the biggest player in social media, was declaring that what gets talked about on Facebook is indeed a part of word of mouth was somewhat surprising, though gratifying for those of us who have always believed in its power. But saying that Facebook enabled word of mouth on steroids? This is a redundant statement, in the sense that word of mouth is already marketing on steroids, and it ignores history to boot. As we've seen, word of mouth, whether offline or online, is an inherently steroidal dynamic and has been since before Elihu Katz and Paul Lazarsfeld first identified the two-step flow of mass communications hypothesis back in the 1950s. Word of mouth doesn't need Facebook to make it happen, any more than the sun needs the Earth to orbit around it. People have always relied on their social networks for ideas and news and information about products. Facebook is an important channel, but it's not the center of the word-of-mouth universe. Facebook is just one channel among many where that conversation goes on.

Also we've found that Rose's point about online mirroring offline isn't true. People simply behave differently online, especially in terms that are relevant to brands. Not only does the overwhelming amount of brand-related conversation occur offline, as we have discussed, but other behaviors are vastly different depending on whether someone is online or off, from the tonality applied, to the brands that people choose to talk about, to a whole host of nonverbal cues that denote meaning differently when conversations take place offline compared to online.

Rose's presentation, while dynamic and exciting, contained some key fallacies and misunderstandings that are rampant in the marketing world, which in the years since Facebook opened itself up to the non-collegiate world has taken up social media as a focal point. Marketers and agencies have rushed headlong into social media. They've hired legions of community managers and installed more senior executives to oversee social strategy. They've devoted more and more spending to Twitter and Facebook campaigns. Many have put social media at the center of their marketing strategies, regardless of whether such a move makes good sense in light of such factors as the brand's attributes, its category, the company culture, or how its consumers like to talk about brands. (You'll recall from chapter 1 that even Facebook's Paul Adams recommends against having a "Facebook strategy" or a "Twitter strategy," and instead recommends a "people strategy.")

Some marketers have been treating social media as a cure-all, thanks to a very hungry investor community that has driven the value of many of these companies sky-high and an industry press that's always been too eager to write off old but dependable marketing models and froth over new ones. As we write this, figuring out how to put a value on your brand's Facebook fans became the new Holy Grail, replacing one-to-one marketing, accountable advertising, engagement, and a long list of other bygone buzzwords as the quest du jour.

Some of the excitement is justified. You can't care about media and not be a bit wowed by the frenetic pace of growth and innovation at companies like Facebook and Twitter. But being excited without trying to ferret out what's real from what's hype is simply shortsighted. Facebook and Twitter very quickly assembled massive audiences, but behind those big numbers there are still largely unanswered questions about how valuable these audiences are from a commercial perspective. There is also a tendency on the part of many to be seduced by the lure of large numbers without looking under the hood to see what's really going on. As we noted in chapter 1, for example, there are brands with truly huge numbers of Facebook fans, tens of millions. However, a fall 2011 study found that of the total number of fans, only a very small percentage (typically 1 percent or fewer) are active.

To assume that because someone created a Facebook account she will want to be bombarded by marketing messages—even from friends—is wrongheaded, and can result in a lot of wasted energy, not to mention money. But at the same time, there is something to be said for the statistics that Facebook's Rose quotes in his speeches. They are compelling, and they should be part of today's consideration set for marketers. Success for any brand is a matter of striking the right balance for social media.

All in all, we believe that understanding social media is crucial for any business. In the customer service arena especially, social media is vital. But we caution against the belief that corporate Twitter feeds and Facebook fan campaigns are going to replace traditional marketing. To act rashly based on the hype is foolhardy. Though it may gain you a quick PR hit in the industry press and show some people that you "get it," evidence shows that it will come back to bite you in the long run.

How Does Apple Do It?

If you don't believe us, consider the case of Apple, which almost every audience we speak with correctly describes as a standout brand from a word-of-mouth perspective. Struggling miserably at the turn of the century, Apple was dubbed Marketer of the Decade in 2010 by *Ad Age*. How did it get there? In part by ignoring all the trends we're told to associate with twenty-first-century marketing. As of the middle of 2011, Apple did not have a company Facebook page. And Apple has maintained a relatively light Twitter presence, with two feeds, one dedicated to its App store and the other to its iTunes music store. The Twitter feeds are there to promote apps and music; they are not models of consumer engagement.

The lesson is simple and clear. Apple is laser-focused on product innovations, popularizing digital music with the iPod, exploding the computing capabilities of the mobile phone with the iPhone, realizing the potential of tablet computing with the iPad, and perfecting the laptop with the MacBook Air. To promote those innovations, Apple has maintained a traditional approach: clever, high-production value, creative advertising with high pass-along value, bolstered by a massive media budget. Apple's designers and engineers make great, dependable products that command a premium price, and Apple's marketing organization makes the gadgets cool. And Apple invests heavily in its retail stores, a number of which it says "have been designed and built to serve as high-profile venues to promote brand awareness and serve as vehicles for corporate sales and marketing activities."

Apple has long been known for innovative advertising, at least since its "1984" spot, directed by Ridley Scott, took on IBM, and more recently the ads featuring the "Mac" versus "PC" guys. The creative approach is to be hip and catchy. Perhaps more important, Apple's designers make the products noticeable, which allows them, in turn, to cue conversations (an idea we discussed in chapter 2).

The success has been all about marketing and product design fundamentals that spark huge amounts of offline conversations, not following every new trend that comes along. According to TalkTrack, Apple is the sixth most talked-about brand in America, fifth in the United Kingdom, and fourth in Australia, making it one of the few brands that hit the top-ten list in all three of these markets. And if we were to combine the Apple brand along with its subbrands—iPod, iTunes, iPad, and iPhone—Apple would be, corporately, number one in the United States, the United Kingdom, and Australia. That's quite an achievement for a company that eschews social media.

Of course, not every company has a visionary like Steve Jobs, or an Apple-size marketing budget, or a massive audience of fans who eagerly anticipate (and talk about) every move the company makes or is expected to make. Most everyone else has to work harder when it comes to getting consumers to talk about their products. Increasingly social media will be one of the ways to do that. But making social media a strategy rather than a tactical channel decision can be dangerous, as we saw with Pepsi and its Pepsi Refresh Project. By overcommitting to social media, Pepsi allowed Coke and Diet Coke, which continued to pound the airwaves with heavy presences on everything from the Super Bowl to *American Idol*, to capture the number one and two slots in market share. From Pepsi's perspective, the long-running Cola Wars, usually a competitive race, were being won in no uncertain terms by the enemy.

PepsiCo responded to the Coke coup by announcing it planned to spend 30 percent more on TV than in recent years, with much of it in support of Pepsi-Cola. Part of the increased spending was to get Pepsi back into the Super Bowl, with a push for Pepsi Max, a diet cola. Pepsi's Super Bowl offerings in 2011 included men, one of them the actor Matthew McConaughey, enjoying Pepsi's taste without calories, and then being punished humorously for their less virtuous, womanizing behaviors. Those ads did well, earning Pepsi Max the seventh largest increase in word of mouth the week after the Super Bowl among forty-two advertisers measured in our TalkTrack Super Bowl study. Later in the year Pepsi execs were telling the *Wall Street Journal* about plans for a new campaign for the flagship Pepsi brand and signed on as a sponsor for the *X Factor*, Simon Cowell's new TV reality show in the mold of *American Idol*, at a reported cost of $60 million. Big-time advertising and sponsorship was back.

After the change, in January 2011, Shiv Singh, head of digital for Pepsi's North American operations, told the *New York Times* that Refresh wasn't meant to move cans of Pepsi after all. "It was designed to drive brand health," he said. Reflecting an evolving strategy at Pepsi, in November of that year Singh wrote on the *Harvard Business Review* blog, "Fewer and fewer advertisers will start their strategic marketing planning with a television advertisement in mind. Instead, they'll step back and begin with an engagement strategy that gets operationalized through a series of creative ideas that then get routed through different channels." That may be true of TV, but it also needs to be said for social media as well. The big lesson of Pepsi Refresh is that brands shouldn't begin with social media engagement as their primary goal, but with an idea that, as Singh wrote, can live in a number of different channels. The strategy should be about engaging people with ideas they will want to share with others, and using all appropriate vehicles that will encourage them to do so.

Pepsi learned the hard way that traditional mass media is still a powerful weapon for driving engagement, word of mouth—and sales.

Social Media's Shortcomings

Let's step back for a moment and look at how social media performs—or underperforms—in marketing contexts.

Since the rise of Twitter and Facebook, brands have adopted social media marketing in a variety of ways. Some, like Pepsi, have done a cannonball into the pool without checking the depth and thrown lots of resources behind social media. Others have taken a more measured approach, using social as a complement to other marketing activities. Still others, like Apple, pretty much stay out of the fray, letting their customers do the chattering on their own while sticking to those marketing and product fundamentals that have driven that company's now astronomical value.

The brands doing it right—and we'll look in depth at a couple later in this chapter—occupy the middle ground. They use social media as a listening channel to see what's being said about them, but not at the expense of knowing what's being talked about offline, in real life. They use it to supplement other media to distribute coupons and promotions or share product news. They use it as a customer-service channel to help communicate with people who have product problems or questions, but not at the expense of in-store or phone-based customer service; those people who want to tweet to get the attention of customer service representatives should be serviced that way, but the vast majority who prefer other channels should not be ignored. If we are going to put people at the center, we need to realize that most people don't have social media at the center of their lives.

With respect to channel mix, the right approach is a hybrid one, as was observed in 2011 by the digital guru Steve Rubel, an executive with Edelman Public Relations. "Social-media marketing," he said, "is getting boring—at least by itself. It still largely sits in a silo and therefore fails to realize its full potential." He continued, "What many fail to see is that the dirty little secret of social media, according to a study by researchers at HP, is that most conversations are driven by media outlets, not individuals." Rubel also pointed to the proliferation of social media how-to books "that read like get-rich-quick schemes."

The brands doing it wrong fail to see through the hype. They're missing some key shortcomings of social media as a marketing tool, as we'll explore next.

Not a Sales Tool

Back in 2009 the computer manufacturer Dell announced that it made $3 million in sales off of one of its Twitter feeds, then about 600,000 followers strong. Anyone waiting for the announcement to herald a new day in social media return on investment is probably still waiting. Few if any major marketers have followed in Dell's footsteps and described to the marketing community just how social media is ringing registers. Marketers these days are more likely to follow Pepsi's Singh and tell you that social is not a sales channel. Singh has also declared that the value of Facebook friends or fans is minimal at best. Sally Dickerson of Omnicom's BrandScience unit, which advises companies on media decisions, goes one step further, declaring the value of a Facebook fan as "zero."

The first thing for companies to note about social media is that there's little to no evidence available showing that it drives sales. Quite the contrary, there's a growing body of evidence showing that it doesn't. One of the most compelling examples we've seen on this was a study of online holiday shoppers from Forrester, the technology research group, and GSI Commerce, a provider of e-commerce and interactive marketing services for the world's premier brands and retailers. Those firms looked at purchase data from fifteen GSI clients during the 2010 holiday season. They found that about eight in ten purchases came after some interaction with digital marketing, but only a small portion of that had anything to do with social media. Traditional digital tactics like search and email marketing were most crucial, followed by affiliate marketing and display ads. Social networks were the least important.

The report concluded, "The truth is that social tactics were largely ineffective in driving sales." In a conversation with the social media news blog Mashable, GSI executive Fiona Dias put it in even blunter terms: "It's been a mystery to me why the media is excited about social media. From a retail and commerce perspective, it seems to have no effect."

Chart 6.1

TOUCH POINTS PRIOR TO CONVERSION USED BY
WEB SHOPPERS

Source: Sucharita Mulpuru, "The Purchase Path of Online Buyers," Forrester Research, Inc., March 16, 2011. Data based on single touch point for hard goods.

Not a Mirror to the Real World

If social media isn't a sales tool, then what is its use for a brand? Social media executives and advocates will argue that social media is more about building trust and engaging with consumers. We agree that Twitter and Facebook can be highly useful as conversation channels. But to have that conversation and earn that trust, consumers first have to be willing to talk about your brand and your product through that channel.

The problem is, as studies have found, online consumers aren't equally interested in all product categories. As we discussed in chapter 1, in 2010 Keller Fay Group contributed to an ambitious academic research project that compared offline conversations about brands with online conversations, and found that just three categories—technology, cars, and entertainment—accounted for two-thirds of all the online conversation about brands. That's a dramatically different situation from offline, where conversation is far more evenly distributed across more categories. For example, whereas beverages account for 13 percent of offline word of mouth, they account for only 3 percent of online conversations. Other categories that see similar gaps are beauty, food and dining, retail, and apparel. Based on this, we'd argue that if you're a tech marketer, an investment in a social media presence makes good sense, although our data make clear that you need to be mindful of offline conversations as well, since far more conversations will be taking place that way, even in tech. If you work for a beauty brand, the most effective social media approach is less clear.

Because online word of mouth behavior isn't an accurate proxy for offline, heavy expenditures of money or human resources in social media shouldn't be an automatic reflex. In an increasingly resource-starved marketing world, why waste time trying to talk to your customer base about something they don't want to talk—or, more accurately, tweet—about? More productive investments can be made in other channels that are known to drive word of mouth, for example, advertising, promotions, or in-store media (as we've shown in chapters 4 and 5).

One very clear indication of just how different are the worlds of offline and online conversations comes from an analysis of the most talked about brands of 2010, as measured in TalkTrack (factoring in both offline and online conversations), versus the most social online brands of 2010, as measured by Vitrue, a social media management company (see Chart 6.2).

Chart 6.2

TOP 10 SOCIAL BRANDS (2010): SOCIAL MEDIA VS. ALL WORD OF MOUTH

	SOCIAL MEDIA	WORD OF MOUTH
1	iPhone	Coca-Cola
2	BlackBerry	Walmart
3	Disney	Verizon
4	Android	AT&T
5	iPad	Pepsi
6	Sony	Ford
7	Apple	Apple
8	MTV	McDonald's
9	Coca-Cola	Sony
10	Samsung	Dell

Source: Social Media data from Vitrue. Word of Mouth data from Keller Fay Group's TalkTrack®, 2010.

What the data show, clearly, is that the two sets of rankings are vastly different:

- Only three brands are in the top ten for both lists: Sony, Apple, and Coca-Cola.

- Only six brands are in the top twenty on both lists (the three mentioned above, plus Samsung, Ford, and iPod).

- Looking across the ten most social brands, the average ranking when it comes to all word of mouth is 82. The biggest disconnect is Android, which is the fourth most social brand online but drops to 400 on the list of most talked-about brands offline and online.

The message is clear. The world of social media is not a mirror image of the real world, as Facebook's Dan Rose says. It's a part of people's world—for some a central part, but for most others, not. For marketers who wish to put people at the center of their campaigns, they need to think holistically about how, where, and when people engage in conversation, and not just about the social silo.

Social Media Is Primarily about People

In 2011 IBM published a report that clearly highlighted a gap in the perceptions of consumers and business when it comes to social media. "Getting closer to customers is a top priority for CEOs," according to the IBM CEO Study. "Today's businesses are fervently building social media programs to do just this. But are customers as enthusiastic?" In a word, no, says IBM: "What we discovered may come as a surprise to those companies that assume consumers are seeking them out to feel connected to their brand."

IBM surveyed consumers about their social media use, asking them to identify the reasons they go to social networking sites. By a wide margin, the top reason, and perhaps unsurprisingly, was to connect with family and friends, cited by 70 percent of the respondents, reinforcing the notion that social networking is about personal (offline) connections. The next most popular reason is to access news and entertainment, cited by about half. You have to go way down the list, to the tenth spot, to find anything about brands, with a quarter of consumers (23 percent) saying they use social media so they can interact with brands.

IBM's researchers then did an interesting reality test. They asked a sample of business people why they think consumers follow their brand's social activities, and then asked consumers why they really did so. The perception gap was stark. Sixty-four percent of business executives think consumers interact with them on social media to feel more "connected" to the brand, when in fact only 33 percent of consumers say that is the case. Sixty-one percent of businesses think consumers follow them to be "part of a community"; in fact that is the least important reason why consumers say they connect with businesses socially. Instead, consumers told IBM, they mainly go to a company's social site to hunt for discounts (61 percent) and—this is better news—to make purchases (55 percent). Both of these categories rank at the very bottom of businesses' perceptions.

Chart 6.3

MISMATCH BETWEEN WHAT CONSUMERS VALUE FROM SOCIAL SITES AND WHAT BUSINESSES THINK CONSUMERS VALUE

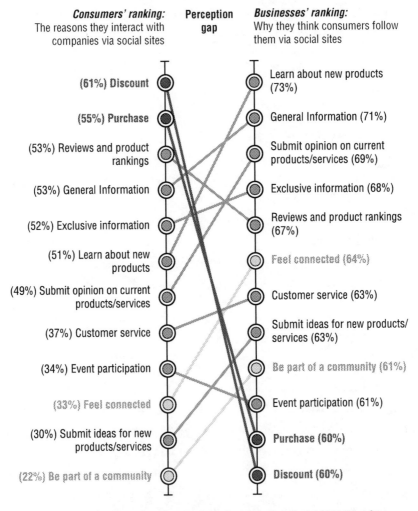

Consumers' ranking:
The reasons they interact with companies via social sites

Perception gap

Businesses' ranking:
Why they think consumers follow them via social sites

(61%) Discount
(55%) Purchase
(53%) Reviews and product rankings
(53%) General Information
(52%) Exclusive information
(51%) Learn about new products
(49%) Submit opinion on current products/services
(37%) Customer service
(34%) Event participation
(33%) Feel connected
(30%) Submit ideas for new products/services
(22%) Be part of a community

Learn about new products (73%)
General Information (71%)
Submit opinion on current products/services (69%)
Exclusive information (68%)
Reviews and product rankings (67%)
Feel connected (64%)
Customer service (63%)
Submit ideas for new products/services (63%)
Be part of a community (61%)
Event participation (61%)
Purchase (60%)
Discount (60%)

Source: Carolyn Heller and Gautam Parasnis, "From Social Media to Social CRM: What Customers Want," IBM Global Business Services, Executive Report, IBM Corporation, 2011.

What can we conclude from this? To the rather modest degree that consumers are interacting with companies in the social media sphere, they're most often looking for two things: to get coupons and to buy stuff. They're also looking for product reviews, which are often closely associated with e-commerce sites as well.

There's good news and bad news here. While there is clear transactional potential, social media isn't shaping up to be a great place to build a brand. Instead it is a place for consumers to get a deal. The other thing worth noticing in this study is how far companies are from understanding consumer motivation in the social environment, which makes the programs that rely on it so often misguided. As the study phrases it, "Businesses hoping to foster closer customer connections through social media conversations may be mistakenly projecting their own desires for intimacy onto customers' motivations for interacting. Interactions with businesses are not the same as interactions with friends. Most consumers are not motivated brand advocates who connect with a company primarily to feel associated with a brand community."

The IBM study should dash the misguided way of thinking in a case study like that of Pepsi Refresh, where product-focused marketing is replaced by gauzy notions of relationships, and should cause marketers to realize the large numbers of people they see on Facebook and Twitter should not be mistaken for an audience clamoring to connect with brands.

Social Media Scales. Or Does It?

In his 2011 speech Facebook's Dan Rose made the point that Facebook "scales" word of mouth. When people at Facebook talk about scale they're usually referring to the more than half-billion people who use the social network. There's no arguing with Rose's point that Facebook has signed up a ton of users. So has Twitter. Foursquare is getting there, and MySpace had a ton and then lost them. The big audiences are certainly assets for traditional forms of paid advertising, particularly when targeted based on the needs and interests of the users. This is a source of great value. But how much of the value comes from consumer-to-consumer advice on these social networking platforms?

It has been estimated that there are 256 billion brand impressions created per year via status updates, tweets, and other mentions on social networking sites, according to Forrester's Josh Bernoff and Ted Schadler in their 2010 book, *Empowered*. They too believe that one of the most attractive things about social media is that it scales. Maybe there is a lot more word of mouth that takes place offline, they say, but if one person tells something to a few real-world friends, the impact is fairly limited; if someone tells something to a few hundred friends on Facebook, the message travels far wider, and faster. At least, that's the argument.

But our research has found that this way of thinking is flawed, and for a large number of reasons, many of which we have already discussed in this book. Among them:

- Face-to-face communication has far greater impact, in terms of perceived credibility and likelihood to take action, than just reading something online.

- The fact that advertising and other forms of marketing spark so much word of mouth means that the right type of campaign, with significant reach, can unleash a huge number of offline conversations, making the question of scale a nonissue, as in the Apple example.

- Most people on Facebook keep in a close contact with only about four people per week, as Facebook's Adams told WOMMA's School of WOM in 2011.

- The greatest impact is created by people's close personal connections, not the far wider number of loose connections, according to McKinsey & Company.

But even beyond these arguments, there remains another big and important question. When marketers salivate over the large numbers of online friends that theoretically read updates when someone is motivated to post a status update about a brand, there is an assumption that every one of a person's online friends (or most of them) reads every update, "like," or "tweet" in social media. That is the assumption in Forrester's estimates of social media "impressions" in *Empowered*. But is this true? As the advertising research pioneer Dr. Daniel Starch observed in a seminal 1914 book, *Advertising: Its Principles, Practices and Techniques*, "For an ad to be effective, it must be seen and read." To understand the extent to which social media scales, we need to know how many of those Facebook status updates or tweets are at least being noticed.

To figure this out, the Keller Fay Group conducted an informal experiment to see if Facebook satisfied Dr. Starch's observation. We posted a version of this message on our own Facebook pages: "Hi friends. Please help me with a research project. If you see this, please just click 'like' on my status. It's that simple. Thanks!" Then we waited forty-eight hours to see how many of our friends noticed and "liked" our post, as requested. The average turned out to be fewer than 10 percent. We then expanded our test to include the Facebook pages of our clients, and quite a number of students at universities when we lecture to marketing classes. The results remained the same. While we would need to conduct a study with a larger and nationally representative sample to draw a definitive conclusion, this test serves as a useful reminder that all the gigantic numbers that get thrown around about the size of various social networks do not lead automatically to an impact that is anywhere near that large.

Just as you wouldn't expect that an entire reported circulation of a newspaper would see an ad, the same is true for newer forms of media. When brands are planning social media outreach campaigns and seek to calculate the potential impact, they should not look at the total audience size but base their calculations on the much smaller percentage of people who are actually going to see the message.

Old Spice: The Right Way to Use Social Media

Having established some of the weaknesses of social media in marketing contexts, let's look at a pair of marketers who have used the channel most effectively.

Over the past couple of years, the case study of choice for the social marketing community has come from Old Spice, the seventy-two-year-old cologne brand that got consumers talking about it again with a wildly successful and effective campaign for its line of body wash products for men. A campaign called "The Man Your Man Could Smell Like" has become something every marketer wants to replicate. Starring a smooth-talking, well-toned former NFL player, Isaiah Mustafa, the effort has captivated customers and the marketing industry alike, winning numerous industry awards and spiking Old Spice sales. Its most lauded execution was an ingenious digital program that had celebrities and everyday folks tweet questions and comments at Mustafa that would then be acted out in near real time and broadcast on YouTube. For a second consecutive year, in 2011 Old Spice was ranked as the most viral brand of the year, receiving nearly 96 million "views" on YouTube, according to the firm Visible Measures. It has been a stunning achievement in writing and production that came with real business results. The campaign's success was immediately interpreted as yet another victory for social media over traditional media. But you don't have to look too hard to see that's not entirely the case. Put simply, the success would not have been possible without an integrated approach that involved smart consumer research and an excellent creative idea delivered in a heavy broadcast presence with a smart social media component.

The insight that powered the campaign came a few years before its implementation, when executives at Gillette, a Procter & Gamble unit, focused on Old Spice–branded deodorants and body washes. They realized that in order to improve sales they had to reach women as well as men. Wives, girlfriends, and mothers, they realized, are important decision makers and influencers for male soap and body wash purchases, and they often do the buying themselves, making more than half of purchases in the category. Our research further shows that when it comes to word of mouth about grooming products, men turn disproportionately to women (not other men) for advice, and they are far more likely to believe and act upon the advice of women.

So beginning in early 2010, Old Spice brand managers decided on a strategy of reaching men and women at the same time, by getting their ads into programming that couples watch together. This not only helped ensure that the ads were seen by a dual audience, but it also increased the chances of a conversation ensuing between the couple, consistent with our advice about TV co-viewing in chapter 5.

The campaign featuring Mustafa launched online over Super Bowl weekend in February 2010 and showed up shortly thereafter in event television programming, like *Lost* and *American Idol* and the 2010 Winter Olympics. It wasn't until July 2010, with the character firmly embedded in the consumer psyche, that Old Spice really laid on the social media marketing. So the campaign was already generating offline word of mouth well before the official social phase began. Between January and March 2010 the brand captured 75 percent of the conversations in its category, with half of those including conversations with women.

In a three-day production Mustafa and the Old Spice and Wieden & Kennedy agency teams created 186 custom messages based on interactions with tweeters and Facebook users, both unknown and famous. Within weeks of being posted, those videos had gotten 40 million views on YouTube, on top of the 30 million views snatched up by the original four TV commercials.

That's genuine reach, the kind that had industry folks crowing that Old Spice had pulled off the most successful social media campaign ever. And it resulted in real sales success in the period following the launch of the campaign. *Adweek* reported on Nielsen data that had Old Spice body wash products up a whopping 107 percent in July, the month that two new TV spots and the online response videos launched, and for the twelve months ending in July 2010 sales were up 11 percent. "Our business is on fire," Old Spice brand manager James

Moorhead told the publication. "We've seen strong results over all of our portfolio. That is the reward for the great work." But Old Spice didn't leave it there. When the 2011 Super Bowl rolled around, Old Spice took advantage of all the good buzz with a new advertisement.

David Hallerman, an analyst at eMarketer, offered a useful insight, writing in *AdAge*, "The overall lesson for brand marketers from the Old Spice campaign is its well-stirred mix of the three media. Paid media, advertising both online and offline, are often essential in encouraging usage of owned media (brand sites or pages) and setting the spark—if the creative is hot enough—for earned media (word of mouth). Therefore, developing a campaign from day one with coordinated plans for all three media types improves the odds of boosting a brand's image, awareness, recognition, and consumer favorability."

The coordination was indeed crucial. Old Spice took strong advantage of the viral and interactive qualities that social media offer, but not at the expense of traditional media or crucial parts of the ad-making process that often get lost in the social media hype, like consumer insights. Remember that the Old Spice campaign was powered by the observation that women were key decision makers and had to be reached. Everything followed from that. And each individual piece was important. That insight led to the hilarious creative idea and execution that developed the character and made the ads worth talking about; the paid media in high-profile programs created awareness and sparked conversation. The social media strategy was the icing on the cake, creating additional online viewing that triggered considerable levels of social media interaction.

This campaign reinforces a concept that Pat LaPointe of MarketShare, the market mix modeling consultants, calls "the rock in the pond" phenomenon, whereby traditional media messages start conversations that then reverberate throughout the social spectrum "like shock waves through a still pond hit by a rock." The ripple effect then adds to the overall impact of the traditional media message and boosts its financial payback. But, warns LaPointe, it's easy to miss this interaction effect if you look at the impact of social media in isolation and not in conjunction with traditional media. "This can cause many marketers to underestimate the real value of the traditional media and over-estimate the digital elements—in some cases by as much as 40 percent."

At its heart, Old Spice created an integrated campaign that worked across media. To label it a social media campaign, though not entirely incorrect, is to miss the whole story of its success.

Zappos: How a Word-of-Mouth Company Uses Social Media

Conventional wisdom in consumer and industry circles holds that Zappos is one of those rare marketers that use social media well. Tony Hsieh, the company's founder and CEO, is seen as something of a Twitter god, using his Twitter feed to promote Zappos as a product as well as his way of thinking about business (also expressed in his book, *Delivering Happiness: A Path to Profits, Passion, and Purpose*) to his many followers. Moreover Hsieh and his lieutenants have encouraged Zappos employees of all seniority levels to start their own Twitter feeds. Social media boosters have eaten this stuff up. Reading the press and the blogs, you'd think that Zappos's fast growth and appeal to Amazon, which purchased Zappos in 2009 for just under $900 million, was largely a function of the company's adeptness on Twitter.

But that's just the conventional wisdom. When you dig down, you find that the story is a lot more nuanced.

In fact Hsieh says that he dislikes the term "social media." He dislikes it so much that anyone who uses it around him at Zappos owes him a dollar. But it's not just the term he dislikes; it's the whole idea of it, "the social media hype," as he calls it. Fundamentally, Hsieh says, Zappos doesn't think about itself as a high-tech company, preferring to consider its strategy a "high-touch" approach.

Aaron Magness, head of business development and brand marketing at Zappos, describes it as a "social company," but he doesn't worry about having a social media strategy. He said, "We have a communications strategy and we ask 'What are the best tools to execute it?'"

Zappos puts a good chunk of the budget a company of its size might spend on marketing into customer service, using it to pay for free customer shipping on both purchases and returns, often via overnight delivery that is intended to surprise and delight customers who are expecting the package to arrive in a few days. This benefit has been a key part of Zappos's appeal and has led to Zappos becoming, in Magness's words, a "word-of-mouth company."

Social media plays into that, but it is not the only tool used; it isn't even the main tool. Social media amplifies the good conversations already happening because of the company's excellent customer service. Magness even says that the ideal way of communicating with consumers is face-to-face. "In a perfect world," he says, "every time someone places an order a Zappos employee would get in their car, drive to the house and thank the customer for the order. Now that's obviously not practical." He adds, "We wish we could talk to every customer to see how their day went." Hsieh considers the telephone to be a very underutilized resource for most companies. "Everyone is trying to figure out how to get their brand to stand out. We think the telephone is one of best branding devices out there." It allows for what he calls "P-E-C": creating a "personal, emotional connection" between the call center rep and the customer. Emotional connection is a critical idea here, because, as we discussed earlier, there is a growing body of research to suggest that emotions are central to people's sharing of stories and word of mouth, as well as their purchasing decisions.

Again, it is not practical to create a strategy that would permit a company representative to talk on the phone with every customer. And this is where Facebook, Twitter, and YouTube factor in: they are logical extensions of Zappos's "customer first" mentality, adding an additional way to listen and talk to customers. What's important is the way Zappos gets there. Hsieh and Magness don't begin with the assumption that social media are the right channels; rather they end up there at the logical conclusion of a process. Furthermore they don't use social media exclusively.

The company takes its call center operations seriously, teaching reps how to satisfy customers and giving them the tools to do so. For instance, there are no time limits on calls, thus avoiding the aggravating experience of being hurried off. Reps are taught to act human and be helpful. Hsieh likes to illustrate this point with a story about a pizza. He was at a hotel with a group one night when someone said he wanted pizza. It was too late to get room service, and Hsieh suggested (only half in jest) that the person call Zappos and ask for a pizza to be delivered. The obvious response from the rep on the phone would be to say "We don't sell pizzas," but at Zappos the culture is to create customer "happiness" and think creatively about how to do so. In this case, the rep found a local pizza place that delivered the pizza. It is in an effort to create such moments of surprise and delight that Zappos spends so heavily on training at its call centers.

So while social media is important to Zappos's customer service reputation, it is not everything, a point worth noting in a marketing world where social media is often thought of as a must-have and where there's pressure to make social media a central part of every campaign. Zappos's way of thinking promotes a holistic approach to media that values the old as well as the new. For Zappos, that has meant a fair amount of advertising, including a heavy presence in magazines.

You read that right. Zappos, darling of the social media world, still believes in print. Stop the presses. Or, rather, start them again.

On a personal level, Magness himself remains a big fan of print magazines, and he discovered that the typical Zappos customer, a married forty-year-old woman with a high household income, shares his enthusiasm. She can still most easily be found flipping through the pages of *Glamour* and *Redbook* and *Us Weekly*, not lingering on Facebook. In response to those who might question an Internet-based company's decision to invest so heavily in print, Magness says, "If you're true to what you're trying to accomplish it's about being complementary rather than trying to take away from what you've done in the past." Knowing that magazines are a medium rich in word-of-mouth influencers (see chapter 3), it should come as no surprise that an investment in magazine advertising, combined with excellent customer service, would be a winning strategy for a word-of-mouth company like Zappos.

Zappos's use of media also extends to TV. In 2010 Zappos launched a TV campaign targeted to channels like Bravo and TLC because they recognized that smart advertising is a powerful conversational spark. And these cable networks, like print, have audiences that are rich in influencers. Zappos, long known as a shoe seller, needed to get across the point that it also sells plenty of clothing. So after conducting an agency review, it took to the airwaves with an offbeat campaign starring a cast of puppets that freaked some folks out. But this was okay with Magness, even though he was surprised by the widespread puppet fear. He used that fear as a talking point for conversations with customers. More important, the ads helped define Zappos as a more diversified retailer in the minds of its existing and potential customers.

Significantly, Magness does not believe that Zappos could get the reach it needs without advertising—in other words, if it had to rely solely on social media. It's worth quoting him at length on this matter, because his perspective really underscores some of the shortcomings discussed throughout this book: "When you look at successful marketing in social media, for the most part what it's around is discount, coupons, offers, things like that. That's not the Zappos brand. We don't offer coupons and we don't discount. As great as Twitter is, it's sort of limiting. You have a better job at telling the story in print than you do in 140 characters. So I don't know if it has the same impact or reach in as authentic way."

It is powerful stuff when the top marketer for what's known as a social media–made brand states that social media alone cannot deliver on the company's business goals. Zappos goes about things in a different way. It doesn't engage in Facebook campaigns with the goal of winning fans. In fact Zappos makes it rather hard to be a Zappos fan. You can't do it from the Zappos website. You have to actually go to Facebook, search for the page, and then push the "like" button.

"We know that if we had two million fans, our reach would be how many times more than what it is today," Magness admits. "But what we also know is that it would be rather diluted. Our fan is someone who has been on Facebook and searched us out. All those Facebook consultants will tell you what the true value of a fan is, when it comes down to it, I don't think people really know. So as opposed to risking our authenticity we'd rather just stay true to who we are and keep plugging away."

What does it mean that Zappos needs paid, traditional advertising to meet its business goals? A major lesson here is not to confuse the industry story with the consumer story. The marketing industry learned about Zappos in part because of its early adoption of Twitter. The customers who keep it in business learn about it because of the great offline word of mouth it receives for its customer service. Customers don't care about its marketing approach. And many of those folks are best reached by paid advertising. Magness confirms this: "If we were to send an email out to all of our customers asking who Zappos's CEO is, I'm willing to bet 95 percent have no idea. But around the Twitter world, everybody knows Tony. It's a different approach. I think the woman reading Oprah's *O* magazine may not know."

To our minds, Zappos and Old Spice represent the way brands should be thinking about social media today. The crucial thing to remember about social media is that it is, at most, a complement to brand and marketing fundamentals. To properly tell the story of your brand and spark conversation, you'll most certainly need the time-tested tools of marketers that have the reach and persuasive power to get the job done.

7

_____

Word of Mouth
as a Channel

D uring the 1990s, as the dot-com boom was taking shape, Jupiter Communications was one of the leading firms marketers turned to when they wanted to understand what impact
the rise of the emerging media technologies would have on the way
consumers were spending their time and money, and the impact all
this would have on their businesses. In fact Jupiter is credited with
being the first to predict just how transformative dial-up access to the
Internet would be, and it was early to predict America Online's domi-
nance in the consumer online services market. Jupiter prided itself on
understanding AOL better than anyone else, and as AOL grew in size
and influence, so did Jupiter. The rest, as everyone knows, is history.
AOL rose rapidly to become the king of the new media hill, with a
large enough market capitalization to take the dominant position in
its 2000 merger with traditional media powerhouse Time Warner, a
deal that still ranks as one of the biggest corporate mergers in history,
even though the merger did not ultimately live up to its fanfare.

Gene DeRose was one of the first hires at Jupiter. An English literature major from the University of Virginia, he joined the company
in 1989 as a report editor. Within days of his arrival, however, the
head of research quit, and DeRose was promoted to that position. He
continued to rise quickly, and a few years later he had risen to become

the company's CEO. *Info Week* credited DeRose with making Jupiter "one of the fastest-growing, most influential voices in the new-media advisory market."

At its peak Jupiter was working on behalf of 2,000 clients who were paying $50,000 each. It sponsored high-profile and well-attended conferences, where DeRose moderated discussions with many of the leading new media executives of the day, including Steve Case, Mark Cuban, and Barry Diller. He and his analysts appeared regularly on CNN and other news outlets, and were regularly quoted in the *New York Times,* the *Wall Street Journal, BusinessWeek,* the *Economist, Ad Age,* and *Variety.* DeRose led Jupiter through an initial public offering and merged it with an Internet audience measurement service called Media Metrix. It seemed like the sky was the limit. Jupiter had become a $100 million revenue per year company. But when the dot-com bubble burst in 2000, its value began to decline sharply, and it was eventually sold at fire sale prices. DeRose was out of work soon thereafter, with his pride wounded but his reputation as a technology visionary and entrepreneur still intact. That meant he could take the time, and the money he had earned from the IPO, to think about his next gig.

Despite Jupiter's ultimate fate, DeRose remained inspired by the Internet and the role that it could have in the marketing plans for everyday consumer-facing companies. But he also recognized that there was untapped power in the everyday conversations of average people. He was inspired by Meetup.com, a company founded in 2002 that empowers people to use the Internet to find other like-minded people in their communities who want to "meet up" to discuss topics of interest, from politics to cooking and crafts, or to engage in athletic pursuits such as running or biking, and a host of other activities. These meet-ups take place in person, locally. Meetup is a blend of online (to find and organize) and offline (to meet and get together with people in the flesh). As the company likes to say, it helps people to "use the Internet to get off the Internet."

In a 2011 conversation DeRose spoke of having had a desire to launch a company that would provide marketers with access to in-home brand experiences for consumers, fueled by the Internet. The goal was to provide consumers who are naturally social and like to entertain their friends and family with cool experiences that they could enjoy in the comfort of their home. The site would make use of Evite, the online invitation and social planning website, to facilitate the process. For marketers, it would provide something akin to handing out samples, or pop-up stores, or corporate tents at sporting events like golf and NASCAR. If these brand events were to take place simultaneously across the country, DeRose thought, it would be like a big, "stadium-sized pep rally, held in people's homes, with a client's brand featured."

The outcome of this vision is a company called House Party, which launched in 2005. At the core of House Party is a network of consumers across the country who volunteer to host in-home events for their family and friends (generally a dozen or so at a time). They are drawn to House Party through a variety of means, including having been invited to a previous party or knowing a party host, through invitations sent to customers in the database of House Party's client, or through online advertising about upcoming events. They are asked to fill out a questionnaire so that they can be invited to host events based on a match between their specific interests and how well they fit with the theme and purpose of the party.

Each event is sponsored by one of House Party's clients—companies like Kraft, McDonald's, Ford, and Microsoft—in which something new is shared, whether it's a consumer product or service, a TV show or movie, or a good cause. The national outreach of this program serves to create a wave of product experiences and conversations during the lead-up to the party, at the party, and afterward. What's in it for the people who participate as hosts? According to House Party's website, "You can share the stuff you like with the people you like, through a fantastic, free party experience. What's the catch? There is none: Our partners understand that if they share something good with the right people in a fun way, we'll all help spread the word."

For brands, House Party offers "a conversation and recommendation engine, online and off."

Rather than relying on advertising, coupons, in-store activity, or PR to help drive word of mouth, pure play word-of-mouth agencies like House Party provide an organized system for brands that want to activate word of mouth directly to their target customers. In other words, they offer a word-of-mouth "channel," whereas most other approaches offer word of mouth as an outcome of some other kind of marketing. A number of similar companies sprang up in the 2000s, as the word-of-mouth movement was gaining steam. They all go about their business in a different fashion, but what they have in common are the following critical factors: (a) they recruit a network of people who enjoy talking about products and services, and (b) they provide them with access to interesting products and services that they will want to talk about with others. Their success depends on their ability to keep their network engaged, since participants are not paid to participate (more on this below), and to convince brand marketers that the word of mouth that comes via their channel leads to sales at a rate that meets or exceeds what they can expect if they invest in other forms of marketing. They also need to convince the marketing community that they can generate word of mouth at a scale that is meaningful.

Kraft Sparks Talk about Solving the Dinnertime Dilemma

Kraft's Philadelphia Cream Cheese is a venerable old brand, but one that had been seeing flat sales for several years throughout the 2000s. To spark sales, the brand sought to find ways for its consumers to use the product more frequently and on more occasions, not just spreading it on more bagels at breakfast time. Philadelphia marketing executive Richard Bode explains, "We knew through research that our consumer is creative, when inspired."

In support of the goal to increase usage occasions for Philadelphia, the brand introduced a new product in 2011 called Philadelphia

Cooking Creme, an "easy to melt and spoon" version of Philly Cream Cheese that is intended to be used in dinner recipes, such as chicken dishes, vegetables, and any other pan-cooked food. In addition to an "original flavor" version to which one's own flavors can be added, there are varieties that are already mixed with spices, such as Italian Cheese and Herb, Savory Garlic, and Sante Fe (Mexican).

Kraft launched this new product with a large advertising budget, reported to be half of all Philadelphia's entire ad budget. But the effort didn't stop with advertising alone. "This is a product that is so new and different from anything the consumer would have seen or used before," Bode told us, "that advertising alone would not do the trick. They wouldn't really understand what it is and how well it works. We needed people to be able to try it and taste it, and we needed to do that on a large scale so that word would get out." As part of the marketing effort, the Philadelphia team engaged House Party. On a Saturday night in March 2011, more than 10,000 house parties were held simultaneously in the United States, pitched to the hosts as a way to solve the "dinnertime dilemma" with a new product that would help them "fight chicken fatigue." To Bode and his colleagues at Kraft it was "huge" that they could deploy a large-scale, simultaneous trial.

House Party provided the hosts with party packs (paid for by Kraft), including everything they would need for a night of cooking with Philadelphia Cooking Creme—the product itself, recipe booklets, cooking spoons, oven mitts, and a cooking skillet—plus coupons and recipe booklets to share with their guests afterward so they could buy the product should they wish to do so. In addition, the celebrity chef Todd English appeared live on HSN the night of the party, cooking with Philadelphia Cooking Creme. He was connected via Skype video conference calls with selected hosts who engaged with him live during their party and on air.

Each party had an average of thirteen guests in addition to the hostess and lasted an average of three hours. The typical activities at the parties included cooking chicken and/or other foods using the

Philadelphia Cooking Creme, discussing the recipes provided in the recipe booklet along with other favorites, watching Todd English interacting live with the other hosts and cooking his own recipes, and generally enjoying an evening of cooking, eating, and socializing with friends. As expected, people not only talked with each other at the party about this new product to which they were being exposed firsthand, but also talked with others after the event. Those conversations turned into purchases, and a positive return on Kraft's investment. Here is a snapshot of what emerged, which is illustrative of how word-of-mouth marketing is supposed to work.

A total of 138,000 people attended the parties live, and in addition to talking with each other each attendee also talked with 8.1 other people on average about the party, according to statistics compiled for House Party by an independent research agency, ChatThreads. Each of those people talked to 3.5 people on average. As a result of this conversational cascade, the series of House Parties with 138,000 people in attendance ended up yielding approximately 6 million offline conversations about Philadelphia Cooking Creme. These are all conversations between people who had personal experience with the product via the parties, or who knew someone who had a personal experience. In addition, there were another 2 million impressions via social media.

But talk is just talk if it doesn't drive people to buy the product and lead to profitability for the brand marketers who invest in word-of-mouth programs. House Party's research found with this program that a dollar investment in word-of-mouth marketing yielded $2.75 in profit. Stated differently, each individual person-to-person conversation about this event was able to generate 26 cents in profit. That is the direct return on investment. According to Philadelphia's Bode, the investment in word-of-mouth activation also made the investment in advertising more effective.

Procter & Gamble Invests in Word of Mouth

Tremor is another word-of-mouth agency, offering a similar value proposition to clients wishing to generate word-of-mouth advocacy, although it executes its programs differently than a company like House Party. Tremor is a part of Procter & Gamble, serving both internal P&G brands as well as external clients.

Tremor was started in 1999 by Claudia Kotchka, a one-time accountant with Arthur Andersen who, after deciding she was "bored silly" as an accountant, joined the marketing department at P&G in 1978. She rose through the ranks, and by 1991 had become the first nondesigner to run the art and package design department. A decade later the newly appointed CEO, A. G. Lafley, tapped her to become a change agent within the company as he sought to drive innovation at P&G, in part by making design a major element of the new product and innovation process. Her charge from Lafley was "to help him open up the cloistered halls of P&G and inject design thinking into every corpuscle of the company," according to *BusinessWeek*, which described Kotchka as "a giant in design and second only to A. G. Lafley himself in spreading the culture of design thinking throughout P&G. Her energy and brilliance have made all the difference in helping to transform the culture of a giant corporation into an innovation-centric organization."

Just prior to taking on the role of vice president of design and innovation, Kotchka had started Tremor, a network of influential teenagers who would be invited by P&G to share information and stories, with each other and with P&G. It began as a portal, using early social networking software. A major area of focus for this new network was in feminine care, where P&G (which manufacturers brands such as Tampax and Always) felt it needed to establish a different type of relationship with this group of young consumers.

When Kotchka left Tremor for her new role she was succeeded by Steve Knox, another long-time P&G executive (whom we discussed earlier in chapter 2). Under Knox's leadership, Tremor expanded from an initial network of 8,000 girls to a network of hundreds of thousands of teen girls and boys. Over time and with experience, Knox and his colleagues came to believe that there could be a much bigger opportunity if they expanded beyond just using an online portal as the venue where conversations could take place, and instead sought to tap friend-to-friend communications no matter where they took place, offline or online. They also introduced a methodology for screening by which teens would be part of the Tremor network, with a reliance on influencers, or what Tremor calls "connectors." Consistent with the themes we discussed in chapter 3, these are teens with broad social networks and an interest in discovering and telling others about relevant new ideas. By 2004 Tremor had expanded its panel further to include a network of 500,000 moms called Vocalpoint. Just like the teens, the moms in the panel are selected based on their status as "connectors." (The teen panel was eventually phased out, and moms are Tremor's main focus today.)

The core of the Tremor/Vocalpoint philosophy is that the right message shared with the right audience will spark word-of-mouth advocacy for brands. The right message, says Tremor, is one that disrupts schemas (a concept we discussed in chapter 2). Messages that disrupt schemas are ones that consumers don't expect to hear and that they feel compelled to discuss with their friends and families. The right audience, says Tremor, is one made up of word-of-mouth influencers, people with wide social networks who are eager to keep up with what is new in the marketplace and who like to share with others what they learn. Tremor works with its clients to create disruptive brand messages that are then shared with its panelists, often via product samples or high-value coupons, who in turn are encouraged to share what they have learned with their friends, family, and others in their real-world social network. These conversations can happen at the time, place, and venue of the panelist's choice—online or offline, one-on-one or in group settings, on weekdays or weekends. Tremor then measures the results and often compares them with "matched samples" of people who were not exposed to the same messages to determine the effectiveness of the program.

To illustrate how a word-of-mouth campaign from an agency such as Tremor works, and the impact it can have on sales, let's consider a word-of-mouth program for the introduction of the Gillette Venus Breeze (a P&G product) in 2009. The objective of the campaign was to introduce the new Breeze, a razor for women that integrated shaving gel with the razor itself, thereby eliminating the need for a separate gel product. The launch included a mass advertising campaign with the message "Reveal the Goddess in You," which Gillette executives felt did a good job in creating awareness. However, they determined that they needed to amplify their message through word of mouth from consumers who had firsthand experience with the product.

True to their process, the Tremor team started by determining what might be a disruptive, personal message that could trigger conversations. Tremor's research found that the schema that most women expect when it comes to shaving is a two-step process, starting with shaving and followed by the application of lotion to prevent dry skin. Because the Venus Breeze razor provides lotion while a woman is shaving, the disruptive WOM message from Tremor was "a new and unexpected way to get soft, creamy legs without lotion." The word-of-mouth campaign started with a mailer to relevant women in the Vocalpoint network, who received a sample of the product to use themselves and coupons to share with their friends.

What was the impact, and how did the WOM campaign relate to the media investment? To determine this, Tremor compared results in markets that ran only the media campaign to markets that ran media plus the WOM campaign. The Tremor campaign sparked 4 million conversations and converted 1 million women into new, active Venus Breeze users. Further, the WOM campaign was responsible for nearly a third of Venus's 13 percent annual sales growth, with the remaining growth attributable to other Breeze marketing. Putting together all the major performance metrics, Tremor determined that each dollar invested in the WOM campaign produced a profit of three dollars for the brand through new users and increased sales.

To Tell or Not to Tell: The Ethics and Efficacy of Transparency in Word of Mouth

As word-of-mouth marketing began developing as a discipline in the late 1990s and early 2000s, the issue of ethics started to become a major topic of discussion and debate. If people were to be encouraged to try new products with a House Party or a Tremor program, or through a program designed by another word-of-mouth agency, should there be payments to the people who were part of the program? And whether or not they were paid, should they be upfront and open about telling the people to whom they recommended the product that they were part of a formal word-of-mouth program? Or should they keep quiet about it and act as if they were just having a natural and spontaneous conversation about a new product?

The founders of the Word of Mouth Marketing Association made ethics a cornerstone of the new trade association when it was launched in 2005. There had already been a few high-profile stumbles when companies tried to fake word of mouth, the most visible of which was in 2002, when Sony Ericsson was readying the launch of its T68i, a mobile phone that could double as a digital camera, a highly innovative capability at the time. They undertook a marketing campaign at tourist venues such as New York's Empire State Building and Seattle's Space Needle, where actors were hired to play tourists, take pictures of each other, and then ask passersby to take their pictures. The purpose was to provide product demonstrations, allowing the unsuspecting tourists who are asked to take the picture to think they have stumbled upon a cool new product.

This type of activity, known as guerrilla marketing, was becoming increasingly popular. But a question was brewing about where the line needed to be drawn between clever marketing and deception. Commercial Alert, a consumer watchdog group founded by Ralph Nader, learned about the Sony Ericsson program and came down hard against it, calling it "deceptive" because "people will be fooled into thinking this is honest buzz." The agency that developed the campaign defended it by saying that the campaign wasn't "undercover" selling because the actors simply demonstrated the product and did not give a sales pitch. The *Wall Street Journal* chimed in with this not-so-positive headline: "That Guy Showing Off His Hot New Phone May Be a Shill—New Campaign for Sony Ericsson Puts Actors in Real-Life Settings."

"Shill" is exactly the word that the emerging word-of-mouth industry wanted to avoid. The industry knew that e-marketers had already been taken down that path when spammers took over and gave e-marketing a bad name, and it wanted to avoid at all costs a situation where word-of-mouth marketing would be similarly tainted. One of the first missions of the Word of Mouth Marketing Association was to take a firm stand on behalf of honesty and against deception. To accomplish this, it created an ethics code that all members would be required to adhere to as a condition for membership. Honesty and transparency were (and still are) bedrock principles.

The bottom line of the WOMMA Ethics Code is this: There should be no "faking it" in word-of-mouth marketing. If a company or agency wants to deploy a network of consumers to help spread the word about a new product or service, or create relationships with bloggers who will write about them, that is perfectly fine and, as we have seen, can be very productive. But companies should not hide the fact that they are doing so; in fact they should be upfront and honest about it. Consumer users should not be told what to say; instead they should be encouraged to give their honest opinions, and if there is any exchange of goods or services or fees, that too should be disclosed.

The 2005 WOMMA Ethics Code (with its periodic updates) became even more relevant when, in 2009, the Federal Trade Commission updated its Guides Concerning Use of Endorsements and Testimonials in Advertising and made certain elements of disclosure and transparency matters of law. The Guides had last been updated in 1980. A lot had changed in the world of marketing and marketing technologies since then, and the FTC expanded the purview of its Guides to apply not just to traditional forms of paid advertising, but also to consumer-generated media such that any "material connections" between advertisers and endorsers must be disclosed. Therefore cash payments or other consideration (including free products) provided by advertisers to the people who have been engaged on their behalf must be disclosed as a matter of law.

These revised Guides turned honesty and transparency from the right thing to do into a legal requirement. Right after their release, WOMMA's general counsel, Tony DiResta, helped interpret the new FTC rules for WOMMA members:

> Advertisers as well as endorsers (which include bloggers or other agents of the messaging) can be held liable. The FTC says that "advertisers who sponsor these endorsers (either by providing free products—directly or through a middleman—or otherwise) in order to generate a positive word of mouth and spur sales should establish procedures to advise endorsers that they should make the necessary disclosures and to monitor the conduct of those endorsers."
>
> In response to a request for a clarification by WOMMA, the FTC notes that not all communications touting a particular product or service constitutes an "endorsement" that requires any disclosures. Rather, it is "sponsored speech" that is covered by the Guides.

There is nothing in the FTC's Guides that in any way prohibits word-of-mouth marketing. The only thing that is prohibited is word-of-mouth marketing where honesty, transparency, and truthfulness are not the bedrocks. WOMMA encourages its members, and any marketer that seeks to tap the power of word of mouth, to ask itself these three questions, which it calls the "Honesty ROI," referring to return on investment:

HONESTY OF RELATIONSHIP
How will we ensure bloggers or other agents who work on our behalf disclose their relationship and participation in this marketing program?

HONESTY OF OPINION

What measures are in place to ensure we are not influencing bloggers to say anything other than their own honest and genuine opinions?

HONESTY OF IDENTITY

Does this program mislead the public in any way that could damage the reputation of our company?

To be compliant with the WOMMA Code of Ethics and the FTC Guides it is now standard best practice for marketers who run word-of-mouth or social media programs to actively encourage their participants to be explicit about their affiliation and to disclose whether they receive free products or cash. One of the interesting questions that disclosure raises, however, is whether or not it diminishes the effectiveness of the word-of-mouth campaign if participants are required (as a matter of good ethics, and now the law) to disclose that they are part of a word-of-mouth network and have been given a product to try and then talk about. Or, in the Internet context, will opinions be less meaningful to readers if a blogger discloses that he or she has been given a new product to try and then blogs about it?

In 2006 Walter Carl, then a professor at Northeastern University (and today the founder and chief research officer of the previously mentioned firm ChatThreads), conducted an interesting and revealing piece of research on this topic. Carl studied people who were on the receiving end of advice and recommendations from people who were part of a word-of-mouth network called BzzAgent (discussed in chapter 2). He looked at the reaction and response from those "conversational partners" who were told by the BzzAgents that they were part of a network and therefore given a product to try and encouraged to talk about it within their social circle, versus those that were not informed. The main conclusions of the research were very encouraging for word-of-mouth marketers who believe in transparency and disclosure. Carl found, "Participation in an organized and transparent word-of-mouth marketing program does not undermine the effectiveness of word-of-mouth communication. In fact, for the overwhelming majority of conversational partners, the research found 'it did not matter that they were talking with someone affiliated with a marketing organization. Instead what mattered was that they trusted the agent was providing an honest opinion, felt the agent had their best interests at heart, and was providing relevant and valuable information.'" In other words, people can find comfortable and natural ways to let others know they are part of an organized word-of-mouth network that provides them with access on occasion to new products or services, and there is a new one they have tried that they really like and recommend. Carl continues, "Disclosure has practical business benefits. The number of people a person told after speaking with a word of mouth marketing agent actually increased when the conversational partner was aware they were talking with a participant in an organized word-of-mouth marketing program."

In the vast majority of cases where a person learned about a brand or product from another source of information (such as a print, radio, TV, or web advertisement), talking with the word-of-mouth marketing agent increased the believability of that other source of information. This last research finding by Carl helps to illustrate the important relationship—one based on trust and credibility— that we have talked about in this book between word of mouth and advertising.

Word-of-Mouth Marketing Is for Services Too

Thus far the cases we have shared about how organized word-of-mouth marketing campaigns work have been for consumer goods. But lest we leave the wrong impression, these techniques can work just as effectively for services. Consider the Australian word-of-mouth agency Soup and their work on behalf of Commonwealth Bank of Australia (CBA), one of the country's biggest banks.

CBA was suffering from significant customer satisfaction challenges when a new CEO, Ralph Norris, took the helm in 2005. The problems were everywhere. "The drivers were things like queues," says Norris, "product competitiveness, staff knowledge and training, follow-up, people taking ownership, issues around levels of error rates." He set out to turn things around and make CBA "Australia's favourite bank." The rallying cry within the bank and to its customers was "Determined to be different. Determined to be #1." The bank's pledge: "We've spent the last four years improving every aspect of our business, refining systems, processes and training, to support our goal of being number one in customer satisfaction."

To help get out the word, they ran advertising on TV, in print, and online promoting their changes in customer service. But the bank wanted to go further, for a number of reasons. They felt that although the advertising was successful from an awareness perspective, it had limited believability given the bank's prior challenges with customer satisfaction. Also, they wanted to live up to their slogan "Determined to be different," and they felt that a word-of-mouth campaign was the ultimate demonstration that they could "walk the walk." In short, they believed that word-of-mouth marketing, in which consumers would honestly express their opinions, would give greater credibility through grassroots conversations and recommendations that reinforced what they were saying via advertising.

This is where word-of-mouth marketing and the Soup agency came into the picture. Keller Fay and Soup had undertaken a Talk-Track study in Australia in 2010, which revealed that about one-third of Australians talk about financial services on a typical day and that an overwhelming number of those conversations take place face-to-face. It's not a highly talked about category relative to others, but a third of a nation's population talking about the category on any given day means there is a sizable base of natural word of mouth to build upon. We also knew that there is a fairly even split between conversations that are positive and those that are negative or a mix of positive and negative, and that it is far more likely for conversations about financial services brands to carry no recommendation at all than to have any type of active advocacy. This puts financial services in a different position than many other categories where active advocacy is stronger. Both of these latter two findings led Soup to tell CBA that there was a good opportunity to build a word-of-mouth campaign that could stand out from the daily conversations about banks and other types of financial institutions that were already taking place in Australia.

The goal of the program was to use word of mouth to illustrate the bank's commitment to customer service by providing influential CBA customers with firsthand experience of the new customer service offering. Armed with this experience, they could then spread word of mouth and encourage reappraisal among their social networks. It was the first time this type of word-of-mouth campaign was run in Australia on behalf of a bank.

Several thousand "Soupers" (people who belong to Soup's word-of-mouth network) were recruited to participate, based on their being CBA customers and word-of-mouth influencers in the area of banking and finance. Several hundred were invited to attend an hour-long behind-the-scenes event held after normal closing hours in eighteen branches across the country. Attendees in groups of between ten and twenty-five were addressed by senior banking executives, given a tutorial on how online banking works, shown the customer relationship management system and how it helps the bank to give customers better service, and given a demonstration of how the money-counting machines work. The rest were given "secret shopper" tasks to test the bank's claims by using its online and telephone services and by visiting local branches. Both sets of people were then encouraged to talk honestly with their network of friends and family about what they had experienced personally.

The result was over 600,000 offline conversations about CBA and its improved customer service, along with more than 50,000 online posts. More than 40,000 people switched banks or increased their holdings at CBA as a result of a conversation. On a per customer basis, Soup and CBA determined that for every dollar invested in the campaign, the bank generated thirty dollars in revenue (calculated on a net present value basis of a new customer over three years).

Social Marketing Meets Social Commerce

We have talked throughout this chapter, indeed throughout this book about the ways word of mouth and social media drive purchase considerations and sales. Our research shows that when consumers receive word-of-mouth advice, they find it to be highly credible, and these conversations lead to high levels of purchase intention. And as discussed in chapter 5, word-of-mouth conversations that take place in a store are far and away the most likely to include active recommendations to buy or try the brand being discussed, and earn the highest levels of purchase intent.

Recognizing the power that can come when word of mouth takes place at the point of sale, there is a movement afoot to bring together two important and fast-growing marketing trends—social marketing and shopper marketing—and find the nexus between them. Social marketing is all about tapping the credibility that comes when consumers recommend products and services to others. Shopper marketing is when the discipline of brand marketing gets brought directly into a retail environment, such as in-store displays, ads, promotions, and product packaging, together with their online equivalents for shoppers who search the Web in advance of going to the store or do their purchasing online.

Two companies that are melding social marketing and shopper marketing in interesting, albeit very different, ways are BzzAgent and Bazaarvoice, an Austin-based technology company that enables online customer reviews and other forms of online content about products and services on e-commerce and brand websites. Their stories illustrate the impact that can be seen when word of mouth connects with what has come to be known as "the first moment of truth," when the shopper is at the point of retail and needs to decide whether to buy one brand or another.

BzzAgent was one of the earliest and most visible word-of-mouth agencies, founded in 2001 by Dave Balter, who had a background in loyalty marketing and marketing promotion. In 2001 Balter came to believe that word of mouth was powerful and widespread but not well understood by marketers, and that word of mouth could be the basis for a new approach to marketing. He had a belief that people (a) love to talk about products and (b) want to be part of a community. He launched the BzzAgent network to allow marketers to accelerate and measure the impact of word of mouth, while giving consumers what he felt would be a fun way to try new products and influence brands. It is what he calls "a new twist on a very old network: the social grapevine." As with Tremor, House Party, and Soup, the core approach of BzzAgent is to send product samples to its agents along with suggested talking points, and encourage them to try the product and then talk about it honestly with their social network, either offline or online.

Since his company's launch, Balter has been a vocal and visible advocate for the emerging discipline of word-of-mouth marketing. He and his company have been profiled widely in the press, including a 2004 cover story in the *New York Times Magazine* titled "The Hidden (in Plain Sight) Persuaders." He has published two books, *Grapevine: The New Art of Word-of-Mouth Marketing* in 2005 and *The Word of Mouth Manual: Volume 2* in 2008. Declaring itself the fastest growing word-of-mouth marketing company, BzzAgent secured significant financing in 2006 from venture capital companies, one of which declared, "Just as the Internet and interactive marketing have exploded in the past 10 years, we believe that word-of-mouth marketing will be the next 'must have' program for every company with a consumer-focused product, brand or service."

We all know that when venture capitalists put money into a company, they expect to get it out one day. So it came as no surprise when, in 2011, ten years after its founding and five years after the venture capitalists funded it, BzzAgent announced that it was sold. What was surprising was to whom: a company called dunnhumby, Ltd. which is a wholly owned subsidiary of the giant British retailer Tesco. Many had speculated that a marketing agency like BzzAgent would be sold one day to one of the large ad agency holding companies as another marketing communications channel, or maybe to a large media organization as part of the growing trend for media to go beyond traditional advertising by offering a more integrated set of marketing options to advertisers. But Tesco? How would that work? According to Balter, the partnership means "we are finally connecting the dots between social media and shopper marketing." You see, dunnhumby is a leading player in the business of loyalty marketing and runs the frequent shopper program for Tesco in the United Kingdom, Kroger in the United States, and many others around the world.

But why connect those dots? Balter explains: "The concepts of social media and shopper marketing are already intrinsically linked: both deal with the engagement of consumers and their loyalty behavior. But they come at the concept from different ends of the spectrum. Social marketing allows a marketer to find loyal customers and to begin an open dialogue with them, and then shopper marketing is where you create the value. We're past the primordial stage of social, where being 'present' as a marketer was enough and significant ROI [return on investment] was hard to determine. In the future, the strongest social marketing programs will be evaluated by exactly what occurs in store." In short, BzzAgent's expectation is that the marriage of social and shopper marketing will be appealing to the marketplace because "shopper marketing—with its focus on crafting offers based on intimate knowledge of consumers—works better when accelerated through the peer recommendations that thrive in social media. And because the ROI of social media can be demonstrated more powerfully through loyalty program data than any other method."

The challenge, Balter believes, will come at the organizational level. "While these two channels inherently deal with the same concepts," he says, "there is currently a huge gap in the ability for them to work together. Right now, marketers are managing their social marketing programs in one corner (usually through the digital or promotions marketing) and shopper marketing in another corner (usually through the trade marketing function), and so these two concepts are disconnected. But imagine if you were to link these together: to tie the scale and trust of the social channel with the ability to drive in-store purchase behavior that shopper marketing provides."

A different way to integrate word of mouth, or social marketing, with shopper marketing comes via ratings and reviews and other forms of consumer-generated content on the websites of retailers and brands. And the data that prove the impact are compelling.

The first retailer to offer what has now become a very popular and credible online resource was Amazon, which was founded in 1995 and launched its ratings and reviews capability almost immediately thereafter. For many years Amazon was alone in this offering. Its popularity proved that people desire to share consumer-to-consumer feedback and make purchase decisions based on what other consumers (even strangers) had to say, rather than relying solely on expert opinion from reviewers. Further, a very popular feature of Amazon, and one of the keys to its success, was its use of algorithms to suggest that if you are interested in "x" you might want to know that people who bought that product also bought "a," "b" and "c," another form of word-of-mouth marketing.

Recognizing that ratings and reviews need not be the purview of online bookselling alone, Bazaarvoice was founded in 2005 to provide software and related services that other online retailers could use to deploy ratings and reviews on their websites. The company's name is intended to evoke the idea of the bazaar, the initial marketplace. Bazaars were once lively centers of towns, the core of a vibrant community, a place where friends, neighbors, and merchants all came to share opinions. Bazaars were places where conversation and commerce came together. Bazaarvoice is thus the "voice" of the marketplace. Today Bazaarvoice's software powers ratings and reviews and other forms of consumer-generated conversation about brands for many of the world's leading retailers, including Walmart, Macy's, Best

Buy, and Costco, as well as brands that wish to post ratings and other forms of consumer content on their own websites, such as P&G, Dell, and Samsung.

There is abundant research to support the view that consumers trust ratings and reviews highly. Nielsen has found that consumer opinions posted online are second in credibility only to recommendations from people consumers know personally. Advertising on TV, in magazines and newspapers, online and in email, along with other forms of marketing communications, all fall below.

What is less well-known, but becoming more apparent, is the powerful outcomes that accrue to retailers and brands when consumer conversation is joined with social commerce. For example, the electronics manufacturer Epson has found that shoppers who interact with reviews show higher intent to purchase, conversion, and revenue per visitor than shoppers who do not interact with user-generated content. According to Bazaarvoice, visitors who interact with reviews on Epson's e-store pages were 67 percent more likely to convert to purchase than visitors who did not interact with reviews. These visitors also had a 25 percent higher average order value. These statistics enabled Epson to determine that revenue per visitor was twice as high for visitors who interacted with reviews compared to those who did not.

Another example of the power of online ratings and reviews comes from CheapCaribbean.com, which offers all-inclusive Caribbean vacations. When Bazaarvoice compared visitors who interacted with user-generated content on the site to those who did not, they found they were more than twice as likely to book a trip, and their average order value was 10 percent higher. The bottom line of these two statistics: a 144 percent lift in revenue per visit.

The impact of ratings and reviews on sales isn't isolated to online sales. For example, Rubbermaid collects ratings and review information on their site. In addition to offering that feedback to consumers online, they also decided to add review star ratings and a review snippet to a free-standing insert with a coupon and distribute them via circulars, thereby bringing online-generated reviews into the print advertising channel. To assess the impact, Rubbermaid compared two versions of an advertisement for the same product; one included reviews and one did not. Both ads had the same offer and were distributed to the same list. The result: the free-standing insert that included reviews saw a 10 percent higher redemption rate.

These examples help to illustrate that word of mouth is not just about informing and satisfying customers. It also drives immediate sales when the ratings are available at the point of purchase, either on an e-commerce site or via signage at a store where the product is displayed. When there is an opportunity for social marketing to intersect directly with purchasing (either online or offline), there is a tremendous opportunity to drive important business outcomes, most critically greater sales conversion and higher sales revenue.

There is a saying that you've probably seen in stores and elsewhere: "If you are happy, tell your friends; if not, tell us." And indeed there is a substantial amount of positive word of mouth that springs organically from happy customers telling others. Some conversations come as a result of people using or seeing the product in use, or seeking out information because they are in the market. Sometimes it is a byproduct of well-planned and well-executed media and marketing activity, as we have seen in earlier chapters. But sometimes word of mouth needs to be deployed as a channel in its own right: Find people who like to talk about brands (including those who have been organized into a network for this very purpose), give them firsthand experiences with a product or service and a "disruptive" message, and then encourage them to share their opinions honestly, with full disclosure about their involvement with your campaign. Evidence shows that the results can be dramatic, and the financial impact on your business can be even more exciting.

8

Negative Word of Mouth:
A Cause for Alarm or
a Customer's Greatest Gift?

One of the watershed moments in the annals of word of mouth belongs to Dell Computer. In June 2005 a high-profile blogger, Jeff Jarvis, ranted online about poor service from Dell related to his newly purchased "lemon." His first online headline was "Dell Lies; Dell Sucks." He blogged regularly, for several weeks, documenting his frustrations in getting help from the company from whom he had also purchased a "complete care" service plan along with his new computer. Not until he wrote directly to the chief marketing officer of the company (and significantly, not until after he did some very public complaining) did he get the satisfaction of a refund. He chose a refund rather than a replacement because by the time the company acted he had lost faith in Dell and wanted to buy an Apple computer instead.

It's important to note that Jarvis is not your average citizen journalist who decided one day to launch a blog and hope people would discover it; he was at one time a writer for *TV Guide, People,* and the *San Francisco Examiner,* was the Sunday editor of the New York *Daily News,* and created *Entertainment Weekly.* As a result of all this, his blog buzzmachine.com had (and still has) a strong following. And his rants went viral, big time.

Unfortunately for Dell, it hadn't been listening closely to social media commentary about the brand, and thus was not initially aware of growing discontent about its customer service. The Jarvis posts changed this, as they reached thousands of people, which, in turn, encouraged a tsunami of additional online complaints from fellow customers. All of this activity eventually got Jarvis's posts ranked number five on Google for searches on "Dell Sucks," according to Jarvis himself, who offered this information in one of his rants. A few years earlier, Jarvis would have represented just one unsatisfied customer and seemingly a small risk to Dell's business. But in an age of consumer-generated media, a highly networked blogger can cost a company like Dell many millions of dollars in lost business and reputation.

Jarvis himself said it best in one of his later posts during the episode:

> The age of caveat emptor is over. Now the time has come when it's the seller who must beware. A company can no longer get away with consistently offering shoddy products or service or ignoring customers' concerns and needs.
>
> For now the customers can talk back where they can be heard. Those customers can gang up and share what they know and give their complaints volume. Of course, they can use their reviews and complaints to have a big impact on a company's reputation and business.
>
> Public relations has to take on a new meaning. It can no longer be about the press and publicity, which just separate companies from the public they are supposed to serve. Public relations must be about a new relationship with the public, with the public in charge.
>
> All that is quite obvious to any of us. But it is far from obvious to too many big companies . . . like Dell.

This episode struck a nerve with Dell. It was a company that had been formed around the concept of being direct, and having direct relationships with customers was supposed to help it ensure the best possible experience. Further, back in the mid-1990s Dell had established one of the first online communities hosted by a company, when it saw that its products and services were being discussed in Com-puServe's, AOL's, and Prodigy's online forums. In response it decided to launch its own online community. According to Manish Mehta, Dell's vice president of social media and community, this move was not initially popular at Dell, as it had the potential to act as a lightning rod for negative feedback. "However, the negative conversation self-regulated over time thanks to satisfied Dell customers joining and be-coming advocates for the company," Mehta recalled. "From this early start, Dell saw the value in engaging with customers one-on-one, and even in encouraging customers to engage with one another, online and unfettered." Dell, by its own admission, was slow to react as cus-tomers like Jarvis sought an even more direct relationship with the company on the Web 2.0. The "Dell Hell" posts sparked a big change at Dell, and indeed at all companies that witnessed what happened to Dell. It is now a widely accepted best practice that brand managers have a system in place to monitor consumer sentiment online, if for no other reason than to uncover customer service and product prob-lems and to respond to them. Dell does that now, and many other companies do as well.

The reengineering of the customer service process began at Dell in April 2006, when Michael Dell charged the company to proactively find dissatisfied customers in the blogosphere and connect them with someone at Dell who could help. By July Dell had launched its efforts with its Direct2Dell blog. Initially there was a team of two or three employees charged with reaching out to consumers online; by 2011 that team had grown to more than sixty members. In August 2010 Dell launched the Social Media and Community Training Program (SMaC U), which provides training and certification for any Dell em-ployee who wants to engage on behalf of Dell in the social media space. Approximately 10,000 employees had received some type of training as of mid-2011, and 2,500 are officially certified, which per-mits them to interact with customers within their area of expertise. In December 2010 Dell opened the Social Media Listening Command Center at its Austin headquarters, which it describes as "a further step to embed social media across the company to build stronger customer connections." The Center tracks on average more than 22,000 daily topic posts related to Dell, as well as mentions of Dell on Twitter.

At the low point in 2006, Dell says at least half of the online conversation about the company was negative. By 2007 Dell calculated the negative online conversation had been reduced to 23 percent. According to our data at Keller Fay, the quality of Dell's overall word of mouth (offline and online) is now positive 61 percent of the time and negative 10 percent of the time. (The remainder is either a mixture of positive and negative, or neutral.) This places Dell very close to the average for the technology category.

Besides the example of Dell, there are many other widely published case studies relating to negative word of mouth. AOL and Comcast have been widely criticized for poor response to customer service problems. Whole Foods has received harsh criticism because its CEO was posting highly satisfied comments online, masquerading as a customer. JetBlue was widely pilloried for leaving passengers stranded on a runway for more than ten hours, ultimately leading to changes in federal policy and the resignation of their CEO. KFC and Taco Bell received terrible news coverage for a viral video that showed rodents infesting a restaurant. For many companies, word-of-mouth marketing is as much about dealing with the negative as with the positive.

Just as companies misunderstand a number of important aspects of consumer word of mouth and how it relates to their business, they also misjudge how much word of mouth about their product is negative. Among marketers and executives, the percentage estimates vary widely. Some assume it is 30 percent, others 50, still others 66. Informed by stories like "Dell Hell," most believe negative word of mouth is a stronger force in the market than positive word of mouth. This has been especially reinforced by some literature on word of mouth, notably in the book A *Satisfied Customer Tells 3 Friends and an Angry Customer Tells 3,000*, by Pete Blackshaw, who coined the term "consumer-generated media" to describe consumer opinion and other content shared online.

The answer to the simple question "What percent of WOM is negative?" surprises almost everyone. In TalkTrack, we have found that it is just 8 percent. It is a number that has been remarkably consistent over the five years we've been tracking word of mouth. People are shocked that of all the conversations that occur about brands, such a seemingly trivial amount could be negative.

In fact, though, the other 92 percent of conversations are not all positive. Sixty-six percent of all brand WOM is described by respondents as truly positive, another 11 percent is "neutral" about the brand, and 15 percent is a mixture of positive and negative. Based on this last category, one could describe 23 percent as containing some amount of negative sentiment, including both the 8 percent negative and the 15 percent mixed. There is some variation by industry, with telecommunications usually ranked last in terms of the share of positive word of mouth, but even this industry earns much more positive than negative conversations. Meanwhile categories such as children's products, packaged food, and beauty products tend to have the most positive and least negative word of mouth.

Our general finding alone does not contradict Blackshaw's book title. It is not uncommon for people to respond to our data by saying, "Well, maybe there's more positive word of mouth, but the negative is more powerful, driven by more emotion, and therefore more viral." The assumption here is that angry customers tell more people about their bad experiences than satisfied ones tell about their good experiences. Sometimes, perhaps, but not usually, and here's why.

In TalkTrack surveys, people who are on the receiving end of word-of-mouth advice are asked to assess the credibility of the opinions they heard and their likelihood of acting on them. Consistently people exposed to positive opinions assign greater credibility than those exposed to negative ones. When people hear something positive about a brand, 66 percent of them assign very high credibility to it, rating it 9 or 10 on a credibility scale ranging from 0 to 10. That compares to only 47 percent who give the same credibility rating to negative opinions about brands. Similarly, negative WOM is less viral

Chart 8.1

POLARITY OF WOM CONVERSATION BY CATEGORY
(Ranked by net advocacy score)

	MOSTLY POSITIVE	MOSTLY NEGATIVE	MIXED	NET ADVOCACY (positive minus mixed and negative talk)
Children's Products	74%	5%	11%	58
Food/Dining	73	6	11	56
Beverages	72	5	11	56
Personal Care/Beauty	72	5	11	56
Household Products	71	5	11	55
Retail/Apparel	71	5	13	53
Media/Entertainment	71	6	14	51
Travel Services	68	7	13	48
All-Category Average	66	8	15	43
The Home	64	8	15	41
Automotive	62	9	17	36
Technology	63	9	18	36
Sports/Hobbies	63	10	18	35
Health/Healthcare	55	12	17	26
Financial Services	51	14	16	21
Telecommunications	51	15	22	14

Source: Keller Fay Group's TalkTrack®, July 2010–June 2011.

Chart 8.2

POSITIVE WOM IS MUCH MORE CREDIBLE THAN NEGATIVE WOM

Percentage rating WOM highly credible, 9 or 10 on 0–10 scale

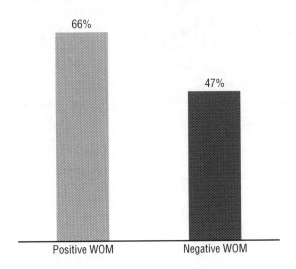

INFORMATION FROM POSITIVE CONVERSATIONS IS MORE LIKELY TO BE SHARED

Percentage rating WOM highly likely to be passed along, 9 or 10 on 0–10 scale

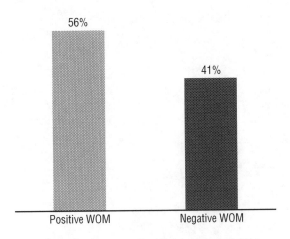

Source: Keller Fay Group's TalkTrack®, July 2010–June 2011.

than positive WOM, with 56 percent saying they are highly likely to tell others about something positive they've heard through word of mouth, compared to 41 percent for something negative.

The work of Jonah Berger and Katherine Milkman, two Wharton School academics whose research was covered in chapter 2, reinforces this point. In a study published in 2011, Berger and Milkman undertook a major content analysis project in which they studied differences in *New York Times* articles that were widely shared online versus those that were not. A key conclusion of their experiment was that "positive content is more viral than negative content."

Even when faced with such evidence, people still wonder why. Why is word of mouth so often positive and so rarely negative? And why does positive WOM travel further than negative, despite anecdotal evidence to the contrary? We believe there are several answers. The first has to do with human nature: most of us are fundamentally positive people and prefer to engage with each other about things we like rather than dislike. Indeed some neuroscientists have identified and described an "optimism bias" that is commonplace among human beings. Tali Sharot, a research fellow at the Wellcome Trust Center for Neuroimaging at University College London, has written, "With the development of non-invasive brain imaging techniques, we have gathered evidence that suggests our brains are hard-wired to be unrealistically optimistic."

There also is a very practical reason. Word of mouth is ultimately about making affirmative buying decisions. That's "the ask" in word of mouth, as in "I'm thinking about buying a new car, or looking for healthy food to buy, or a great place to take my family on vacation. What do you suggest?" While it is very helpful to be steered away from a bad product or service, it's even more helpful to be steered toward something good to buy. Many conversations about negative experiences are immediately followed by the next logical question: "So what brand *should* I buy?" And the answer to that question is almost always positive.

While we have provided quite a bit of evidence to support the "positive is more powerful" thesis, we do not mean to suggest that negative word of mouth is an unimportant phenomenon or should be taken lightly. Negative consumer sentiment can be toxic for businesses if it is sustained; it needs to be addressed and minimized. And the lessons such sentiments teach, which are so well described in Blackshaw's book, represent an essential part of the core curriculum for any brand marketer today. But think of these lessons as a form of preventive medicine: taking good care of your brand on a day-to-day basis is vital to warding off—or to helping you to recover quickly from—a more serious illness.

Advertising amid Crisis

Unfortunately the first decade of the twenty-first century provided plenty of opportunities to study word of mouth for companies in crisis. Indeed whole industries—pet food, peanut butter, financial, and auto companies—have faced extremely serious crises. Each of these has led to dramatic shifts in word-of-mouth conversations as measured by our surveys—more talk overall, and much more negative sentiment shared between consumers.

The Great Recession of 2008–2009 was led by a meltdown in the financial sector—big banks, investment companies, and insurers—who risked their very survival, and the economy as a whole, by over-leveraging themselves, especially in the mortgage markets. TV news viewers and newspaper readers during the second half of 2008 were shocked by a series of dramatic headlines and news stories about the near collapse of the financial sector. "Lehman Files for Bankruptcy; Merrill Is Sold" read the headline in the *New York Times* on September 14. Two weeks later, as anxiety accelerated, readers awoke to an equally alarming *Times* headline: "House Rejects Bailout Package, 228–205; Stocks Plunge." Even though Congress and President Bush finally did adopt a $700 billion bailout plan for the financial sector, this seemed only to fuel public anger and anxiety—particularly at the idea of so much taxpayer money being used to save banks that hadn't been wise enough to save themselves—helping to set up a landslide election victory for Barack Obama a month later.

During the fall of 2008 consumer word of mouth about financial services companies responded in dramatic fashion to events as they unfolded in the news. Our research found that across all financial companies, positive word of mouth plummeted from over 50 percent of all conversations to less than 40 percent in the fall of 2008, when the meltdown was in full swing. Negative WOM doubled from about 15 percent of conversations to nearly 30 percent. There was a second, similar pattern in the spring of 2009, when more bailout bills were passed. People were talking more about financial companies, and they weren't saying many nice things.

Several companies saw truly massive changes in the quality of their word of mouth. Between early and late 2008 negative word of mouth about Merrill Lynch, which survived only by being acquired by Bank of America, quadrupled from 13 to 54 percent. And AIG, the big insurer at the center of the crisis, saw its negative word of mouth multiply by a factor of seven, from 11 to 76 percent. Word of mouth might be mainly positive under normal circumstances, but the financial crisis of 2008–2009 surely was not a normal time. The crisis proved that word of mouth is highly sensitive to events.

The rise of negative word of mouth was in response to news reports, of course. Normally advertising is a leading driver of word of mouth about financial companies and news stories are secondary, according to our research. But at the worst points in this particular crisis, news stories soared as a driver of financial company conversations, moving ahead of advertising. Financial companies were clearly not in control of the conversation. Not surprisingly these news-related conversations were more negative than positive. Nearly half of conversations referencing a news story were negative about the financial company or brand at the peak of the crisis, versus less than a third that were positive. Negative news stories were fueling negative consumer conversations about financial companies.

Chart 8.3

FINANCIAL CRISIS CAUSED A DRAMATIC DECREASE IN POSITIVE AND INCREASE IN NEGATIVE TALK: SUMMER 2008, WINTER 2009

Polarity of financial services conversations, 8-week rolling average

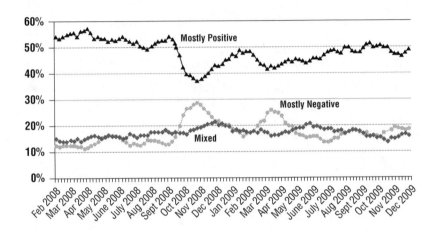

AT PEAK OF FINANCIAL CRISIS (2008–2009), NEWS DROVE MORE WOM THAN ADVERTISING

Percentage of financial brand conversations containing media/marketing references, 8-week rolling average

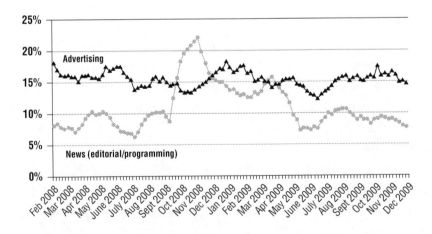

Source: Keller Fay Group's TalkTrack®, February 2008–December 2009.

But what about conversations that related to advertising by financial companies—did they turn negative too? The answer to this question was surprising. According to an analysis undertaken by Keller Fay and the media agency MediaVest, when consumers talked about the bank-related advertising they had seen, the conversations were mostly *positive*. Even at the worst of the crisis, about 50 percent of ad-influenced conversations were positive, against about 20 percent that were negative. Although not quite as positive as before the crisis, it appears nonetheless that advertising has the ability to serve as a bulwark against the negative during a crisis.

Chart 8.4

FINANCIAL CRISIS 2008–2009: NEWS-BASED DISCUSSIONS TOOK A HARDER WOM QUALITY HIT THAN AD-BASED

Percentage of positive financial brand conversations by media/marketing reference, 8-week rolling average

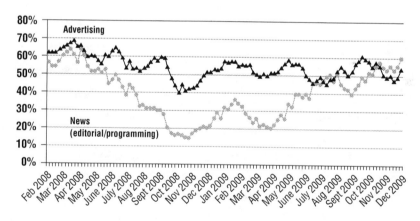

Source: Keller Fay Group's TalkTrack®, February 2008–December 2009.

This is an important insight because virtually every major financial company had an agonizing decision to make about whether to continue advertising or to cut back during the crisis. Arguments for reducing ad spending were many and varied: Save funds that were in short supply; avoid antagonizing taxpayers and politicians who in some cases became majority shareholders in companies; keep one's head down in the face of an existential threat; avoid wasting money since people won't be receptive (or persuaded) anyway.

Yet the companies that fared best from a word-of-mouth perspective were the ones that kept up their advertising. The data that Keller Fay analyzed in conjunction with MediaVest showed that the companies that maintained or increased ad spending experienced a softer "word-of-mouth crisis" and rebounded faster than other companies—because they were able to counteract the negative press with messages over which they had more control. The best advertising in these circumstances acknowledged the crisis and the stress on customers, but also provided reassurance.

The group of companies in our analysis that maintained or even increased spending at this time included BB&T Bank, Chevy Chase Bank, E*Trade, The Hartford, M&T Bank, Morgan Stanley, Regions Bank, Scottrade, Sharebuilder, Suntrust, TD Ameritrade, & US Bank. Charles Schwab and JP Morgan Chase adjusted their messaging to help reassure customers. The Schwab ads were based on the tag line "I've got less cash and a lot more questions." Chase ran a campaign that focused on "the way forward." Both companies recognized that advertising during the crisis could not be "business as usual." They had to adjust to the new consumer reality and offer some of the reassurance that was in such low supply. For the stable ad spenders, the crisis was over—from a word-of-mouth perspective—in the first quarter of 2009. But for the financial companies with large cutbacks in advertising, the negative word-of-mouth experience continued for another year. So even in a "word-of-mouth era" it is clear that advertising plays a vital role in steering the consumer conversation, and marketers surrender this valuable tool at their peril.

The "Gas Pedal" Crisis

The American automobile industry also suffered during the Great Recession, as General Motors and Chrysler fell into government-managed bankruptcies and bailouts. Our research found similar dynamics at work for these two companies as we had seen just a few months earlier for the financial companies. But it was an entirely different type of crisis at another auto company, Toyota, that offers the best lessons for how to recover from negative word of mouth related to a serious crisis.

In late 2009 and early 2010 Toyota experienced the worst possible problem for any brand: an alleged product flaw that was being blamed in the press for some serious customer injuries. Worse, the company was perceived as being initially slow to acknowledge and respond to public concern. Following a gradual lead-up to the problem, the crisis came into full view in January 2010, when the company made two major product recall announcements and suspended sales and production for a week. On February 5 the president and CEO of Toyota Motor Corporation, Akio Toyoda, apologized for the loss of confidence in his company's products. On February 24 he did so again before a committee of the U.S. House of Representatives.

The consumer word-of-mouth reaction was swift. The number of Toyota impressions nearly doubled, from about 72 million per week to 123 million per week for the next two to three months, and the sentiment of those conversations turned sharply negative. The share of Toyota conversations that were positive dropped from around 70 percent before the crisis to less than 30 percent, while the share that was truly negative about Toyota rose from less than 10 percent to over 40 percent. Consumers were being exposed to 50 million negative conversations about Toyota per week at the worst of the crisis, compared to fewer than 4 million per week in normal times.

Chart 8.5

TOYOTA'S WOM SOARED DURING ITS GAS PEDAL CRISIS
Weekly impressions, in millions

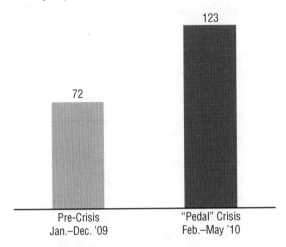

Source: Keller Fay Group's TalkTrack®, January 2009–May 2010.

TOYOTA'S POSITIVE TALK LEVELS DROPPED TO UNPRECEDENTED LOWS
Polarity of Toyota conversations, 8-week rolling average

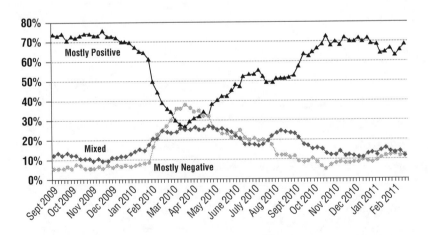

Source: Keller Fay Group's TalkTrack®, September 2009–February 2011.

Impressively Toyota recovered—almost fully—from this low point. By November 2010 positive sentiment about Toyota had returned to its pre-crisis level of about 70 percent, and negative was once again below 10 percent. But the recovery wasn't entirely complete, as people's word-of-mouth recommendations were not quite as strong and advocacy-oriented as before. Most consumers talking about Toyota recommended their friends and family "consider" the brand as opposed to making a strong "buy it" recommendation. Also, very negative "avoid it" recommendations were still at almost 10 percent in late 2010, rather than around 5 percent, which was more typical on a pre-crisis basis.

Yet even with these qualifiers, the rebound was truly impressive, considering how negative the conversations about Toyota had turned during the spring and early summer of 2010. Not only had the conversations returned to a strongly positive orientation, but sales also held up well enough for the company to maintain its number one position globally. Why? We believe there were two critical factors: the strength of the brand prior to the crisis and the effectiveness of Toyota's crisis communications plan.

In 2009, before the crisis, Toyota had the second best word-of-mouth sentiment of the nineteen major auto manufacturers measured in our surveys, with 71 percent positive talk, only 5 percent negative, and 11 percent mixed positive and negative. As a summary score, we have a metric we call "Net Advocacy," which subtracts negative and mixed WOM from the percentage of WOM that is positive. Before the crisis Toyota was at a positive score of 55, behind only BMW (at 60), and well ahead of the auto industry average of 34. At the worst of the crisis Toyota fell to dead last on the list, behind eighteen competitors, but a year later it was once again highly ranked, at number five.

Chart 8.6

TOYOTA'S GAS PEDAL CRISIS: WOM QUALITY FELL SHARPLY, BUT
RECOVERED ALMOST COMPLETELY

Net advocacy (positive minus mixed and negative WOM) by make;
before, during, and after crisis

	NET ADVOCACY (positive minus mixed and negative talk)	RANK (among auto companies)
Pre-Crisis Jan.–Dec. 2009	55	2
"Pedal" Crisis Feb.–May 2010	–25	19 (last place)
Post-Crisis Sept. 2010–Feb. 2011	46	5

Source: Keller Fay Group's TalkTrack®, January 2009–February 2011.

For many years we have pointed to Toyota in speeches and work-shops as one of the great success stories of word of mouth. It has been a talkworthy brand because it has been very good at cultivating loyal and motivated advocates, and it has provided consumers with things to talk about, such as Toyota's vaunted product reliability, green hybrid models and features, forward-looking designs—and a strong safety reputation. This strong marketing, branding, and word of mouth served it well during the crisis, according to the team at Toyota and its ad agency of nearly four decades, Saatchi & Saatchi Los Angeles.

Tim Morrison, a thirty-year Toyota man, is responsible for market-ing at Toyota USA as the corporate manager of marketing communica-tions. He has long believed in the power of word-of-mouth advertising, having used the strategy in a campaign he launched in 2001, when he was the general manager of the New England region. At the time, he and his team were looking for a campaign that would "sell the product and not the deal," an acknowledgment that much of automotive adver-tising is about short-term discounts and price promotions. Confident of the product and aware of the many fiercely loyal customers that Toy-ota had cultivated over the years, Morrison's team settled on the theme

"Ask somebody who owns a Toyota." The campaign's call to action was to have a conversation—and Morrison had the confidence that most of the time this would lead to a strong recommendation to buy a Toyota. Morrison credits the campaign, among other factors, for nearly doubling Toyota's share in the New England region from between 12 and 13 percent in 2000 to number one among automotive retailers by 2007 at between 22 and 24 percent.

Morrison's "Ask Somebody" campaign in New England was possible because the brand had long been, and continues to be, committed to high standards, continuous improvement, and innovation, among other key principles encoded in the firm's famous "Toyota Way." The foundational elements of the "Toyota Way" include meeting challenges with courage and creativity, continuous improvement, fact-finding and careful decision making, respect for people, and teamwork. It is in part because of the company's commitment to these principles that its customers are extremely loyal, and this turned out to be hugely valuable to the firm when the "gas pedal" crisis hit.

"Toyota owners paused, but didn't jump away from Toyota," Morrison said in June 2011. He added, "They have decades of positive experience with us, and this created a disconnect between the negative news they read about the crisis, and their own experience with Toyota." While Morrison acknowledges that some non-Toyota owners "may have crossed us off their shopping lists" during the height of the crisis, the current owners did not abandon the company (nor did they stop offering good recommendations for it). Morrison believes many other carmakers, without so many long-term, loyal customers, wouldn't have survived a similar crisis as effectively.

The company had evidence that Toyota owners continued to support the company even in the early weeks of the crisis. The company used the social media platform Digg to run a "Digg Dialogg" in which Toyota owners and other interested people could ask questions of Jim Lentz, the president of Toyota Motor Sales USA. The Digg software ranked the questions according to popularity. The two most popular had nothing to do with the crisis, instead asking Lentz what car he drives and about the future of electric vehicles at Toyota. Two of the six questions involved the recall crisis, demonstrating that the people most involved with Toyota were interested in a variety of topics, not just the recall.

Besides its loyal customer base, Morrison credits the rebound to some critical communications decisions made by the company in the midst and aftermath of the crisis:

- High-level accountability: The CEO publicly apologized and promised to make things right.

- Broad communication: Toyota significantly increased its brand-related advertising, while also maintaining product-specific advertising. Total ad spending increased by about 40 percent, according to Kantar Media. Specifically the company took advantage of large audiences for the opening ceremonies of the 2010 Winter Olympics to say "Our company hasn't been living up to the standards that you've come to expect from us or that we expect from ourselves."

- Promotion: As a way to keep current customers in the fold, they offered zero percent financing for sixty months and described the program as a "way of saying thanks."

- Grassroots communication: Toyota distributed special funds to every dealer in the country in order for them to develop their own local communications programs, such as open houses to answer questions and concerns. The company also continued to heavily organize local events to engage new car buyers at retail locations such as Best Buy and Bass Pro Shops and at music festivals.

- Engagement with customers via social media: Toyota created a marketing program called "Auto-Biographies" that involved customer-created content to celebrate people's relationships with their Toyotas and spur advocacy. According to Kimberley Gardiner, who leads social media for Toyota, the new platform had just been built when the recall crisis hit, and it became a way for people to express themselves. "We tried not to be too heavy handed about it," she said, allowing people to talk about why they love their Toyota at a time when the news media was running with a very different story. Some of these advocate stories turned into an authentic testimonial campaign with TV commercials and print ads for the Camry and Corolla makes.

The decision to communicate so extensively was not automatic. Like other companies coping with crisis, Toyota had to wrestle with decisions about where resources could be most effectively allocated— and indeed whether to communicate at all in the midst of such negative news. Saatchi & Saatchi LA, Toyota's agency since 1974, played a critical role in the decision to make a major investment in advertising, and two papers on word-of-mouth research from Keller Fay Group were central to making the case. The first paper, "Advertising amid Crisis," was described earlier in this chapter; it provided an estimate of the degree to which Toyota's word of mouth had shifted negative as a result of negative news coverage. The second paper related to a statistical analysis by the media agency Universal McCann, described in chapter 5. In that analysis, UM estimated the cost required to move word of mouth by 1 percentage point. Saatchi's "return on marketing investment" team observed that the negative news in the press behaved a great deal like ad spending by a competitor. By bringing together the data from the two published papers, it was possible to estimate the negative value of all the news coverage: about $1.9 billion, according to Saatchi executives.

This insight was a factor in convincing Toyota to significantly increase paid brand messaging in order to offset the negative news, according to Toyota's Morrison and senior executives at Saatchi LA. Given how quickly word of mouth turned positive again after just a few months, it would seem that their approach clearly worked.

Profiting from Negative Word of Mouth

Negative word of mouth is something worth avoiding and minimizing, as the financial industry and Toyota examples show. But negative word of mouth can be valuable in terms of teaching marketers valuable lessons—and pointing the way toward improvement.

In chapter 7 we discussed the company Bazaarvoice, whose software powers online ratings and reviews for big marketers like Samsung and Procter & Gamble and major e-retail sites such as Bestbuy.com and Walmart.com. Bazaarvoice provides online shoppers with immediate opportunities to report on what they like and don't like about products they bought online, posted right on the site where they purchased the product or to the manufacturer's site. The reviews are tied to a precise product that has been purchased and include a standard 1 to 5 star rating score as well as other feedback. These reviews are available to all site visitors, as well as to client companies.

Marketers' fear of negative word of mouth has been a challenge for Bazaarvoice from its founding. Why would a marketer want to publish the negative opinions of its customers? For marketers, there can be a huge temptation to want to suppress negative reviews. Bazaarvoice cofounder and CEO Brett Hurt says that his company has never suppressed a bad review, apart from editing out profanity or comments against a religion or ethnic group. But Hurt acknowledges that most new clients are at first concerned about the risk of negative reviews.

From an overall perspective, the problem of negative reviews is rather small. About 80 percent of product reviews worldwide earn 4 or 5 stars out of a possible 5, confirming the Keller Fay finding that most word of mouth is positive. Chart 8.7 presents data from Bazaarvoice consumer reviews in twenty-seven countries, in which average ratings range from a low of 3.85 in Spain to a high of 4.5 in Chile. The United States, the source of the largest number of reviews, is in the top half, at 4.3.

Chart 8.7

CONSUMERS WORLDWIDE RATE PRODUCTS HIGHLY

Average consumer ratings, by country (on a scale of 1 to 5)

RANK	COUNTRY	AVERAGE RATINGS
1	Chile	4.5
2	Puerto Rico	4.4
3	Australia	4.4
4	New Zealand	4.4
5	Mexico	4.4
6	United Kingdom	4.3
7	Germany	4.3
8	Ireland	4.3
9	United States	4.3
10	Canada	4.3
11	South Korea	4.3
12	Belgium	4.2
13	France	4.2
14	Netherlands	4.2
15	Norway	4.2
16	Brazil	4.1
17	Japan	4.1
18	India	4.1
19	Switzerland	4.1
20	Austria	4.1
21	Sweden	4.1
22	Denmark	4.1
23	Finland	4.1
24	China	4.0
25	Italy	4.0
26	Portugal	3.9
27	Spain	3.9

Source: Bazaarvoice.

While most customer reviews are positive, some are not. In Hurt's view these negative reviews are "a gift." Certainly, that is the view of L.L. Bean, the outdoor apparel company based in Maine. A client of Bazaarvoice, Bean has a tradition of excellent customer service that goes back to the company's founding in 1912 with the invention of the Maine Hunting Shoe. Since the beginning, the company has had a famous guarantee: "Our products are guaranteed to give 100% satisfaction in every way. Return anything purchased from us at any time if it proves otherwise. We do not want you to have anything from L.L. Bean that is not completely satisfactory."

It's hard to believe that there is a company that replaces its products after failing from normal wear and tear—but L.L. Bean does. "We are one of the very few brands in which the customer decides the guarantee. We don't put a time frame on it. You decide if it is fair, and that's the definition we are going with," said Bean CMO Steve Fuller at a conference of Bazaarvoice clients in 2011.

In addition to the customer guarantee, the company has a tradition of seeking out customer feedback. In 1936 the founder, Leon Leonwood Bean, said, "We welcome criticism of our merchandise or service, either favorable or unfavorable." Part of this strategy is to have all their call center customer service representatives located in the company's home state of Maine—"in Bangor, not Bangalore," according to CMO Fuller.

Surely the original Mr. Bean could not have anticipated the invention of the Internet and the scale and speed with which such feedback would one day be delivered. But one imagines he would have welcomed it, as has the current management of L.L. Bean. Bean has over 300,000 ratings and reviews on file via Bazaarvoice, and they use these reviews in a wide variety of ways. Of course, they are available on the website as a guide to the next purchaser's decision. In addition, they are used in advertising, as in this headline from a recent ad: "I am in love with this doormat. Is it wrong to love a doormat?"

As a management tool, the ratings and reviews are distributed, in aggregate, in a report distributed to company managers every Monday, alongside financial performance metrics. On Thursdays a report of "winners and losers" is also made available, to show which products are performing best and which are performing worst. And it's the negative reviews that are particularly interesting.

Fuller says that six negative reviews are a key action threshold for management. If there are fewer than six bad reviews (a one- or two-star rating), then the relevant company manager is responsible for responding to the customers and making things right. Most often Bean finds there has been an error in the way the product was described on the website or in the catalogue, and this is quickly fixed.

But if a product gets six or more negative reviews, the matter is escalated and leads to one of three actions: (1) the product is liquidated because the price was too high relative to the value of the product; (2) the inventory is given away to charity because the product does not meet Bean's standards; or (3) in rare cases, the product isn't even good enough to give away with the L.L. Bean name on it, and therefore the product is destroyed. In 2010 Bean destroyed half a million dollars' worth of merchandise, in every case because the product was made "out of spec" by the supplier. "There's nothing more powerful than to go back to a supplier with a fistful of negative reviews," says Fuller.

Online ratings and reviews have in this way allowed a company with a long-standing reputation for outstanding service and focus on customer satisfaction to extend its tradition to the Internet age. But online reviews also played a key role in helping a very modern company recovering from a reputation problem: Dell.

In Search of Dell Heaven

We began this chapter with the story of "Dell Hell," the blog-fueled crisis that caused Dell to become more progressive in the way it manages social media feedback. After the initial crisis in 2005, Dell spent the next year making a large investment in customer service and customer care and helped to lead other companies in embracing the new reality of consumer-generated media.

By 2007, though, the company decided to take its efforts to an entirely new level. Alex Gruzen was running the small and medium-size business product group at Dell between 2004 and 2010, during which time he became a client of Bazaarvoice. In the beginning it was obvious to Gruzen why an e-retailer like Amazon would want to offer ratings and reviews: the products weren't owned by the retailer, and the reviews helped shoppers make a quick decision about which product to buy. But putting ratings and reviews on the Dell.com website seemed less obvious and much riskier: all the products were Dell's, and some were bound to be reviewed negatively.

Gruzen described having a "holy shit moment" upon discovering the company had products with ratings of 3.2 stars. He wondered, "Who is going to buy that?" He says the company was presented with a choice: either they could remove the negative reviews and lose credibility, or they could change all their management processes to incorporate feedback in real time and authentically raise their product ratings. The company chose the latter strategy.

This decision was critical for several reasons, the first one being credibility. It is commonly assumed that if consumers find zero negative reviews about a product online they are going to doubt that the positive ones are legitimate. It's actually better to have a few negative reviews to add credibility and to allow people to read a variety of perspectives. It's also the ethical and legal thing to do. The Word of Mouth Marketing Association and the Federal Trade Commission have both published guidelines on online consumer opinions, and both are strongly on the side of transparency and authenticity, as are we. (See chapter 7 regarding ethics in word of mouth.)

For Dell, jumping into online ratings and reviews sparked a revolution for the company. In 2008 Dell's average rating was just 3.7 stars across all its products. Gruzen set a goal to get average ratings up to 4.0 for 2009, and achieved it. Dell then set, and achieved, ratings of 4.3 by early 2010, and 4.5 by the end of 2010, incorporating these as targets in executives' management goals. Gruzen acknowledges the changes did not come easily. They involved a cultural change.

To help achieve these goals, Dell launched a "Five Star Challenge," which required that every product team create a plan to grow review ratings from an average of four stars to five stars. Gruzen and his team incorporated consumer feedback into the product development process. Says Gruzen, "I have been doing product development for twenty years, and never before did I have feedback that was specific to a certain product, and delivered fast enough so that we could act on it. Feedback within ten days meant Dell could fix a product in the factory in the first month of manufacturing. At other companies, we measured quality by the number of warranty parts needed in the field. But once we started realizing the power of consumer feedback, we changed our main quality metric to the five-star rating, with feedback delivered in real time. Bazaarvoice had an engine for feedback; we had to find the causes of problems, and feed the information to new product teams. You could see real-time improvements to the product. Fixing problems in the current product year was a breakthrough."

Negative word of mouth—it's rarer than you think, but when you get it, fear not: embrace it instead. Make smart decisions about the root causes and all the tools at your disposal to react and respond. Agreeing with Bazaarvoice's founder Brett Hurt, Dell's Gruzen says, "Negative information from a customer is the greatest gift you can have."

9

Imagining a
New Social Marketing

Throughout this book we have made a case that sparking conversations is a critical success factor for all marketing, and that any channel, or form of marketing, has the potential to unleash the power of social influence. We have seen that being social is fundamental to our humanness, and we've seen how impactful other people can be on the decisions we make in our lives. And we have shown that the opportunity for social marketing extends far, far beyond the myriad social media tools that are available to marketers today. Online social media drives only a small amount of the much larger and more varied range of conversations that take place each day about products, services, and brands. All types of advertising, public relations, direct marketing, promotion, and customer service activities can and should be used to generate positive word of mouth, advocacy, and socially influenced decisions. Marketing and advertising are most effective when thought of as part of a two-step flow in which information and messages from media are shared and discussed with other people before decisions are made.

The fact that word of mouth and social marketing can be initiated and executed from virtually any part of an organization creates large strategy and implementation challenges for management. When faced with a new strategic opportunity, the instinctive solution within most organizations is to declare, "We need a dedicated team to do that!" And this, almost always, leads to the question of who owns the initiative. In what department shall it reside? Indeed there are a remarkable number of articles and blog posts under the title "Who Owns Word of Mouth?" or, more commonly, "Who Owns Social Media?" The difficulty companies have had in answering this question has led to turf and budget battles that have undermined companies' ability to capitalize fully and completely on the opportunity to become more social.

In our work we've encountered companies in which word-of-mouth and social marketing initiatives have been entirely owned by public relations, digital marketing, or customer service departments, by customer relationship management, departments responsible for product sampling, or even market research departments. In some cases, these departments have veto power over the use of word-of-mouth marketing strategies, tools, and vendors by anybody else in the company. Many companies have gone through long, drawn-out and sometimes painful reviews to evaluate all vendors in the word-of-mouth or social arena in terms of their ability to meet the needs of every functional corner of an organization. In our view this approach is bureaucratic and has inhibited organizations from truly embracing social marketing and maximizing their marketing performance.

Most of the above-mentioned departments have strong claims. Public relations points out that word of mouth is earned media, in that marketing has to be interesting enough to encourage somebody to talk about it, just as stories for the press must be interesting enough to journalists and editors to earn media coverage. Digital marketing departments argue that they have the most expertise in Web 2.0 social media tools and techniques, and thus are best able to motivate and manage consumer conversations online. Departments that own customer databases assert that they own their organization's best sources of intelligence on their customers; hence they are best placed to identify and communicate with customers who are brand loyalists and potential advocates of the brand. Customer service and market research point out that they have unique capabilities to listen to the voice of the customer in an age when marketers need to listen before they speak in a two-way dialogue with customers and prospects. The advertising and media departments—and the agencies serving them—can reasonably claim that they have the greatest expertise in developing and delivering content that will be worth talking about. Even human resource departments may have a claim on word of mouth: some have suggested that every single employee, whether they use Twitter or just talk about their employer on the sidelines of a soccer field, is a potential ambassador, or detractor, for the organization, deserving of social media training and empowerment.

The question of how to manage social strategies is important. In a 2011 survey of brands that are members of the Word of Mouth Marketing Association, two-thirds cited a "lack of coordination" as an obstacle to pursuing a word-of-mouth marketing or social media strategy.

Another perspective comes from a survey undertaken by Altimeter Group, a research-based advisory firm that specializes in disruptive technologies. Founded by Charlene Li, the author of the books *Open Leadership* and *Groundswell* and a former vice president at Forrester, Altimeter has been among the most advanced in thinking about how companies can adapt to the new social marketing. In late 2010 Altimeter partner and principal analyst Jeremiah Owyang was on the speaking circuit, describing how companies were adapting to social marketing. He reported that in a survey of businesses, Altimeter found a split between companies that house social media under marketing (41 percent) and under corporate communications (30 percent). He also analyzed the management strategy adopted by companies, identifying five approaches. The leading one, called "hub and spoke," puts expertise in a central support role that provides guidance to other operational units of the company, a strategy adopted by 41 percent of the companies Altimeter surveyed. The next most popular (used by 29 percent) was a "centralized" strategy in which one department is responsible for all social activities. The least popular was a "holistic" approach, used by just 1 percent, in which "everyone in the company uses social media safely and consistently across all organizations."

Chart 9.1

SOCIAL MARKETING STRATEGIES: ONLY 1% OF COMPANIES
EMBRACE A HOLISTIC APPROACH

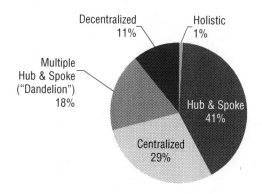

Source: Jeremiah Owyang, Altimeter Group, "Social Business Forecast: 2011,
The Year of Integration."

The fact that so few companies embrace a holistic approach underscores how far the business community still needs to travel in the way it thinks about social marketing. To the extent that they have a strategy, many are focused predominantly on online social media, such as Facebook, Twitter, blogging, and online customer reviews. Few are focused on the larger social marketing opportunity that encompasses social conversation via all channels and a new, more social approach to every form of marketing. Altimeter's research also left unanswered who *should* own social marketing.

Several experts reject the corporate ownership question altogether. Another Altimeter principal analyst, Brian Solis, has argued that the ownership of word of mouth shouldn't be internal to corporations— that word of mouth is owned by all the brands' customers and external influencers, in keeping with the new "consumer-centric" marketing model. We agree with this assessment, yet it is not an entirely satisfying point of view, because it leaves open the question of who *within* a brand organization is responsible for managing those many external relationships, as leaving them to chance seems rather risky.

Another answer we've heard to the "Who owns it?" question is a company's chief executive officer or chief marketing officer. It's hard to quarrel with this answer, since surely the buck stops in the c-suite for all important things, but it's also true that these are people with rather busy jobs; they may own social marketing, but it's a fact of life that it will have to be delegated to others in order to get much done. Which leads us back to the original question: To whom?

We would like to offer this answer: social marketing shouldn't be owned by anyone. Rather it should be a fundamental way of doing business for all functions and therefore deployed by all. This surely will sound to some like a cop-out, but it's a carefully considered point of view. Just as we believe that social marketing is far greater than a matter of deploying a new set of so-called social media tools, we also believe that social marketing shouldn't be thought of mainly as a channel or as a single corporate function. Social influence is, quite simply, the way markets function, and therefore it's the way businesses should function. Social influence needs to be a philosophy—a paradigm, if you will—that all parts of the business enterprise need to embrace. Arguing over who owns social marketing is a bit like arguing over who owns a whole series of fundamental truths that large organizations accept and support today, such as the notion that the customer is always right; that companies must be accountable to their shareholders, communities, customers, and employees; that revenues should exceed costs; that motivated employees produce better results than discouraged ones. These are things that we all learn as fundamental to working in a business environment of virtually any kind.

The same is true for social influence; everybody needs to incorporate social thinking in what they do. In this sense, we would endorse the holistic management strategy described by Altimeter, although with this caveat: social influence should be defined much more broadly than as "online social media." The rapid growth in enthusiasm for social media has brought attention to social marketing as a concept—but it's also skewed our perception of what social marketing means. Social is not about a technology or a channel; it's about people, and how we all make decisions every day.

The truth is, consumers make decisions socially—they always have, and they always will—and business practices need to be designed accordingly. Until it becomes second nature to businesses, every department should be charged with having an overt social strategy. If a company decides it needs to hire a social marketing guru to champion the idea, give him or her a long leash. A social guru ought to teach and encourage social strategies and tactics widely, throughout an organization.

What does this mean in practical terms? Several companies we've been following closely are well along on their journeys to marketing in a more social way, one that embraces social media but has embedded the principle of being social far more broadly. Best Buy has done it by training a large number of front-line employees to think socially and to focus on social objectives. General Mills has done it by capitalizing on its long-standing social assets, while embracing principles of a "modern campaign" that places more emphasis on earned and owned media without minimizing the importance of paid media. Kimberly-Clark has reengineered the marketing process to increase collaboration, emphasizing talkworthy commercial ideas. All three companies admit they are still at the early stages of a process they know will continue to evolve, yet all are worth emulating by anyone who believes that social influence needs to be given much more weight in how organizations manage themselves and go to market.

Best Buy's Twelpforce Connects Employees to Customers

As we discussed in chapter 8, Dell is a company that has embraced the idea that social influence needs to be an important component of how it goes about its business. Dell has now trained some 10,000 employees in social marketing, and they have dramatically improved customer satisfaction and advocacy through these efforts. The same is true of the tech retailer Best Buy, which has harnessed the power of its massive army of retail associates to strengthen relationships with customers. Both companies have integrated social into their management practices, and they've done it on a large scale.

Best Buy has long understood the value of conversation with customers in a real-world setting, hence its well-trained and carefully branded Blue Shirts (its army of in-store salespeople) and its investment in the Geek Squad, a meticulously marketed company subsidiary with space in all Best Buy stores, which employs thousands of agents who help people set up and troubleshoot their electronics purchases. The Blue Shirts and Geek Squad agents have been a huge part of the phenomenal Best Buy sales growth from $9 million in 1983 to more than $50 billion today. But, of course, these sales and service experts only converse with people who have already elected to talk to them.

As Best Buy CMO Barry Judge told us, "When we think about social marketing it's about taking the brand proposition beyond the store. I mean, with the store, your doors are open and you can hope people come in and allow you to help them. But the genius of social is that it allows you to get outside of your store and find people who are already having conversations about consumer electronics—and participate in them and share your knowledge and help them."

It was thinking like this that prompted Best Buy to launch the Best Buy Community, an online arena where customers could seek help from Best Buy advocates such as Blue Shirts and Geek Squad agents, as well as interact with other customers. They also launched Best Buy Twitter channels in multiple languages and launched blogs that covered electronics and allowed users to raise specific issues, converse, and get answers.

Then, in July 2009, Best Buy started really trying to scale this dialogue, by launching its Twelpforce initiative, which essentially gave all customer service agents the ability to chat with and help anyone on Twitter. Instead of just helping people who had visited a Best Buy destination, the company's huge army of tweeters could spot conversations already going on between two customers and offer their thoughts or contribute to the chat. As Judge put it, "Twelpforce really emerged from that concept of 'Well, we'd help them if they came to the store, so why not try to get outside of the store and help people.'"

Judge continued, "Social differentiates us. We have the blogs and Twitter, and I think it's appreciated and understood by our customers, but it's still relatively fringe. It's not like mainstream people would understand. I think Twelpforce is a platform that we can do a lot more with. We won Direct Marketer of the Year for the Twelpforce, and we won a Titanium Cannes Lion for the best digital idea in the world. . . . But it's more an internal tool than it is something that's really . . . getting a lot of traction with consumers. We've got a platform and we've proven it's interesting, but it's just like anything else—you've still got to put some muscle behind it so that people know what you're doing."

One way to look at the return on investment in this case is that the Twelpforce team had answered over 30,000 questions from consumers as of the middle of 2010, according to Best Buy. And importantly, it drove customer complaints down by over 20 percent because it got to some of the potential complainants and resolved the problem before the customer felt the need to pick up the phone to reach a Best Buy call center. More than half a million customers visit the Best Buy Community sites every quarter, and they post more than 20,000 messages during that period.

TalkTrack surveys show additional evidence of initial success for Best Buy. In the first half of 2010 word of mouth about the company that made reference to the Internet as an information source rose to about a third of conversations, double what it was in the prior year, likely reflecting, in part, the increased use of the Internet as a conversation channel with the Twelpforce. Our research also finds a reduction in purely negative word of mouth about Best Buy over this same time, consistent with fewer complaints.

Barry Judge knows that this is just step one in terms of word-of-mouth marketing for Best Buy. What he's essentially achieved so far is to integrate digital social tools into customer service, amplifying the number of conversations between his paid advocates and his customers. What he hasn't done yet is maximize the benefit of all the consumer-to-consumer conversations that happen.

"It's true," Judge says, "so far we've seen social as being much more about the employees and about doing customer service in a scalable way that takes the conversation beyond the stores. We've done less around the new ways people are going to get information, which is clearly from their friends and social networks. We're talking about that, thinking about that, and I think it's coming quick. How do we do even more to participate in a conversation?" Best Buy continues to refine this incredibly beneficial strategy.

General Mills Increases Its Emphasis on Earned and Owned Media

General Mills is one of the world's largest food companies. Started with a pair of flour mills in the 1860s, today it sells a mix of old brands that have stood the test of time—Betty Crocker, Pillsbury, Cheerios, and Green Giant, to name a few—with relative newcomers such as Fiber One, Nature Valley, and Yoplait Yogurt. As with so many brand marketers that we have profiled in this book, General Mills recognizes that the changing dynamics of the consumer marketplace demand changes in the way the company markets its products. Social influence now plays a very important role in the design and execution of the company's marketing programs.

Keller Fay's involvement with the General Mills journey from a "traditional" to a "social" company began when the CMO, Mark Addicks, invited Ed to address the company's marketing organization in 2006 about the power of word of mouth and the forces that drive it. We then consulted with General Mills as it designed and began developing new social programs such as Pssst and MyBlogSpark. Pssst is an advocacy network of about 200,000 influential, "everyday" consumers who told General Mills they were interested in receiving news, behind-the-scenes information, and new product samples, and who are then encouraged to spread the word to their social network via offline conversations or online posts on social networking sites. It is an in-house version of programs we talked about in chapter 7 by word-of-mouth agencies such as Tremor/Vocalpoint (which is owned by P&G but works non-P&G brands as well) and BzzAgent. MyBlog-Spark is a network of about 5,000 bloggers who blog about food and who have agreed to receive information and news from General Mills or give feedback about new product and marketing concepts that are being considered. They are then encouraged to blog (honestly) about anything they receive that interests them. General Mills says this network affords them the opportunity to "join the conversation with influential consumers online."

CMO Addicks says that General Mills' journey to creating a holistic social strategy for the entire organization started long before the advent of the Internet. To see this, one needs only to look at Betty Crocker, a key name in General Mills' brand stable. For those who don't know, Betty Crocker was never a real person. The character was created in 1921, when a promotion for Gold Medal flour flooded the company with questions about baking. To answer the questions in a more personal manner, a fictitious cooking expert was created. Her last name honored an outgoing member of the board of directors (William Crocker), and her first name was adopted because it sounded friendly. Since then Betty Crocker has had her own radio programs (beginning in 1924) and TV shows (1954–1976), published hundreds of cookbooks, and sold magazines at checkouts, and a 1945 *Fortune* magazine study found she was the second most famous woman in America after Eleanor Roosevelt. "Long before Martha Stewart, there was Betty Crocker," said *Advertising Age* when it honored her as one of the icons of the "Advertising Century."

Also in the 1940s, Addicks told us, Betty Crocker received thousands of letters each day, seeking her advice about cooking. Each one was answered. And hundreds of thousands of people would visit the company's Minneapolis headquarters—often as part of their vacation—to tour the Betty Crocker kitchens. The brand enjoyed the type of relationship with consumers that the most social of brands aspire to have with consumers today. To Addicks, this isn't just a good story. It's an important reminder that people had social relationships with brands long before there was Facebook, Twitter, or even email. He believes technology is an enabler, but not the reason people establish social relationships with brands. "Don't follow technology, follow the consumer" is one of Addicks's mantras.

Inspiration for one of General Mills' current programs came from another one of their legacy brands, Bisquick, a brand that General Mills launched in 1930. To celebrate the fiftieth anniversary of Bisquick in 1980, it published a special-edition cookbook, *Betty Crocker's Creative Recipes with Bisquick*. At the same time, it launched the Bisquick Recipe Club, which provided its members with a free newsletter and cookbooks and encouraged them to share baking tips and recipes with their friends and family. At its peak, hundreds of thousands of baking enthusiasts were part of the program. The program ended in 1985, however, because it became too expensive to keep it going in light of the rising cost of postage and fulfillment.

In the early 2000s Addicks was meeting with a large retailer when the opportunity presented itself to tap into the retailer's loyalty card database to launch an e-mail marketing campaign. The question was what to do. Remembering the success of the Bisquick Recipe Club, that idea was refreshed and reintroduced. Over 80 percent of the people who were invited to join accepted. They might receive Saturday morning breakfast ideas, or ideas for how to make heart-shaped cookies for Valentine's Day. Today this has evolved into the Recipe of the Day from Betty Crocker, available on BettyCrocker.com. Recipes are also available from Betty Crocker via Facebook and Twitter for those who prefer those vehicles.

"Whenever it makes sense," Addicks said, "we try to modernize an old idea. I firmly believe that what is old will be new again. We just have to rejuvenate great ideas from the past." He considers it one of the benefits of having such a rich corporate history and legacy brands. It also helps him to inspire confidence in his team that they can launch new social marketing ideas successfully.

In 2010 Addicks started preaching to his organization about the importance of what he calls "the modern campaign." He developed the principles by studying what other highly successful companies were doing by benchmarking with them, when possible, or studying them from afar. He was particularly interested in the best practices of those brands (from within the food industry and outside of it) that consistently outgrow their category average over a three-year period. From this exercise emerged the operating principles of the modern campaign.

The biggest change, says Addicks, is the order in which the company now prioritizes among earned, owned, and paid media. In the past lip service was given to all three, but paid media was at the heart of both marketing strategy and execution. The ad agency was at the center of new ideas, and other disciplines needed to follow their lead. Today Addicks says earned media is the most important priority, because he believes that consumers value most what they hear authentically. Fiber One bars are an example of a product for which General Mills says that consumer conversation was critical to its launch. In fact its research found that online consumer conversation correlated quite well with unit sales during the launch phase. Owned media is the next most important because it is where consumers go to seek out information. The General Mills legacy, with brands such as Betty Crocker, thus becomes a very important asset for the company when it comes to owned media, which today has been expanded to include heavily trafficked websites, Facebook pages, and Twitter feeds, in addition to popular cookbooks and other forms of more traditional media. Paid media is now third in the General Mills pecking order. It is still incredibly important to the company, says Addicks, but it no longer leads, nor do the people who create the ads.

We believe that the General Mills experience sheds light on a particularly important insight, which is the degree to which earned and owned media can work together. Since we launched TalkTrack, we've been impressed by the frequency with which people talk about something they have seen on a brand website when they talk about a brand. In fully 5 percent of all conversations about brands—that's about 750 million word-of-mouth impressions each week—somebody mentions something he's seen on a brand's website; that's higher than the number who mention an Internet ad, a newspaper or magazine ad, indeed any other type of paid media other than a TV commercial. Brand websites should not be forgotten or minimized as marketers search for ways to engage with today's social consumers.

Like a brand website, the product package is another form of owned media. In about 4 percent of all conversations—around 600 million times per week—people are exposed to a conversation about something seen on a product package, which in the case of food products might include recipes or nutritional information. For Betty Crocker that number is double the average rate, with 9 percent of conversations in 2010 and 2011 referring to something on the product package.

Why do owned media loom so large when it comes to earning word of mouth? We think the reason is that these owned touch points are one of the best ways brands have for connecting with consumer influencers, and particularly brand advocates. People who love and advocate for a particular brand are always looking for information to share about it. That information could come from a Facebook page, but it's more likely consumers are going to visit bettycrocker.com and share the recipe ideas they find with their friends.

Regardless of the channel, these owned media are the ideal place to put information you want your advocates to know about. And once they find something interesting, it's in their nature to want to share it with others, so it's important to make it easy for them to do so. When a company designs its websites, social media sites, newsletters, packages, and even coupons, brands should use "forward thinking." This means designing content that will be easy to find, digest, and forward to other people.

Addicks's experience also suggests an important mantra for managing "the modern campaign," with its emphasis on earned and owned media: "Good ideas can come from anywhere." A winning idea, he says, might still come from the creative agency, as it used to. But it can also come from PR, package design, the multicultural team, digital, or couponing. He expects his teams and his agencies to work together. He also is looking for a different set of skills within his marketing department. "We want people who are deeply skilled," he says, "but we also want people who are broadly skilled. We are training people to think more broadly and not to be niche specialists anymore."

It all comes back to the need for a deeper and better understanding of the consumer and what makes her tick. The goals of the modern campaign are *engage, convert, advocate*. What does this mean in practice? According to Addicks, "Consumers are always sorting their priorities for how they spend their time and their money. We need to engage with them at the right time and the right place." In fact, he says, "where, when and how you market to the consumer is often as important, if not more so, than what you say, because it helps her to determine how well you understand the consumer." Addicks's observations about "where, when, and how" have important implications for media planning, as we discussed in chapter 5. Increasingly it is possible to target messages to reach people when they are most likely to be interested—a recipe timed with meal planning, for example—and also most apt to share it with somebody who is close by. Beyond targeting for demographic segments, it's important to target those media channels, times of day, and locations that are most likely to promote engagement with the brand and its message.

Once they have engaged with the brand, the goal is then to convert consumers to purchase a General Mills product. And finally, the company wants consumers to advocate on behalf of the brand—to become brand champions. This means that the product must be remarkable enough to be worth talking about, and that the company provides tools and experiences that can be easily shared. "We need to understand what consumers want to know and what they want to do, and then we need to determine how we can be of help," says Addicks. "If we can do that, then we are of service and we will achieve all three goals: engage, convert, advocate."

Kimberly-Clark: Starting an Unlikely Conversation

As we discussed in chapter 2, it hasn't been easy to dispel the widespread belief that word-of-mouth marketing works only in "exciting" categories, like technology, cars, restaurants, travel, and movies. We hope that by now we have convinced you that word of mouth can also work for everyday products and brands in categories like children's products, beverages, and beauty products. But tampons? Yes, word of mouth can work for tampons and other feminine hygiene products too. As we discovered in writing this book, the phenomenally successful launch of the tampon brand U by Kotex in 2010 can teach many of the most important lessons for the new social marketing. And the lessons go beyond how to design and execute a great social marketing campaign—they also teach us how corporations should manage themselves differently in this social marketing era.

Kimberly-Clark, the big consumer packaged goods company based in Irving, Texas, manufactures and markets a wide variety of household and personal care products, including feminine protection items, a rather quiet category that had seen very little innovation in decades. Traditionally it's a category that people are *not* supposed to talk about. Or if they do, conversations are generally limited to private whispers between mother and daughter, between sisters, or among one's closest girlfriends. Advertising and marketing in the category have long been based on breezy images of snowy, white purity and euphemistic language about "freshness" and "protection." In her humorous autobiography *Bossypants*, the comic actress Tina Fey pokes fun, seriously, at the time-honored Madison Avenue approach to menstruation. Recalling her first menses, she writes, "I had noticed something was weird earlier in the day, but I knew from the commercials that one's menstrual period was a blue liquid you poured like laundry detergent into maxi pads to test their absorbency; this wasn't blue, so . . . I ignored it for a few hours."

Kimberly-Clark executives believed that society's unwillingness to talk honestly about vaginal health and menstruation was a serious matter, with the potential to lead to bad health decisions and outcomes by teenagers unable to get the information they needed. This view was supported by a Harris Interactive survey they commissioned among U.S. and Canadian females ages fourteen to thirty-five. Among those polled, 70 percent said they believed "it's about time society changes how it talks about vaginal health issues," while fewer than half (45 percent) said they felt empowered to make a difference. About half (52 percent) said they felt society looks down on talking about vaginal health.

The crucial idea behind U by Kotex was that feminine protection should not be a taboo subject. Not only should women feel comfortable talking about it, but the category could even become fashionable. U by Kotex's packaging and applicators would be colorful, and its marketing would break the cycle of euphemistic advertising and communications about the category. Tampons—and vaginal health generally—would become acceptable topics for conversation. The launch campaign was designed to encourage honest conversations and to provide essential health and how-to information to young women.

First launched in Australia in 2007, U by Kotex was launched in the United States in March 2010, jumping from zero to a 5.5 percent share of the tampon market by the following spring, while also increasing the overall Kotex share by 2.5 points, to a total of 18.2 percent, and expanding the entire tampon category by 2 percent. This was a stunning success in a market that hadn't seen a serious product innovation since Tampax Pearl ten years earlier. Indeed U by Kotex was named 2011 USA Product of the Year, based on a survey of 60,000 shoppers. In 2011 the Brand Power Index, created by NBC Universal, named Kotex and Harley Davidson two brands that were gaining the most traction among women, drawing on data

from Keller Fay Group and two other sources. The campaign succeeded by getting young women to talk about the surprisingly fun
and fashionable colors, the silliness of traditional feminine protection
advertising, and the social importance of having honest conversations
about women's health.

And it worked. According to TalkTrack surveys, the Kotex family
of brands increased their share of category conversations among females thirteen to forty-four from 20 percent in 2008 to 32 percent in
the first half of 2011. The peak talk levels came when the new brand
was featured on *The Tyra Banks Show* and Khloé Kardashian made a
"declaration of real talk" in support of the brand on national media; at
that time, WOM levels for Kotex were four times higher than before
the campaign among females ages thirteen to twenty-four—the prime
target market for the brand.

Chart 9.2

KOTEX'S TALKSHARE™ EXPERIENCED A SHARP JUMP IN EARLY 2011

Brand's share of feminine care WOM among women 13–44

	2008 (%)	2009 (%)	2010 (%)	1ST HALF OF 2011 (%)
Kotex	20	22	25	32
Always	34	41	32	30
Tampax	32	28	32	29
Playtex	14	8	11	9

Source: Keller Fay Group's TalkTrack®, January 2008–June 2011.

Based on discussions with key marketing and product development executives at Kimberly-Clark, including Chief Marketing Officer Tony Palmer, plus launch team members from the agencies
involved, we've observed that there are several key components to the
company's success not only with U by Kotex, but also with a series
of other brands, including Poise for adult light bladder leakage. The
most important factor is the "commercial idea."

The Commercial Idea

The mystique of Madison Avenue has long been linked to a popularized image of the creative process. Since the days of "Mad Men" in the 1960s, fans of the ad world have prized that "eureka moment," when an up-and-coming ad executive, or perhaps the creative director, offers a clever idea that seems to perfectly connect a brand to a current in the popular culture, with a dollop of entertainment and a sprinkling of wit. The idea is then perfectly captured and revealed in a compelling storyboard, leading to the classic "That's it!" reaction from a tough-as-nails client. Usually absent from this story is the product itself. Indeed there is a tendency to most appreciate the brilliant campaign that succeeds even in selling a boring product.

Most marketing executives at Kimberly-Clark, however, talk about the importance of the "commercial idea," meaning the underlying business idea and the consumer benefit, not the idea behind a clever television commercial. CMO Tony Palmer says, "We've changed the way we view innovation. No longer do we simply consider innovation as coming in the form of a new product, but also through the development of the promise of our brands, creation of commercial ideas that are actionable and drive sustainable revenue growth, and the strategic selection of communications channels." In other words, creativity is woven through the entire product development life cycle, not something that's tagged on at the end, when the campaign has been assigned to the ad agency. Kimberly-Clark wants products that sell themselves based on the quality of the idea embedded in their conception and design; the ad campaign is a means to communicating the commercial idea to the intended target.

In our view, this is much like aiming at the outset for a talkworthy idea, something that's going to be worth consumers talking about, recommending, and sharing with each other. "Right from the start, we believed it was about word of mouth," said Kimberly-Clark's Jay Gottlieb, vice president of adult and feminine care marketing, recalling the development of U by Kotex.

The design department played a central role in launching U by

Kotex. Jennifer Westemeyer, the design director for adult and feminine care, said the inspiration for U by Kotex came out of consumer research, in particular from watching how females emptied out their purses containing feminine care products. "We listened with our eyes, not our ears." She said that executives concluded they needed a product that addressed the "individual nature of females," and that "variety was important—a decision to be different with their colors and fashion choices." The result was a wide array of U by Kotex designs and colors for tampons, pads, and liners.

Another key to the strategy was social, to "break the cycle of shame," according to Melissa Sexton, who does integrated marketing planning for adult and feminine care. "We recognized there was little innovation in the category, a lack of education, and we had to ask why we hadn't taken ownership of that. Our go-to-market strategy was to raise consciousness, to shake the tree, causing disruption. We wanted our brand to give a voice to women."

The campaign itself was all about disruption: a tampon that was fashionable and talkworthy and commercials that poked fun at the genre. "Why are tampon ads so ridiculous?" asked one commercial. A particularly humorous spot showed an attractive young woman on hidden camera outside a grocery store, looking for a stranger willing to go into the store to buy her tampons so she didn't have to leave her unlocked bicycle on a city sidewalk. The entertainment comes from the reaction of earnest young men explaining to her why they are not willing to buy her tampons. One gives the incredulous young woman a counteroffer: "I'll buy you toilet paper."

Collaborative Process

Kimberly-Clark executives talk about U by Kotex as just one example of a new product and campaign development process that has changed fundamentally at the company, as evidenced also by the ground that is being broken by Poise, the company's successful light-end incontinence brand that has Whoopi Goldberg and Kris Jenner (mother to the Kardashian children) as some of its spokespeople.

According to CMO Palmer, the company has "created a central Global Marketing Organization, combining marketing, market research and analytics, innovation, and technology, and communications, under one umbrella" that "places the consumer at the center of everything we do." Adds Marketing VP Gottlieb, "It's hard to look for solid reporting lines" at Kimberly-Clark because "we are matrixed and it's all brand-driven," whereas other companies tend to be more organized around functional areas. He says this is important because "sparks of inspiration can come from anywhere," a sentiment echoing what we heard from General Mills. Palmer calls the new approach "integrated marketing planning" that involves everyone, inside and outside the company.

Indeed Kimberly-Clark has elevated the role of certain key agencies to help in providing ideas. In the U by Kotex launch, the digital agency Organic and the public relations agency Marina Maher Communications were invited to participate very early on. Founder and CEO Marina Maher told us that Kimberly-Clark brought MMC "on board almost two years before the product actually launched. We worked collaboratively with our marketing and advertising colleagues to develop a holistic communications strategy that helped credential the brand and create a groundswell of interest from media, customers and women." Maher was proud of the U by Kotex campaign, not only for its results, but also because of its social significance. Writing in her blog just after MMC won Silver Anvils in 2011 for both the U by Kotex and Poise campaigns, she recalled a similar achievement in 1996, when MMC won the same awards for the launch of the Wonderbra. "In 1996 it was about overcoming discomfort above the belt. In 2011, we tackled below the belt—menstruation and light bladder leakage. . . . These topics were so taboo that television networks refused to run TV commercials that used the term 'down there'— although they had no problem running ads for Viagra that warn men to consult their doctors if they 'experience an erection that lasts more than 4 hours.'"

The MMC and Organic executives working most directly on the campaign were passionate about achieving business and social results. "There is so much shame around the subject of the vagina, and it affects women's health and self-esteem. As you think of young women growing up, it has a big affect on them," said Diana Littman Paige of MMC. Amy Carjaval of Organic added, "We had to point out that something was wrong." Honesty was a key value that rallied everyone involved with the campaign.

The response from consumers was impressive. Thousands of comments came back through social media and the brand website (www.ubykotex.com), which was designed and managed by Organic. Carjaval provided us with a few examples:

- "The U by Kotex products really make having your period girly and fun, which is impossible usually. Thank you for making 'that time of the month' cool!"—A.I., via Facebook

- "I gotta admit whoever came up with the U by Kotex concept, packaging and advertising is a genius. It was time for a shakeup in how ladies view feminine products. It was like telling teens and young women: Don't hide it. Own it. Kudos."—Sherelle, via Facebook

- "I love this product soo much that I feel like showing it off."—Monique, via ubykotex.com

- "Hope you know you've change my life. . . . Just everything you've done for people with your website. All the advice you've given us . . . it's just helped a lot."—R., via Twitter

Here are two of the face-to-face conversations reported in the TalkTrack surveys:

- "That this new invention of U by Kotex is just amazing for the people that like comfort-ability, security and don't like to feel embarrassed."—Female, 18

- "I was talking about how the tampons from Kotex have a cute and fun packaging, and are small and discreet." —Female, 15

Kotex's brand website is a place not only for expressing opinions and for connecting with the brand, but also for health information and product advice, including videos on how to use a tampon. Thus the campaign is an outgrowth of the product and the desire to enable women's self confidence—to "champion a woman's pursuit of fearless femininity," in the words of company executives.

In a July 2008 interview with the marketing journal *Marketing-NPV*, Palmer recalled how marketing worked early in his career: "It was about throwing a 30-second spot on the air. You'd shoot an ad, put it on the air, then you go to the sales force and say this is our ad, now take a photograph of it and put it up at the point of sale, and let's see what we can do with it in digital. . . . The challenge today is to re-sequence that. You come up with a brand promise. . . . Then you decide what your channels are going to be. Then you get into creative execution. You don't start with creative execution. . . . And that, to me, is a big, big change for the industry. At Kimberly-Clark, we're a long way down the path."

Sequencing is something we've been talking to our clients about since we started the Keller Fay Group. It starts with finding what's talkworthy, then deciding which consumers to target, then picking the best media channels, some of which might be traditional and some of which might be social networks.

Social 2020

Best Buy, General Mills, and Kimberly-Clark, along with quite a few other companies described in this book, are changing their go-to-market strategies to become more consumer-focused. Social influence provides a valuable framework because it's all about engagement. How do you engage consumers sufficiently so they will want to spend valuable time and attention with you, and then talk about you, share your content with friends and family, and even create their own content related to your brand? The fact that social influence is also fundamental to how human beings live and make decisions increases the importance of and the power of a social strategy even more.

In writing this book, we have had a unique opportunity to study companies at the vanguard of the new social marketing. Drawing on this experience, as well as our research and more than a decade of being deeply involved in the word-of-mouth marketing field, we want to end with these observations about the forces that are at play today and will continue to revolutionize marketing and business over the next decade.

The Science of Social

We believe we are just at the beginning of our understanding of how emotion and social influence are hard-wired into the human brain. Our species has evolved to be supremely social; we are constantly being affected by social cues around us. Emotions are transferred almost unconsciously from person to person; social norms, aspirations, and personal preferences are transferred as well. Social influence is most powerful between people who are close to us in terms of both relationship and proximity. Face-to-face interactions are by far the most powerful, and conversations that occur face-to-face will always be more credible and more likely to spur action than those that occur in other ways.

The rise of online social media is an outgrowth, not a cause, of our social nature, and though their effects are important, they are more limited than many marketers believe. The rapid rise of online networking tools, especially Facebook, offers proof that the desire to connect with others is fundamental to being human. Facebook's Mark Zuckerberg's greatest contribution was recognizing that people's craving for connection was being underserved in the marketplace. Marketers, though, need to employ a varied set of tools if they are going to capitalize on this insight, and need to be careful not to put all their eggs in the basket of a limited number of online social media networks.

We foresee big advances occurring at the intersections of psychology, sociology, anthropology, and neuroscience that will provide new insights and tools that will improve the effectiveness of marketing and communications. Advertising testing, for example, may increasingly involve biometric response measurements to identify images and words that are best at triggering an emotional or social response. These scientific advances will almost certainly reinforce some of the oldest lessons: the power of a story, the engagement delivered by a surprise or "cognitive disruption." They will also reveal new insights about what motivates sharing that will need to be incorporated into the process of developing and executing marketing programs.

Targeting for Influence

Companies have long segmented customers based on their value, as defined by those that spend the most or the most often: frequent shoppers and heavy spenders are traditionally seen as the most valuable customers. We believe that "social value" is a characteristic that can be measured and nurtured—and it's probably the most important metric associated with any current customer of a brand. Your most valuable customers are not necessarily the ones who spend the most money directly on your brand, but the ones who bring the most new customers into the fold through word-of-mouth advocacy. Understanding which customers have the highest social value, and what motivates them, will become an important part of the "insights agenda" for companies.

New technologies will make it increasingly possible to identify those customers and prospects that have the greatest influence on the purchases of other consumers. In addition, there will be more novel marketing tactics and programs that are designed to encourage those influencers and advocates to self-identify as they are attracted to programs that allow them to be "in the know" before other people, like to join loyalty programs, and are people who seek out and share the information with others.

We believe that brand advocates—influencers who are also loyal—are among the most important assets of any brand. They should be a greater focus of marketing research to discover exactly what features and benefits of a brand are the reasons for their recommendations. Marketers may find that often the messages used by their strongest advocates are the ones that should be used more in marketing communications to everyone.

Social Advertising

We anticipate that the wall separating traditional advertising from the nascent field of word-of-mouth advertising will be torn down, as the advertising profession discovers the connection between stimulating conversations and advertising effectiveness.

The creative side of the advertising business will increasingly design communications with the intention of triggering conversations. There are several proven creative strategies for generating conversation with advertising. One is to use advertising to provide a megaphone for authentic consumer recommendations, as Wendy the Snapple Lady did by bringing to life the fan letters of real consumers in television advertising. Contests that put real consumer-created advertising on television, as Doritos did for a Super Bowl commercial and as Toyota did in its "auto-biography" campaign, are consistent with the megaphone ad strategy. Ads that feature ratings and reviews and a review snippet, as Rubbermaid does in free-standing inserts delivered in newspapers, are another example.

Another approach is the "reminder" strategy, designed to stimulate current or former customers to retell their stories of delight to friends and family. Reminders can work especially well for the travel category, which can generate intensely, emotionally satisfying experiences that may fade from memory without a reminder. The strategy, though, can work in any category, as Toyota's New England division demonstrated with its "Ask Someone Who Owns a Toyota" campaign.

One of the most effective creative strategies for generating word of mouth is based on disruptive messaging that marketers can use to drive conversation from people who are seeking to regain their equilibrium after being exposed to something that does not fit their normal expectations. Chick-fil-A, the restaurant chain that sponsors white tablecloth "Daddy-Daughter Date Nights," provides a fine example of disruptive messaging, as do the Domino's pizza commercials that actually admit there was a time when the product wasn't very good.

There may also be room for more exclusive "in the know" messaging that prompts conversations between people who are in the club and those who aren't, as Target did with the mysterious use of its logo in print ads upon its arrival in the New York market. Google uses this philosophy when it rolls out new product launches (most recently for Google+); the only way to become a user is to be invited by others who are already users, thereby creating a buzz in which people clamor to be invited to use the new Google service.

Humor, and especially parody, is another approach that can lead to productive conversations, provided the product is at the center of the conversation. The Crispin Porter + Bogusky campaign that turned baby carrots into snack food effectively parodied both health and junk food advertising; the same can be said of the commercials for U by Kotex that parodied traditional feminine hygiene advertising. Humor also is used to generate conversations about any number of Super Bowl ads we see every year. The key, though, is to make sure that the humor supports the brand and its message; ads fail if their only tangible success is to win conversations about the celebrity featured in the commercial or industry awards at red-carpet events.

All Media Are Social

Just as the creative side of the advertising business has begun designing for social, so too will media planners think more about the how, when, and where of reaching consumers at moments most likely to lead conversations and engagement. Media planning will begin to focus more not only on how many people are reached directly by an ad, but how many influencers are reached and how many "brand talkers" are reached, with the idea that they are more likely to share with others what they learn from an ad. Advertising's impact will incorporate word of mouth, which the media agency UM says is closer to sales impact than metrics such as brand recall.

We believe that co-viewing of television represents an underappreciated opportunity to give consumers something to talk about, whether as a prompt to share their own stories about a brand experience, or simply by helping to fill a conversation void. Programming that tends to get high levels of co-viewing—sports, children's programs, soap operas, reality shows—deserve to have advertising designed to prompt conversation, which will increase the effectiveness of the advertising.

A similar strategy can be used in lots of other media: Internet ads that are timed to be seen when people are likely talking to other people, such as at the beginning of the work day, when people are logging on to computers and greeting each other at work; where people are likely to attend events together and able to be exposed to shareable messages on billboards; or on radio formats and times of day when people are prone to be listening together. Ads in public places—bars, restaurants, airports—may also be valuable vehicles for prompting and feeding content to conversations.

The Internet's greatest social asset, in our view, is not social networking sites per se, but rather the ability of the Internet to be utilized as an information source during or soon after a conversation. Searching the Internet in midconversation helps people fill in critical blanks related to a brand they are talking about, such as the price of an item or where it can be purchased, or comparing features and benefits in conversational real time.

The Owned Media Revolution

In the 1990s major brands like Kraft were publishing their own magazines as a way to build stronger ties between the brands and their most loyal consumers. As well, product packages and labels have been valuable owned media assets that undoubtedly could be better leveraged as a place to distribute shareable content. The Internet age has provided even more cost-effective ways for brands to publish content that will be consumed and shared by brand advocates, with an emphasis on brand websites but also on video-sharing sites, social media fan pages, and the like. These tools are incredibly powerful because they connect brands with their most valuable customers: their advocates. A brand's advocates are drawn to owned media assets that provide content that can advance their own knowledge, which they can then share with their friends, family, and coworkers. A key metric for evaluating owned media should be the extent to which visitors and readers share the content, and such content should be designed for easy sharing.

As General Mills has done in placing greater importance on owned media, such as those related to the Betty Crocker brand, all marketers should nurture their owned media and not overlook them in search of the next new thing. Innovation should be built on the foundation of what works today, not at the expense of it.

The Word-of-Mouth Channel

Most often word of mouth comes about organically as a result of superior product or service performance or an innovation that meets an important need. We have also seen that it can come as a result of visual cuing, in which the visibility of the product or its marketing activity increases the likelihood that it will be talked about, both in the short term and over a sustained period of time. But your efforts need not end there: word of mouth can also be a channel unto itself—so long as it's done in an ethical way that is transparent. Consumers are becoming savvier about word of mouth and are interested in participating in programs that are interesting, worthwhile, and fun.

When designing these programs, remember the key motivations that draw people to programs like this: (a) to learn about the latest products and (b) to share what they have learned with their friends and family and give feedback to manufacturers. People like being one of the first to know about new products and marketplace innovations, so make sure "insider knowledge" and "you can be the first to know" are cornerstones of your offer. Make it as easy for people to share their stories—and thereby your story as well—through all available channels. Consumers use an array of channels when they communicate; the most frequent forms of conversation are offline, so get your product into people's hands so they can try it and show it to others. Consider offering coupons that can be physically shared, and give people opportunities to invite their family and friends to events or parties. They will use online vehicles for sharing as well, whether email, posting updates or photos to their social networking sites, or contributing to rating and review sites, so make it easy for them to do so.

Word-of-mouth networks are magnets for influencers, whether in the form of local outreach that helped propel the winning candidates to the White House in 2004 and 2008, or in organized programs offered by agencies such as House Party, BzzAgent, or Tremor, or a well-conceived online community. And we're not talking about the very small group of people with an oversize network of followers on social media, to whom it will be hard (and getting harder) to pitch your story in the hope they will write about it or retweet something you send. No, we are talking about the everyday influencers who have disproportionate influence with their personal social networks and whose word-of-mouth advice carries four times the weight of what the average person has to say. They are your key constituency in today's social era, and these programs will help you to attract and remain engaged with them.

Turning Negatives into Positives

Fears of negative word of mouth have been the most important deterrent for many companies: "If we cede control to consumers to share their stories, they might say negative things about us." It's true, they might. But the fact is, as we've shown, these fears are overblown. There is a much better chance that the things people say about your brand or company—whether at home, in the workplace, at their kid's little league game, online in ratings and reviews, or wherever they choose to talk—will be positive rather than negative. The idea that people are much more likely to share negative experiences than positive ones is a myth and is not borne out by the evidence, including multiple different sources we have written about in this book.

Of course, negative word of mouth does occur, and when it does it actually has value in several ways: it helps to identify problems that need to be fixed and to reinforce a company's reputation for caring about product quality, as in the case of L.L. Bean. Or it can be a galvanizing force for companies that wish to raise their quality bar, as we saw from Dell and its journey from "Dell Hell" to the rapid success that came as a result of its "Five Star Challenge." In a short period of time Dell went from fearing negative word of mouth to embracing it: "Negative information from a customer is the greatest gift you can have."

Negative word of mouth opens the door to better communications with customers and suppliers, and it even lends credibility to positive messages that are more prevalent. Companies should be open to hearing criticism and addressing it, not running from it.

Managing for Word of Mouth

We've looked at a wide variety of companies that are at various stages of adopting social marketing strategies and integrating them into their management practices. It strikes us that one of the greatest obstacles companies face in the social marketing era stems from the practical difficulties that brands have delivering on the promise of becoming our "friends." If brands become friends, it is natural that we will want to have conversations with them and that we will want to introduce them to our other friends. But can we depend on those brand friends to remember previous conversations we've had with them? Can we depend on them to behave with our other friends in a manner consistent with those relationships? Are they friends that we are proud to include as part of our social circle, and are they reliable friends we can count on to be there for us, through thick and thin?

Companies that own and manage brands are large and complex, run by hundreds, thousands, sometimes hundreds of thousands of people. With companies it is almost certain that the right hand won't know what the left hand is doing, whereas real-world people and friends have control of both hands. To be a true friend, companies need to think and learn to act holistically so that they can be in better, more consistent control of this relationship. They can't wish to be friends through a single communications channel while it's business as usual throughout the rest of the organization.

Some of the more effective social brands are ones that deliver consistency, thanks to a strong culture—think Apple, General Mills, Toyota—that makes sure all hands are operating with a common set of goals and expectations. Other successful brands have used large investments in information technology and well-honed customer service departments—think Best Buy, L.L. Bean, Zappos—to ensure high-quality interactions between employees and customers. And still others have created a product or brand promise that is so compelling—think MillerCoors' cold activation cans or Kotex's fashionable line of feminine products—that it can't help but spark conversation and generate positive recommendations.

What all of these companies, and the others we have written about in this book, have in common is that their success is driven by their ideas and their flexibility; they demonstrate a willingness to change their structures and ways of doing business in light of today's social consumer; their efforts are often enabled by—but not driven by—technology; and most important, they truly put the consumer, real people, at the center of their planning, their strategies, and their execution.

Facebook and other social media have blazed a trail toward a future in which social influence will be a critical factor in marketing, in business, and in our culture. But theirs is not the only pathway, nor even the primary one, toward the success that can be achieved through the inherently social nature of human beings. While we should all point ourselves in the direction of a social future—as the Gold Rush Forty-niners were once admonished to "go west"—it would be foolish to exclusively follow the siren call of online social networking tools. Social influence represents a profound change in the way we think about human behavior and decision making, but there are hundreds of potential social strategies one can choose, and the most lucrative of these are based on the power of connecting face-to-face.

Acknowledgments

It seems only appropriate that a book about social influence should acknowledge the fact that many people have influenced us, our research, our thinking, and this book.

We thank our colleagues at the Keller Fay Group, who work so tirelessly to help us produce the ongoing TalkTrack research and the custom studies that provide the research foundation for this book, and have helped to uncover the insights that we share here. In particular we wish to thank Heather Evans, Laura Keane, Christina Gerber, Siobhan Counihan-McGee, Ben Schneider, Stephanie McQuay, Jim Schaffer, and Steve Thomson. Jonah Bloom and Matt Creamer were instrumental in conducting a number of the executive interviews that became the basis for case studies featured in the book, and we thank them for their support and suggestions. Matt also provided invaluable editorial assistance as we worked to organize certain chapters to tell stories in a clear and readable manner.

We feature quite a number of people in this book, many of whom have been our longtime clients or business partners. In addition, we found ourselves meeting fascinating new people because our research identified their companies as having great word-of-mouth success stories to tell us. To those that are featured by name in the book we thank you all for your generosity and willingness to let us share your knowledge and perspectives. In addition, there are many people and organizations not named in the chapters themselves who need to be recognized here. We wish to thank Greg Pharo of AT&T; Julie Propper of ESPN; David Witt of Hershey's; Peter Stork of House Party; Clive Sirkin, Michelle Froah, and Claire Miller of Kimberly-Clark; Debra Gaynor of Marina Maher; David Shiffman of MediaVest; Tony Cardinale of NBC Universal; Ron Fournier of the National Journal; John Lisko, Conrad Nussbaum, and Kurt Ritter of Saatchi & Saatchi LA; Sharyn Smith and Michele Bray of Soup; Kate Sirkin of Starcom MediaVest Group; and Jack Wakshlag and Gregg Liebman of Turner Broadcasting.

We also benefitted greatly from many years of interaction with colleagues and friends convened by the Word of Mouth Marketing Association. WOMMA was founded in 2004 and has grown to become the central networking and thought leadership hub for those of us who believe in the fundamental importance of word of mouth and social media. We thank both the WOMMA staff and the many people who contributed their time and money to make sure WOMMA is a vibrant and dynamic association.

We are also appreciative of the support provided by our friends at Loeb Partners—Tom Kempner, Bruce Lev, and Norman Mintz—as well as Jay Wilson, who believed in us when our idea for a research company to focus on word of mouth, both offline as well as online, was no more than a business plan.

Free Press published Ed's first book, *The Influentials*, and we are delighted to have had the opportunity to work with them again. Our editor, Dominick Anfuso, and editorial assistants Sydney Tanigawa and Maura O'Brien were enthusiastic boosters of our ideas and the story we wanted to tell, and helped us find the best ways to tell the story of the power of "good old-fashioned, face-to-face word of mouth" while also being "fresh, contemporary, and modern." We hope our readers feel we achieved that goal.

Our agent, Richard Pine from InkWell Management, immediately embraced our ideas from the first time we discussed them with him and has been an expert guide for us in navigating the world of book publishing. In that same regard, we benefitted from the support and counsel of our publicists, Lynn Goldberg and Angela Hayes of Goldberg McDuffie, and of our speaker's agent, Tom Neilssen of BrightSight Group. All of these people have made invaluable suggestions to us about the overall success of our effort and we are thankful to them.

We both have many personal debts to people who have helped to shape our careers. We are deeply indebted to the late Burns W. "Bud" Roper and to William J. "Jay" Wilson, to whom we have dedicated this book. Both sons of market research industry pioneers, they followed in their fathers' footsteps and then welcomed us as members of a third generation in a great profession that is always innovating and evolving. Each of us spent close to two decades working for their companies—"Roper" and "Starch," which came together as Roper Starch Worldwide (and successor companies)—where we met and collaborated with some of the brightest people we've ever known. Even before we started our careers in research and writing, we were inspired by important teachers along the way, in particular Michael O'Leary and Bud Roper for Brad, and George Gerbner for Ed.

Finally, the creative process that leads to the formation of a new company and the writing of a book like this one can only flourish with support at home. In this regard, we are deeply appreciative of the love and support provided to us by Ed's family—Karen, Isabel, and Meredith Keller—and by Brad's—Brendan and Allison Fay. They are the people with whom we spend the most "face-to-face" time, and thus represent the most important influences in our lives.

Notes

INTRODUCTION: THE SOCIAL MEDIA GOLD RUSH

ix *During the American Gold Rush*: H. W. Brands, *The Age of Gold: The California Gold Rush and the New American Dream* (New York: Doubleday, 2002).

x *More than 90 percent of the conversations*: TalkTrack surveys collect data across fifteen categories in the United States: automotive, financial services, health and health care, food and dining, beverages, technology, telecommunications, travel services, personal care and beauty, household products, the home, children's products, shopping, retail and apparel, media and entertainment and sports, recreation and hobbies. People who have previously agreed to participate in online research surveys are asked to participate in a survey about "conversations." Upon agreement, they are given a two-page diary to use during a single "study day," during which they record the number of conversations in each category and write down the names of any brands or companies that come up during those conversations. They are then invited to take an online survey, which starts with respondents reporting the categories and brands that were involved in their conversations that day. Respondents report on conversations occurring offline or online (the mode of conversation can be face-to-face; on the phone; by email; by IM or text message; through an online chat room, blog, Twitter, or social networking site; or some other type of conversation). Brands with a sufficient number of mentions are coded and tracked over time, while brands below the threshold fall into "other" within the appropriate category. Keller Fay Group collects responses from a fresh sample of seven hundred respondents each week, designed to be representative of all persons ages thirteen to sixty-nine. Quotas are used to make sure the sample represents accurately different segments of the population, and for the same reason weights are applied on the factors of gender, age, race or ethnicity, educational attainment, and region.

CHAPTER 1: THE SCIENCE OF SOCIAL

1 *The beverage and snack giant PepsiCo*: Mike Esterl, "Diet Coke Wins Battle in Cola Wars," *Wall Street Journal*, March 17, 2011, 12, http://online .wsj.com/article/SB10001424052748703899704576204933906436332.html, accessed December 19, 2011.

2 *In a tacit admission of error*: Ken Wheaton, "A Not-So-Secret Recipe for Pepsi to Regain Its Footing," *Advertising Age*, March 28, 2011, http://adage.com/article/cmo-strategy/a-secret-recipe-pepsi-regain-footing/149578/, accessed December 19, 2011.

4 *MarketShare then ran sophisticated*: Dave Cavander, abstract from a forthcoming paper, "Social Voice as Brand Amplifier: A New Framework for Understanding the Interrelationships of Paid, Owned and Earned Media," by MarketShare provided to Keller Fay Group on October 28, 2011.

4 *MarketShare is not the first*: Elihu Katz and Paul Felix Lazarsfeld, *Personal Influence: The Part Played by People in the Flow of Mass Communications* (New York: Free Press, 1955).

5 *These conclusions are achieving consensus*: Malcolm Gladwell, *Blink: The Power of Thinking without Thinking* (New York: Little, Brown, 2005); Daniel Goleman, *Social Intelligence: The New Science of Human Relationships* (New York: Bantam Books, 2006); Mark Earls, *Herd: How to Change Mass Behaviour by Harnessing Our True Nature* (Hoboken, NJ: Wiley, 2007); Nicholas A. Christakis and James H. Fowler, *Connected: The Surprising Power of Our Social Networks and How They Shape Our Lives* (New York: Little, Brown, 2010); Tina Rosenberg, *Join the Club: How Peer Pressure Can Transform the World* (New York: Norton, 2011); David Brooks, *The Social Animal: The Hidden Sources of Love, Character, and Achievement* (New York: Random House, 2011).

7 *The transfer of emotions*: Pam Belluck, "Hearts Beat as One in a Daring Ritual," *New York Times*, May 2, 2011, http://www.nytimes.com/2011/05/03/science/03firewalker.html, accessed December 19, 2011.

8 *While there has been some debate*: A number of critiques have been made of the Christakis-Fowler analysis of the Framingham Study, winning both "respect and skepticism," as summarized in Andrew Gelman, "Controversy over the Christakis-Fowler Findings on the Contagion of Obesity," *The Monkey Cage Blog*, June 10, 2011, http://themonkeycage.org/blog/2011/06/10/1-lyonss-statistical-critiques-seem-reasonable-to-me-there-could-well-be-something-important-that-im-missing-but-until-i-hear-otherwise-for-example-in-a-convincing-reply-by-christakis-and-f/, accessed December 19, 2011.

9 *The high school in Montgomery Township*: Nadine M. Connell, Pamela M. Negro, and Allison N. Pearce, "Montgomery High School Report," Social Norms Project, New Jersey Department of Education and Rowan University Center for Addiction Studies and Awareness, January 2011.

11 *A Google search quickly yielded*: Terry Connolly and Lars Aberg, "Some

Contagion Models of Speeding," *Journal of Accident Analysis and Prevention* 25, no. 1 (1993): 57–66, http://www.ncbi.nlm.nih.gov/pubmed/8420535, accessed December 19, 2011.

12 *David Brooks points to research*: David Brooks, "Nice Guys Finish First," *New York Times*, May 17, 2011, http://www.nytimes.com/2011/05/17/opinion/17brooks.html, accessed December 19, 2011.

13 *Huge sums of money*: Lauren Indvik, "Social Networks to Capture 11% of Online Ad Spending in 2011," *Mashable*, January 18, 2011, http://mashable.com/2011/01/18/emarketer-social-network-ad-spending/, accessed December 19, 2011.

14 *For further reading on this subject*: Stephen D. Rappaport, *Listen First! Turning Social Media Conversations into Business Advantage* (Hoboken, NJ: Wiley, 2011).

14 *In the late 1980s and 1990s*: Ed Keller and Jon Berry, *The Influentials: One American in Ten Tells the Other Nine How to Vote, Where to Eat and What to Buy* (New York: Free Press, 2003).

14 The Influentials *led to an invitation for Roper*: "A Brief History of WOMMA," Word of Mouth Marketing Association, 2011, http://womma.org/about/history/, accessed December 19, 2011.

19 *In 2009 two Israeli marketing professors*: Data sources included social media data from NM Incite, a joint venture of Nielsen Online and McKinsey; offline word of mouth from Keller Fay Group; brand equity data from Y&R Brand Asset Valuator; and custom research performed by Decipher Inc. for Peres and Shachar. "Multichannel Word of Mouth: The Effect of Brand Characteristics," was presented by Renana Peres and Ron Shachar at the WIMI Multi-Channel Conference in December 2010, sponsored by the Wharton School of the University of Pennyvania and the Marketing Sciences Institute. The presentation can be found at https://www.communicationsmgr.com/projects/1387/docs/PeresShachar_WIMI%202010.pdf, accessed December 19, 2011. Also, in October 2011, Peres provided the authors with a working paper "On Brands and Word of Mouth" authored with Shachar and Mitch Lovett of the University of Rochester that extended their analysis of the same data.

22 *This phenomenon of looking*: Personal interview with Artie Bulgrin of ESPN, July 13, 2011.

23 *Consider this in light of a study*: "Replies and Retweets on Twitter," Sysomos Inc., September 2010, http://www.sysomos.com/insidetwitter/engagement/, accessed December 19, 2011.

24 *While the viral power of social media*: Peter L. Berger and Thomas Luckmann, *The Social Construction of Reality: A Treatise in the Sociology of Knowledge* (New York: Anchor Books, 1966).

24 *Forty-five years later, despite*: Jacques Bughin, Jonathan Doogan, and Ole Jørgen Vetvik, "A New Way to Measure Word-of-Mouth Marketing," *McKinsey Quarterly*, April 2010, https://www.mckinseyquarterly.com/ghost.aspx?ID=/A_

new_way_to_measure_word-of-mouth_marketing_2567, accessed December 19, 2011.

24 *According to a 2010 report on word of mouth*: Bughin, Doogan, and Vetvik.

25 *In 2011 a social media marketing agency*: Jackie Cohen, "Report: The 100 Most Engaging Brands on Facebook," *All Facebook*, October 4, 2011, http://www.allfacebook.com/facebook-engaging-brands-2011–10, accessed December 19, 2011. See also University of South Australia, "Big Brands being Snubbed by Facebook Fans," *PhysOrg.com*, January 30, 2012, http://www.physorg.com/news/2012-01-big-brands-snubbed-facebook-fans.html, accessed January 30, 2012.

25 *Despite the enormous reach*: "Smaller Categories Still Saw Growth as the U.S. Liquid Refreshment Beverage Market Shrank by 2.0% in 2008 Beverage Marketing Corporation Reports," *Beverage Marketing*, March 30, 2009, http://www.beveragemarketing.com/?section=news&newsID=111, accessed December 19, 2011.

CHAPTER 2: CONVERSATION STARTERS: WHAT MAKES A BRAND TALKWORTHY?

27 *When Steve Hershberger, a social marketing consultant*: Personal interview with Steve Hershberger of Flat12 Bierwerks, October 18, 2011.

29 *Indeed for every one of the first sixty months*: Unless otherwise noted, all Keller Fay TalkTrack® data in this book are based on the twelve months ending June 30, 2011, during which time we conducted 37,343 online interviews with nationally representative samples of Americans ages thirteen to sixty-nine, collecting data on 356,934 conversational mentions of brands and companies. In this section projected estimates are weekly.

30 *Half of the ten biggest WOM brands*: These brands—Verizon, AT&T, Walmart, Ford, and McDonald's—are among the top ten in terms of measured-media spending, according to *Advertising Age*. Bradley Johnson, "Ad Spending Is on the Rise, but Growth Rate May Slow," *Advertising Age*, December 20, 2010, 8–10.

31 *After all, they might have read Seth Godin's*: Seth Godin, *Purple Cow: Transform Your Business by Being Remarkable* (New York: Do You Zoom, 2003), 2–3.

32 *If we were to expand our analysis*: The top forty most talked-about brands for the twelve months ending June 30, 2011, in order, are Coca-Cola, Walmart, Verizon, AT&T, Pepsi, Apple, Ford, Sony, McDonald's, Dell, Chevrolet, Target, NFL, HP, Sprint, Toyota, Samsung, Nike, iPhone, T-Mobile, Microsoft, Honda, iPod, Mountain Dew, Dr Pepper, Bank of America, Sprite, Dodge, JP Morgan Chase, Macy's, NBA, Kohl's, JCPenney, Home Depot, Burger King, LG, Dove, Taco Bell, Lowe's. From Keller Fay Group, LLC.

32 *We teamed with the word-of-mouth agency BzzAgent*: "The Steak Is the Sizzle: A Study on Product Attributes That Drive Word-of-Mouth Success," Keller Fay Group and BzzAgent, July 2006, http://www.kellerfay.com/wp-

content/uploads/2011/01/Keller-Fay-WOM-Drivers-Study-July-2006.pdf, accessed December 19, 2011.

34 *From the time we conducted:* Jonah Berger and Eric Schwartz, "What Drives Immediate and Ongoing Word-of-Mouth," *Journal of Marketing Research* 48 (October 2011): 869–880; Jonah Berger and Katherine Milkman, "What Makes Online Content Viral," *Journal of Marketing Research,* forthcoming.

35 *One of Berger's major studies:* Jonah Berger and Eric Schwartz, "What Drives Immediate and Ongoing Word-of-Mouth?" *Journal of Marketing Research,* forthcoming, marketing.wharton.upenn.edu/documents/research/ BzzAgent.pdf, accessed December 19, 2011.

37 *To understand how this comes together:* Personal interview with Andy England of MillerCoors, January 21, 2011.

38 *But it is also true that the brewer:* The Brand Show, with Ethan Whitehill and Lou Thurman, guest Keith Villa, podcast transcript from February 4, 2011, http://twowest.com/podcasts/thebrandshow/2011/transcripts/thebrandshow_ BlueMoon_Keith_Villa_110204.pdf, accessed December 19, 2011.

38 *The orange helps provide the cue:* Tim Manners, "Blue Moon Beer," *Reveries.com,* November 2006, http://www.reveries.com/2006/11/blue-moon-beer/, accessed December 19, 2011.

38 *With wide-mouth venting, package designers:* "Coors Light Announces a Better Way to Vent," Coors Brewing Company Press Release, April 7, 2008, http://www.reuters.com/article/2008/04/07/idUS104809+07-Apr-2008+BW20080407, accessed December 19, 2011.

39 *Cold-activated cans have been another hit:* Stuart Elliot, "Coors Light Uses Cold to Turn Up Heat on Rivals," *New York Times,* April 27, 2009, http://www.nytimes.com/2009/04/27/business/media/27adnewsletter1.html, accessed December 19, 2011.

40 *In his 2011 keynote:* David Brooks, Keynote Address, Advertising Research Foundation's Audience Measurement 6.0 Conference, June 12, 2011.

40 *He echoed the comments of another ARF speaker:* Jonah Lehrer, *How We Decide* (New York: Houghton Mifflin, 2009), 17.

42 *Writing on his blog:* Emanuel Rosen, *The Anatomy of Buzz: How to Create Word-of-Mouth Marketing* (New York: Random House, 2000) and *The Anatomy of Buzz Revisited* (New York: Crown Business, 2009).

42 *"Last year," wrote Rosen:* Emanuel Rosen, September 29, 2009, "The Biggest Misconception about Word of Mouth," *The Anatomy of Buzz* blog, http://anatomyofbuzz.blogspot.com/2009_09_01_archive.html, accessed December 19, 2011.

42 *TOMS also gives people ways:* TOMS online comments can be found, at http://www.toms.com/review/product/view/id/14730, accessed December 19, 2011.

43 *This is the same theory put forth:* Chip Heath and Dan Heath, *Made to Stick* (New York: Random House, 2007).

43 *According to the Heaths*: Heath and Heath, 67–68.

43 *Its mission is certainly not distinct*: Chick-fil-A, "Company Fact Sheet," 2011, http://www.chick-fil-a.com/Company/Highlights-Fact-Sheets, accessed December 19, 2011.

44 *And yet according to our surveys*: Chick-fil-A had 84 percent positive talk, 3 percent negative, and 5 percent mixed. Those were the best figures among eighteen quick-service restaurants measured in TalkTrack.

44 *Its restaurants have never*: "Chick-fil-A's Closed-on-Sundays Policy," Chick-fil-A Press Release, June 2011, http://www.chick-fil-a.com/Media/PDF/ClosedonSundaypolicy-b.pdf, accessed December 19, 2011.

45 *Steve Knox, a senior advisor*: Steve Knox, Anthony Pralle, Kate Sayre, and Jody Visser, "Harnessing the Power of Advocacy Marketing," Boston Consulting Group, March 2011, 7, http://www.bcg.com/documents/file74205.pdf, accessed December 19, 2011.

45 *Knox is a strong proponent*: Steve Knox, "Why Effective Word-of-Mouth Disrupts Schemas," *Advertising Age*, January 25, 2010, http://adage.com/article/cmo-strategy/marketing-effective-word-mouth-disrupts-schemas/141734/, accessed December 19, 2011.

46 *Knox drew our attention to a program*: Chick-fil-A, "Daddy-Daughter Date Night," 2011, http://daddydaughterdate.com, accessed December 19, 2011.

46 *L. J. Yankosky, the senior manager of sponsorships and event marketing*: Personal interview with L. J. Yankosky of Chick-fil-A, June 15, 2011.

47 *All this is a far cry*: Personal interview with Steve Knox of Boston Consulting Group, April 18, 2011.

49 *An ad campaign dubbed "Pizza Turnaround"*: DominosVids, "Domino's Pizza at the Door of Our Harshest Critics," January 22, 2010, online video clip, http://www.youtube.com/watch?v=-SwLn8ZPcUk&NR=1, accessed December 19, 2011.

49 *CP+B's chairman, Chuck Porter, talked about*: "Getting to Powerfully Creative Ads through Creative Business Strategies" was presented by Chuck Porter at the Advertising Research Foundation's Re:Think 2011 Conference on March 20–23, 2011. The presentation can be found at http://www.youtube.com/watch?v=53ynSlan1kk, accessed December 20, 2011.

50 *A 2011 article in the* Financial Times: David Gelles and Alan Rappaport, "Domino's Eats a Slice of Humble Pie in Push to Boost Sales," *Financial Times*, May 6, 2011, 9.

CHAPTER 3: INFLUENCERS: THE PEOPLE AT THE
CENTER OF THE CONVERSATION

52 *Since the publication of Malcolm Gladwell's*: Malcolm Gladwell, *The Tipping Point* (New York: Little, Brown, 2000), 32.

55 *Not long after this*: See Jeremiah Owyang's blog, *Web Strategy*, http://www.web-strategist.com/blog/2011/02/21/klout-for-business-a-sometimes-

useful-metric-but-an-incomplete-view-of-customers/, accessed December 19, 2011.

55 *Rishad Tobaccowala is the chief strategy and innovation officer*: Rishad Tobaccowala (@rishadt), "Klout is not Clout. Little to no offline influence. Easy to game. Bias to Frequency vs Quality," Twitter update, July 16, 2011.

55 *A service like Klout measures*: Klout started by analyzing Twitter only, then added Facebook (only those people who sign on via Facebook Connect). In June 2011 it added LinkedIn, and in August 2011 it added Flickr, Instagram, Last.fm, Tumblr, and Blogger.

55 *The people who are the most active*: Josh Bernoff and Ted Schadler, *Empowered: Unleash Your Employees, Energize Your Customers, Transform Your Business* (Boston: Harvard Business Review Press, 2010), 37–56.

56 *But campaign insiders have a different view*: Jon Carson, in *Electing the President 2008: The Insiders' View*, ed. Kathleen Hall Jamieson (Philadelphia: University of Pennsylvania Press, 2009), 42.

57 *Mary Joyce, who was new media operations manager*: Personal interview with Mary Joyce of the Obama 2008 campaign, July 1, 2011.

57 *Social media grabbed many headlines*: Claire Cain Miller, "How Obama's Internet Campaign Changed Politics," *New York Times*, November 7, 2008, http://bits.blogs.nytimes.com/2008/11/07/how-obamas-internet-changed-politics/, accessed January 31, 2012.

57 *The* Washington Post *ran an article that month*: John F. Harris, "In Ohio, Building a Political Echo: Campaigns Rely on Word of Mouth to Spread Message," *Washington Post*, May 12, 2004, A1, http://www.washingtonpost.com/wp-dyn/articles/A19040-2004May11.html, accessed December 19, 2011.

58 *The motivating factor*: Personal interview with Matthew Dowd of the Bush 2004 campaign, May 12, 2011.

58 *To Dowd, this meant*: Douglas Sosnik, Matthew Dowd, and Ron Fournier, *Applebee's America: How Successful Political, Business, and Religious Leaders Connect with the New American Community* (New York: Simon & Schuster, 2006), 31.

58 *According to Dowd*: Sosnik, Dowd, and Fournier, 186.

59 *The twenty-first century opinion leaders*: Gabriel Weimann, "The Influentials: Back to the Concept of Opinion Leaders?," *Public Opinion Quarterly* 55, no. 2 (1991): 267–279. See also Ronald Burt, "A Note on Social Capital and Network Content," *Social Networks* 19, no. 4 (1997): 355–373; Alexa Bezjian-Avery, Bobby Calder, and Dawn Iacobucci, "New Media Interactive Advertising vs. Traditional Advertising," *Journal of Advertising Research*, July/August 1998, 23–33; Christophe Van Den Bulte and Stefan Wuyts, *Social Networks and Marketing* (Cambridge, MA: Marketing Science Institute, 2007); Jacob Goldenberg, Sangman Han, Donald Lehmann, and Jae Weon Hong, "The Role of Hubs in the Adoption Process," *Journal of Marketing* 73, no. 2 (2009): 1–13.

59 *"The Bush team realized . . ."*: Sosnik, Dowd, and Fournier, 188.

59 *In 2008 the Obama team studied*: David Plouffe, in *Electing the President 2008: The Insiders' View*, ed. Kathleen Hall Jamieson (Philadelphia: University of Pennsylvania Press, 2009), 40. See also Steve Peoples, "Final House Race Decided; GOP Net Gain: 63 Seats," *Roll Call*, December 8, 2010, http://www.rollcall.com/news/-201279–1.html, accessed December 19, 2011.

60 *When our firm launched our continuous study*: Since then, our influencer segmentation work has been conducted in our own syndicated studies in the United Kingdom and Australia; in custom work we have done in Mexico, Korea, Greece, Japan, and Russia; in the IPA TouchPoints study in the United Kingdom; and in a U.S. TouchPoints study being conducted by the Media Behavior Institute.

60 *Through discussions with other members*: Word of Mouth Marketing Association, *The WOMMA Influencer Handbook*, 2008, http://womma.org/membercenter/influencerhandbook.php, accessed December 19, 2011.

65 *"People come to me . . ."*: Keller and Berry, 163.

66 *Influencers like Graham*: Gladwell, *The Tipping Point*, 33. According to Gladwell, one of the keys is "the law of the few": there are certain people "with a particular and rare set of social gifts" who are primarily responsible for the spread of social epidemics. These are the people Gladwell calls "connectors," "mavens," and "salesmen," terms that quickly became part of the lexicon as a result of *The Tipping Point*. For word-of-mouth epidemics to spread, said Gladwell, it requires a combination of mavens ("data banks" who provide the message), connectors (the "social glue" who spread it), and salesmen ("people who persuade others to act on what they hear").

66 *We were given the opportunity*: "Return on Influence: From Buzz to Buy" was presented by Ed Keller and Rachel Swanson at the Advertising Research Foundation's Re:Think 2010 Conference on March 22–24, 2010. The presentation can be found at http://www.slideshare.net/gsweeton/keller-fay-conde-nast-arf-paper-3–2410, accessed December 19, 2011. Barak Libai is a professor of marketing at the Arison School of Business, Interdisciplinary Center, in Israel. Previously he was a faculty member in the Recanati Graduate School of Business, Faculty of Management, Tel Aviv University, and at the Industrial Engineering and Management faculty of the Technion, Israel Institute of Technology, and a visiting professor at the MIT Sloan School of Management. His research deals with customer social effects such as word of mouth and their effect on new product growth and the firm's profitability, growth of markets for new products, and customer relationship management.

67 *For this part of the research we collaborated*: Barak Libai, Eitan Muller, and Renana Peres, "The Sources of Social Value in Word of Mouth Programs," Marketing Sciences Institute, Working Paper Series (2010): 10–103, http://www.msi.org/publications/publication.cfm?pub=1694, accessed December 19, 2011.

68 *About a year later consultants*: Bughin, Doogan, and Vetvik.

69 *Remember Steve Hershberger and his craft beer*: Personal interview with Steve Hershberger of Flat12 Bierwerks, October 18, 2011.

71 *"Looking for ambassadors became . . .":* Personal interview with Robbin Phillips of Brains on Fire, October 25, 2011.

74 *In 2005, after noting that per capita milk sales:* "Marketing with a Whisper," *Fast Company*, January 11, 2003, http://www.fastcompany.com/ fast50_04/winners/stewart.html, accessed December 19, 2011.

74 *It was conceived by a word-of-mouth agency, Fizz:* Personal interview with Ted Wright of Fizz, August 9, 2011.

74 *To begin to address the milk challenge:* Kimberly Smith, *Influencer Marketing Success Stories: Case Study Collection* (MarketingProfs, online, 2011): 18–19. See chapter 5, "Increasing Sales—American Dairy Association Mideast."

CHAPTER 4: WORD OF MOUTH MEETS MADISON AVENUE

80 *That's what surveys show:* Large and growing numbers of consumers expressed these sorts of grievances about advertising in polls. For example, 72 percent of consumers polled in fall 2010 agreed that "advertising on TV is a nuisance because it clutters up the programs"; 82 percent agreed that "advertising encourages people to use products they don't need"; more than 51 percent said that they "often" get up and do something else during commercials; and 52 percent said they ignore the commercials to talk to others in the room. GfK Roper Consulting, Roper Reports U.S., Fall Core Study 2010 and Fall Core Study 2008.

80 *It's also what has led to a cottage industry:* "U.S. Annual Advertising Spending Since 1919," *Coen Structured Advertising Expenditure Dataset*, PQ Media, 2005 figures, http://www.galbithink.org/ad-spending.htm, accessed December 20, 2011.

82 *In the spring of 2010 Jeff Dunn:* Douglas McGray, "How Carrots Became the New Junk Food," *Fast Company*, March 22, 2011, http://www .fastcompany.com/magazine/154/the-new-junk-food.html, accessed December 19, 2011.

83 *Though Bogusky left the agency in 2010:* Personal interview with Rob Reilly of Crispin Porter & Bogusky, April 11, 2011.

84 *All this effort caught on with the media:* Personal interview with Rob Reilly of Crispin Porter & Bogusky, April 11, 2011. See also "Getting to Powerfully Creative Ads through Creative Business Strategies," presented by Chuck Porter at the Advertising Research Foundation's Re:Think 2011 Conference on March 20–23, 2011, http://www.youtube.com/ watch?v=53ynSlan1kk, accessed December 20, 2011.

84 *"Marketing by interrupting people . . .":* Seth Godin, *Unleashing the Ideavirus* (New York: Hyperion, 2001), 15.

85 *At CP+B the process:* Personal interview with Rob Reilly of Crispin Porter & Bogusky, April 11, 2011.

86 *As far as we have been able to determine:* Ernest Dichter, "How Word-of-Mouth Advertising Works," *Harvard Business Review* 44, no. 6 (1966): 147–160.

86 *Dichter is generally considered*: Lynne Ames, "The View from Peekskill: Tending the Flame of a Motivator," *New York Times*, August 2, 1998, http://www.nytimes.com/1998/08/02/nyregion/the-view-from-peekskill-tending-the-flame-of-a-motivator.html?src=pm, accessed December 19, 2011.

87 *His advice was a natural follow-up*: Katz and Lazarsfeld.

87 *Dichter brought his perspective*: Dichter, 147.

88 *Many call this period*: John McDonough, "Why 1960 Is the Golden Age of Advertising," *Advertising Age*, June 23, 2008, C6.

89 *When it launched in 1987, Kirshenbaum*: "How to Create Word-of-Mouth Advertising," Kirshenbaum & Bond company brochure, from the files of Jon Bond, shared with Keller Fay in early 2011. See also http://www.kbsp.com/, accessed December 19, 2011.

89 *Cofounder Jon Bond recalls*: Personal interview with Jon Bond, then of Kirshenbaum & Bond, March 9 and 11, 2011.

89 *For Target, KB was charged with helping*: Tina Rosenberg, *Join the Club: How Peer Pressure Can Transform the World* (New York: Norton, 2011).

90 *Snapple was founded in 1972*: The founders of Snapple were Hyman Golden, Arnold Greenberg, and Leonard Marsh.

93 *Nearly a quarter-century after*: Maureen Morrison, "Jon Bond Joins Social-Media Agency Big Fuel," *Advertising Age*, January 12, 2011, http://adage.com/article/agency-news/jon-bond-joins-social-media-agency-big-fuel/148158/, accessed December 19, 2011.

93 *He left KB in 2010*: In July 2011 Big Fuel sold a majority stake to Publicis Groupe, the ad agency holding company. Kunur Patel, "Behind Big Fuel's Sale to Publicis Groupe," *Advertising Age*, July 18, 2011, http://adage.com/article/agency-news/big-fuel-s-sale-publicis-groupe/228769/, accessed December 19, 2011.

93 *Though the marketing world wasn't prepared*: Jack Neff and Lisa Sanders, "It's Broken," *Advertising Age*, February 16, 2004.

94 *The* Wall Street Journal *published a headline*: Brian Steinberg, "As 30-Second Spot Fades, What Will Advertisers Do Next?," *Wall Street Journal*, January 3, 2006, http://online.wsj.com/article/SB113624334456335918.html?mod=todays_us_marketplace, accessed December 20, 2011.

94 *Yes, digital advertising is growing faster*: Brian Steinberg, "Are Advertisers in Love with TV Again? 2011 Upfront Totals $8.8 Billion to $9.3 Billion, but Doesn't Beat 2004 Benchmark," *Advertising Age*, June 9, 2011, http://adage.com/article/special-report-tv-upfront/2011-upfront-totals-8-8-billion-9-3-billion-tops-2010/228102/, accessed December 20, 2011.

94 *This impressive rebound was consistent*: "Deloitte Technology, Media and Telecommunications (TMT) Predictions 2011" Deloitte Touche Tohmatsu, Ltd., Bucharest, Romania, January 19, 2011, http://www.deloitte.com/assets/Dcom-Romania/Local%20Assets/Documents/EN/TMT/ro_TMT_Predictions_011911.pdf, accessed December 20, 2011.

95 *Our research shows that all of the above*: Our paper "The Role of

Advertising in Word of Mouth" appeared in "What We Know about Advertising: 21 Watertight Laws for Intelligent Advertising Decisions," special issue of *Journal of Advertising Research* 49, no. 2 (2009): 154. The projections are based on brand mentions and census data for people ages thirteen to sixty-nine.

98 *There are a number of mechanisms*: Emanuel Rosen, "Conversation Starter: In a World of Word-of-Mouth Buzz, Marketers Need to Trigger the Talk," *Adweek*, April 12, 2010, http://www.adweek.com/news/advertising-branding/conversation-starter-102037, accessed December 20, 2011.

99 *At no time is this question more important*: Aaron Smith, "Super Bowl Ad: Is $3 Million Worth It?," *CNN Money*, February 3, 2011, money.cnn .com/2011/02/03/news/companies/super_bowl_ads/index.htm, accessed December 20, 2011.

100 *"Close to 50% of viewers . . ."*: Katherine Dorsett, "Rather Watch Ads Than the Super Bowl?," *CNN Online*, February 4, 2011, http://www .cnn.com/2011/US/02/03/super.bowl.ads.commercial/index.html, accessed December 19, 2011.

102 *Chief Marketing Officer Scott Keogh told us*: Personal interview with Scott Keogh of Audi, February 2, 2011.

CHAPTER 5: RETHINKING MEDIA: PLANNING FOR WORD OF MOUTH

109 *Today there are television ratings*: Stuart Elliott, "Effort to Provide TV Ratings by Brand Moves Ahead," *New York Times*, February 10, 2011, http:// mediadecoder.blogs.nytimes.com/2011/02/10/effort-to-provide-tv-ratings-by-brand-moves-ahead/, accessed December 19, 2011.

109 *efforts are under way to improve*: "Turner Expands 'TV In Context,'" *New York Times*, May 20, 2009, http://mediadecoder.blogs.nytimes .com/2009/05/20/upfronts-turner-expands-tv-in-context/, accessed December 20, 2011.

110 *A 2011 study called "How Co-viewing . . ."*: Steven Bellman, John R. Rossiter, Anika Schweda, and Duane Varan, "How Co-Viewing Reduces the Effectiveness of TV Advertising," *Journal of Marketing Communications*, January 2011, www.tandfonline.com/doi/abs/10.1080/13527266.2010.531750#preview, accessed December 20, 2011.

110 *The authors cite a 1965 study*: Robert B. Zajonc, "Social Facilitation: A Solution Is Suggested for an Old Unresolved Social Psychological Problem," *Science* 149, no. 3681 (1965): 269–274.

111 *Reports from the leading U.S. and U.K. advertising trade associations*: Anca Cristina Micu and Joseph T. Plummer, "On the Road to a New Effectiveness Model: Measuring Emotional Responses to Television Advertising," Advertising Research Foundation and the American Association of Advertising Agencies Task Force, March 2007, http://www.aaaa.org/working/essentials/Documents/ tv_road.pdf, accessed December 20, 2011. See also Peter Field, Donald Gunn,

and Janet Hull, "The Link between Creativity and Ad Effectiveness: The Growing Imperative to Embrace Creativity," The Gunn Report and Institute of Practitioners in Advertising in association with Thinkbox, March 2011, http://www.thinkbox.tv/upload/pdf/Creativity_and_Effectiveness_Report.pdf, accessed December 20, 2011.

111 *These conclusions follow*: Donald B. Calne, *Within Reason: Rationality and Human Behavior* (New York: Pantheon Books, 1999).

113 *ESPN had the English-language rights*: Eric Gershon, "At World Cup, ESPN Looks to Become a Global Star," *Hartford (Ct.) Courant*, June 9, 2010, http://articles.courant.com/2010–06–09/sports/hc-espn-worldcup-0609–20100609_1_world-cups-south-africa-soccer-teams, accessed December 20, 2011.

113 *Combined with the efforts*: Richard Sandomir, "World Cup Ratings Certify a TV Winner," *New York Times*, June 28, 2010, http://www.nytimes.com/2010/06/29/sports/soccer/29sandomir.html, accessed December 20, 2011. We also relied on updated, final figures via Nielsen data provided by Artie Bulgrin, senior vice president of research and sales development at ESPN, via email on December 2, 2011.

114 *ESPN believed that in addition*: Nick Green, "Where to Watch the World Cup in LA," *Los Angeles: The Official Guide*, 2010, http://discoverlosangeles.com/play/activities-and-recreation/outdoors-and-sports/where-to-watch-the-world-cup-in-la.html, accessed December 20, 2011.

115 *One of the people in the audience*: "Walking the Path: Exploring the Drivers of Expression," was presented by Alex Chisholm, Henry Jenkins, Stacey Lynn Koerner, Brian Theisen, Sangita Shresthova, and David Ernst at the ESOMAR Worldwide Audience Measurement Conference in June 2003.

121 *In late 2010 Keller Fay did a study*: "Word of Mouth and the Internet," Google and Keller Fay Group, June 2011, http://www.gstatic.com/ads/research/en/2011_Word_of_Mouth_Study.pdf, accessed December 20, 2011.

123 *At a 2011 Advertising Research Foundation conference*: "How Social Are Social Media Audiences, Really?" was presented by Brad Fay and Lauren Hadley at the Advertising Research Foundation's Re:Think 2011 Conference on March 20–23, 2011. The presentation can be found at http://www.slideshare.net/kellerfay/how-social-are-social-media-audiences-really, accessed December 20, 2011.

127 *The ubiquity of television*: David E. Poltrack, "Food for Thought," presented at the UBS Media and Communication Conference, December 6, 2010, as quoted in Dave Morgan, "CBS Audience Five Times Bigger Than Facebook," *OnlineSPIN*, December 9, 2010, http://www.mediapost.com/publications/?art_aid=141044&fa=Articles.showArticle, accessed December 20, 2011.

130 *Around the time Steve Jobs passed away*: Walter Isaacson, *Steve Jobs* (New York: Simon & Schuster, 2011). See especially chapter 29, "Apple Stores."

131 *An increasingly popular approach*: For another example of market mix modeling, see "How WOM Drives AT&T's Sales," presented by Greg

Pharo, Matthew Sato, and Brad Fay at the Advertising Research Foundation's Audience Measurement 6.0 Conference on June 13, 2011. The presentation can be found at http://www.slideshare.net/kellerfay/word-of-mouths-role-in-driving-sales, accessed December 20, 2011.

132 *They won the WOMMY award*: "Determining the Impact of Advertising on Word of Mouth" was presented by Graeme Hutton for the Word of Mouth Marketing Association in April 2011. The presentation can be found at http://www.slideshare.net/WOMMAssociation/does-advertising-affect-word-of-mouth, accessed December 20, 2011.

132 *UM's statistical analysis produced*: Kantar Media Intelligence is a company that provides advertisers with strategic advertising intelligence, used in this study to track advertising expenditures for Sony and its competitors: http://kantarmediana.com/intelligence, accessed December 20, 2011.

134 *According to UM's Hutton*: Brad Fay and Graeme Hutton, "Advertising Worth Talking About," *AdMap*, November 2010, 15, www.kellerfay.com/wp-content/uploads/2011/01/ADMFayHutton.pdf, accessed December 20, 2011.

134 *In a study conducted for NBC Universal*: "Supercharging the Path to Purchase: Using Word-of-Mouth to Drive More Consumers to Buy" was presented by Tony Cardinale and Ed Keller at the Advertising Research Foundation's Re:Think 2011 Conference on March 20–23, 2011. The presentation can be found at http://www.slideshare.net/kellerfay/supercharging-the-path-to-purchase-using-word-of-mouth-to-drive-more-consumers-to-buy, accessed December 20, 2011.

135 *The British trade association for advertising agencies*: "Welcome to IPA TouchPoints," Institute of Practitioners of Advertising, http://www.ipa.co.uk/Content/TouchPoints-Site-Home, accessed December 21, 2011. IPA TouchPoints is a survey of 5,400 British adults age fifteen and older providing information gathered through individual PDA diaries and self-completion questionnaires. Research was conducted from September 2009 through February 2010. Each respondent completed both the PDA-based diary, filling in activities on a half-hourly basis over a seven-day period, and a self-completion paper questionnaire covering usage and attitudes to media, shopping, and lifestyles. The findings presented in this report focus on the diary portion of TP3. The diary records information on a half-hourly basis on the following: location of respondent, who they were with, what they were doing (consuming media, communicating, etc.), what media they were consuming, and their mood. See Field, Gunn, and Hull.

135 *Starting in 2006 they have undertaken*: In 2010 the study also was launched in the United States, where it is licensed by the Media Behavior Institute.

137 *One of the most frequently quoted phrases*: Marshall McLuhan, *Understanding Media: The Extensions of Man* (New York: McGraw Hill, 1964), 7. See also Mark Federman, "What Is the Meaning of the Medium Is the Message?," July 23, 2004, http://individual.utoronto.ca/markfederman/article_mediumisthemessage.htm, accessed December 20, 2011.

CHAPTER 6: ALL THINGS IN MODERATION:
WHERE SOCIAL MEDIA FITS

139 *In investing circles, social media*: Clint Boulton, "Facebook Worth $50B after Goldman Sachs Investment," *e-WEEK*, January 22, 2011, http://www .eweek.com/c/a/Government-IT/Facebook-Worth-50B-After-Goldman-Sachs-Investment-124739/, accessed December 20, 2011. See also Tomio Geron, "New Investment Fund Values Twitter at $4.1 Billion," *Wall Street Journal,* January 4, 2011, http://blogs.wsj.com/digits/2011/01/04/new-investment-fund-values-twitter-at-41-billion/, accessed December 20, 2011; Stu Woo, Lynn Cowan, and Pui-Wing Tam, "LinkedIn IPO Soars, Feeding Web Boom," *Wall Street Journal,* May 20, 2011, http://online.wsj.com/article/SB10001424052748 7048166045763333132239509622.html, accessed December 20, 2011.

140 *One of the regular speakers on behalf of Facebook*: Dan Rose, Keynote Speech, Bazaarvoice Social Commerce Summit, Austin, TX, April 4–6, 2011, http://www.bazaarvoice.com/blog/2011/04/11/mirrors-not-billboards-redesigning-your-brand%E2%80%99s-presence-for-the-social-web-2/, accessed December 20, 2011.

143 *If you don't believe us*: Beth Snyder Bulik, "Marketer of the Decade: Apple," *Advertising Age,* October 18, 2010, http://adage.com/article/special-report-marketer-of-the-year-2010/marketer-decade-apple/146492/, accessed December 20, 2011.

144 *But making social media a strategy*: Natalie Zmuda, "Risk or Opportunity? PepsiCo Pulls Beverage Ads from Super Bowl," *Advertising Age,* December 17, 2009, http://adage.com/article/special-report-super-bowl-2010/ advertising-pepsico-pulls-beverage-ads-super-bowl/141149/, accessed December 20, 2011. See also "A Not-So-Secret Recipe for Pepsi to Regain Its Footing," *Advertising Age,* editorial, March 28, 2011, http://adage.com/ article/cmo-strategy/a-secret-recipe-pepsi-regain-footing/149578/, accessed December 20, 2011.

144 *PepsiCo responded to the Coke coup:* Mike Esterl, "Pepsi Thirsty for a Comeback," *Wall Street Journal,* March 18, 2011, http://online.wsj.com/article/ SB10001424052748703818204576206653259805970.html, accessed December 20, 2011.

145 *After the change, in January 2010, Shiv Singh*: Jennifer Preston, "Pepsi Bets on Local Grants, Not the Super Bowl," *New York Times,* January 30, 2011, http://www.nytimes.com/2011/01/31/business/media/31pepsi.html?_r=1, accessed December 20, 2011.

146 *With respect to channel mix*: Steve Rubel, "In Battle between Social and Mainstream, Hybrid Media Will Be the Winner," *Ad Age* blogs, October 10, 2011, http://adage.com/article/viewpoint/hybrid-media-trumps-social-mainstream/230273/, accessed December 19, 2011.

147 *Back in 2009 the computer manufacturer Dell*: Stefanie N, "@DellOutlet Surpasses $2 Million on Twitter," Dell, June 11, 2009, http://en.community.

dell.com/dell-blogs/direct2dell/b/direct2dell/archive/2009/06/11/delloutlet-surpasses-2-million-on-twitter.aspx, accessed December 20, 2011.

147 *Singh has also declared*: Shiv Singh, "Will You Tie Bonuses to Facebook Fan Counts?," *Going Social Now*, August 22, 2011, http://www.goingsocialnow.com/2011/04/tie-corporate-bonuses-to-faceb.php, accessed December 20, 2011.

147 *Sally Dickerson of Omnicom's BrandScience unit*: Sally Dickerson, "Paid, Owned and Earned—How to Measure Their Effectiveness and Synergy," paper presented at the British Library, London, November 8, 2011.

147 *One of the most compelling examples*: Sucharita Mulpuru, "The Purchase Path of Online Buyers," Forrester Research, Inc., March 16, 2011, http://www.forrester.com/rb/go?docid=58942&oid=1-IJJHSS&action=5, accessed December 20, 2011.

147 *In a conversation with the social media news blog Mashable*: Todd Wasserman, "Social Media Has Little Impact on Online Retail Purchases," *Mashable*, April 27, 2011, http://mashable.com/2011/04/27/social-media-retail-purchases/, accessed December 20, 2011.

149 *One very clear indication*: "The Vitrue 100: Consumer Electronics Reigned Supreme in 2010," *Vitrue*, January 7, 2011, http://www.vitrue.com/the-vitrue-100-consumer-electronics-reigned-supreme-in-2010, accessed December 20, 2011.

151 *In 2011 IBM published a report that clearly highlighted*: Carolyn Heller and Gautam Parasnis, "From Social Media to Social CRM—What Customers Want: A Joint Holiday Shopping Study with GSI Commerce of 15 Retail Websites," IBM Global Business Services, Executive Report, IBM Corporation, 2011, http://www.forrester.com/rb/Research/purchase_path_of_online_buyers/q/id/58942/t/2, accessed December 20, 2011. Data based on single touch point for hard goods among web shoppers.

154 *It has been estimated that*: Bernoff and Schadler, chapter 3, "Peer Influence Analysis."

155 *As the advertising research pioneer*: Daniel Starch, *Advertising: Its Principles, Practice, and Technique* (Chicago: Scott, Foresman, 1914).

155 *The average turned out to be*: It has been pointed out to us that some people may have seen the status update and not clicked "like." Yet it is also true that because these posts got more "likes" than the typical post, they ended up with greater prominence on Facebook than the typical post would get.

156 *Over the past couple of years*: Stroomedia, "Old Spice Responses Case Study," August 8, 2010, online video clip, http://www.youtube.com/watch?v=fD1WqPGn5Ag, accessed December 20, 2011. See also "Online Video: Old Spice the Most Viral Video of the Year—Again," Ad Age Digital, December 28, 2011, http://adage.com/article/the-viral-video-chart-weeks-most-popular-branddriven-viral-ads/spice-viral-brand-year-video/231780/?utm_source=daily_email&utm_medium=newsletter&utm_campaign=adage, accessed December 29, 2011.

156   *The campaign's success was immediately interpreted*: Brian Morrissey, "Old Spice's Agency Flexes Its Bulging Stats," *Adweek*, August 4, 2010, http://www.adweek.com/adfreak/old-spices-agency-flexes-its-bulging-stats-12396, accessed December 20, 2011.

157   *The campaign featuring Mustafa*: Craig Reiss, "Now Look Here, Now Learn from This. . . ," *Entrepreneur.com on msnbc.com*, July 18, 2010, http://www.msnbc.msn.com/id/38282026/ns/business-small_business/t/now-look-here-now-learn/, accessed December 19, 2011. See also Rupal Parekh, "Wieden & Kennedy Is Ad Age's Agency of the Year," *Advertising Age*, January 24, 2011, http://adage.com/article/special-report-agency-alist/wieden-kennedy-ad-age-s-agency-year/148369/, accessed December 19, 2011.

157   *That's genuine reach*: David Griner, "Hey Old Spice Haters, Sales Are Up 107%," *Adweek*, July 27, 2010, http://www.adweek.com/adfreak/hey-old-spice-haters-sales-are-107–12422, accessed December 20, 2011. See also Eleftheria Parpis, "Spice It Up," *Adweek*, July 26, 2010, http://www.adweek.com/news/advertising-branding/spice-it-102895?page=1, accessed December 20, 2011.

158   *David Hallerman, an analyst at eMarketer*: David Hallerman, "What Marketers Can Learn from the Old Spice 'Your Man' Campaign," *Advertising Age*, August 26, 2010, http://adage.com/article/digitalnext/marketers-learn-spice-man-campaign/145603/, accessed December 20, 2011.

158   *This campaign reinforces*: Pat LaPointe, "The Rock in the Pond: How Online Buzz and Offline WOM Can Make a Strong Message Even More Powerful," *Journal of Advertising Research*, September 2011, 456–457.

159   *Tony Hsieh, the company's founder and CEO*: Tony Hsieh, *Delivering Happiness: A Path to Profits, Passion, and Purpose* (New York: Hachette, 2010). See also *The CEO TV Show with Robert Reiss*, August 8, 2011, available online at http://videos.ceoshow.com/tony-hsieh-ceo-zappos-com-innovation, accessed December 20, 2011.

159   *Aaron Magness, head of business development*: Personal interview with Aaron Magness of Zappos, May 11, 2011.

160   *Hsieh considers the telephone*: The CEO TV Show with Robert Reiss, August 8, 2011, available online at http://videos.ceoshow.com/tony-hsieh-ceo-zappos-com-innovation, accessed December 20, 2011.

161   *Hsieh likes to illustrate this point*: Carmine Gallo, "Delivering Happiness the Zappos Way: How the Footwear e-tailer's CEO, Tony Hsieh, Builds a Brand through Public speaking," *Bloomberg Businessweek*, May 12, 2009, http://www.businessweek.com/smallbiz/content/may2009/sb20090512_831040.htm, accessed December 20, 2011.

CHAPTER 7: WORD OF MOUTH AS A CHANNEL

164 *During the 1990s, as the dot-com*: Claire Tristram, "The Up and Comer: Gene DeRose, Jupiter," *Information Week Online*, November 17, 1997, http://www.informationweek.com/657/57iuan4.htm, accessed December 20, 2011.

164 *AOL rose rapidly to become*: Richard Pérez-Peña, "Time Warner Board Backs AOL Spinoff," *New York Times*, May 28, 2009, http://www.nytimes .com/2009/05/29/business/media/29warner.html, accessed December 19, 2011.

164 *Gene DeRose was one of the first hires*: Personal interview with Gene DeRose of House Party, June 16, 2011.

167 *Kraft's Philadelphia Cream Cheese is a venerable old brand*: Personal interview with Richard Bode of Kraft, July 29, 2011.

168 *Kraft launched this new product*: E. J. Schultz, "Kraft Puts Big Bucks behind Philadelphia Cooking Creme Launch," *Advertising Age*, October 26, 2010, http://adage.com/article/news/marketing-kraft-puts-big-bucks-philly-cooking-creme/146710/, accessed December 20, 2011.

168 *As part of the marketing effort*: Third-party research was conducted for House Party by ChatThreads. Research results from a presentation on March 12, 2011, provided to Keller Fay Group by House Party. More information on House Party can be found at http://corp.houseparty.com/, accessed December 20, 2011.

170 *Tremor is another word-of-mouth agency*: The methodology and philosophy of Tremor can be found at www.tremor.com, accessed December 20, 2011.

170 *Tremor was started in 1999*: "Executive Profile of Claudia Kotchka," *Bloomberg Businessweek*, 2011, http://investing.businessweek.com/businessweek/ research/stocks/people/person.asp?personId=25779428&ticker=PG:US, accessed December 20, 2011. See also Jennifer Reingold, "The Interpreter," *Fast Company*, June 1, 2005, http://www.fastcompany.com/magazine/95/ open_design-kotchka.html?page=0%2C1, accessed December 20, 2011; Bruce Nussbaum, "Claudia Kotchka Leaves Procter & Gamble," *Bloomberg Businessweek*, May 22, 2008, http://www.businessweek.com/innovate/ NussbaumOnDesign/archives/2008/05/claudia_kotchka_1.html, accessed December 20, 2011.

171 *They also introduced a methodology*: Steve Knox, "Understanding Word of Mouth: The Science of Advocacy," Proctor and Gamble Tremor presentation, http://www.slideshare.net/jorgebarba/the-science-of-word-of-mouth, accessed December 19, 2011.

172 *To illustrate how a word-of-mouth campaign*: "The Venus Breeze Story: Proving WOM Effectiveness with Disciplined Measurement," WOMMY Award submission presentation, 2009. Provided to Keller Fay by Tremor.

173 *The founders of the Word of Mouth Marketing Association*: "Ethical Education and Oversight," Word of Mouth Marketing Association, 2011, http://womma.org/ethics/code, accessed December 20, 2011.

173 *There had already been a few high-profile stumbles*: Suzanne Vranica, "Sony Ericsson Campaign Uses Actors to Push Camera-Phone in Real Life," *Wall Street Journal*, July 31, 2002, http://online.wsj.com/article_email/SB1028069195715597440.html?mod=todays_us_marketplace_hs, accessed December 20, 2011.

174 *The 2005 WOMMA Ethics Code*: "Guides Concerning the Use of Endorsements and Testimonials in Advertising," Federal Trade Commission, FTC 16 CFR Part 255, October 2009, http://www.ftc.gov/os/2009/10/091005 revisedendorsementguides.pdf, accessed December 20, 2011.

175 *Right after their release*: Tony DiResta, "Three Significant Changes to the Guides," *DiResta the Law*, WOMMA, October 6, 2009, http://womma.org/diresta/2009/10/three-significant-changes-to-the-guides/, accessed December 20, 2011.

175 *WOMMA encourages its members*: "Don't Tell. Do Ask." Word of Mouth Marketing Association, 2011, http://womma.org/ethics/honestyroi/, accessed December 20, 2011.

176 *an interesting and revealing piece of research*: Walter Carl, "To Tell or Not to Tell? Assessing the Practical Effects of Disclosure for Word-of-Mouth Marketing Agents and Their Conversational Partners," Northeastern University, Communications Studies, January 2006, http://www.waltercarl.neu.edu/downloads/ToTellOrNotToTell.pdf, accessed December 20, 2011.

176 *The main conclusions of the research*: The reason some conversations included disclosure that the BzzAgent worked for a word-of-mouth marketing agency and some did not is that this study was conducted before disclosure was required, something the agency subsequently changed. Further, there were times when the agents made a disclosure of their affiliation with BzzAgent but the person to whom they were talking did not recall this, which could be due to the fact that interviewees forget they were told, or the agents thought they made the disclosure but in fact did not. In either case, under those circumstances the Carl analysis assumed that no disclosure was made.

177 *Consider the Australian word-of-mouth agency Soup*: Personal interview with Michele Bray of Soup, July 19, 2011.

178 *CBA was suffering from significant*: David McNickel, "Switched on CEO: Ralph Norris, Commonwealth Bank of Australia," *iStart: Technology in Business*, January 30, 2008, http://www.istart.com.au/index/HM20/AL29454/AR210381, accessed December 20, 2011.

179 *The goal of the program*: Survey statistics from Roy Morgan Research, conducted for Soup, as reported to Keller Fay by Soup.

180 *Shopper marketing is when*: GMA Sales Committee, "Shopper Marketing 4.0: Building Scalable Playbooks That Drive Results," Grocery Manufacturer's Association and Booz & Company, 2010, http://www.booz.com/media/uploads/BoozCo_GMA_Shopper_Marketing_4.0–2.pdf, accessed December 20, 2011.

180 *Two companies that are melding*: Ed Keller has been a member of the Bazaarvoice Board of Directors since 2006.

181 *BzzAgent was one of the earliest*: Personal interview with Dave Balter of BzzAgent, August 1, 2011.

181 *It is what he calls "a new twist . . ."*: Dave Balter and John Butman, *Grapevine: The New Art of Word-of-Mouth Marketing* (New York: Portfolio, 2005), 34.

181 *He and his company have been profiled*: Rob Walker, "The Hidden (in Plain Sight) Persuaders," *New York Times Magazine*, December 5, 2004, http://www.nytimes.com/2004/12/05/magazine/05BUZZ.html, accessed December 20, 2011.

181 *He has published two books*: Balter and Butman; Dave Balter, *The Word Of Mouth Manual: Volume II* (Boston: 2008).

181 *Declaring itself the fastest growing*: "BzzAgent Hive Grows with $13.75 Million in Venture Capital Financing," BzzAgent Press Release, January 13, 2006, http://www.bzzagent.com/downloads/press/BzzAgent_Financing.pdf, accessed December 20, 2011.

181 *So it came as no surprise when*: Cheryl Morris, "BzzAgent Acquired by Tesco's dunnhumby for $60M to 'Connect the Dots between Social Media and Shopper Marketing,'" *BostInnovation*, May 23, 2011, http://bostinnovation.com/2011/05/23/bzzagent-acquired-by-tesco%E2%80%99s-dunnhumby-for-60m-to-%E2%80%98connect-the-dots-between-social-media-shopper-marketing%E2%80%99/, accessed December 20, 2011.

182 *In short, BzzAgent's expectation*: Dave Balter, "Social Media Meets Shopper Marketing," BzzAgent, January 19, 2011, http://www.bzzagent.com/blog/post/social-media-meets-shopper-marketing/, accessed December 20, 2011. See also "The Rise of Social Shopper Marketing: Thought Starters on Connecting Social Media and Shopper Marketing," BzzAgent, January 2011, http://about.bzzagent.com/downloads/BzzAgent_SSM.pdf, accessed December 20, 2011.

184 *There is abundant research*: "Global Advertising: Consumers Trust Real Friends and Virtual Strangers the Most," *NielsenWire*, July 7, 2009, http://blog.nielsen.com/nielsenwire/consumer/global-advertising-consumers-trust-real-friends-and-virtual-strangers-the-most/, accessed December 20, 2011.

184 *For example, the electronics manufacturer Epson*: "Review Users Show 98% Higher Revenue per Visitor for Epson," Bazaarvoice Case Study, November 10, 2010, http://www.bazaarvoice.com/files/pdf/case-studies/epson_casestudy.pdf, accessed December 20, 2011.

184 *Another example of the power*: "Review-reading Travelers Convert 123% Higher at CheapCaribbean.com," Bazaarvoice Case Study, October 6, 2010, http://www.bazaarvoice.com/files/pdf/case-studies/cheapcarribean_casestudy.pdf, accessed December 20, 2011.

184 *For example, Rubbermaid*: "Coupon with Review Sees 10% Redemption Lift," Bazaarvoice Case Study, April 15, 2010, http://www.bazaarvoice.com/

resources/case-studies/coupon-review-sees-10-redemption-lift, accessed December 20, 2011.

CHAPTER 8: NEGATIVE WORD OF MOUTH:
A CAUSE FOR ALARM OR A CUSTOMER'S GREATEST GIFT?

186 *In June 2005 a high-profile blogger*: Jeff Jarvis, "Dell Hell: Seller Beware," *BuzzMachine*, July 1, 2005, http://www.buzzmachine.com/archives/cat_dell.html, accessed December 20, 2011.

187 *It was a company that had been formed*: Christy Kirby, "Dell: A Company Built on Direct and Open Communication," Altimeter Open Leadership Awards, September 13, 2010, http://awards2010.openleadership.spigit.com/Page/ViewIdea?ideaid=47, accessed December 20, 2011.

188 *The reengineering of the customer service process*: "Dell and Social Media," *Brand Autopsy*, September 21, 2007, http://www.brandautopsy.com/2007/09/dell-and-social.html, accessed December 20, 2011.

188 *Initially there was a team of two or three employees*: Personal interview with Bob Kaufman of Dell, May 6, 2011.

188 *In December 2010 Dell opened*: Visit to Dell to tour the Social Media Listening Command Center on May 26, 2011.

189 *According to our data at Keller Fay, the quality*: When one includes both offline and online word of mouth, the average for technology companies is 63 percent positive, 9 percent negative, and 18 percent mixed (positive and negative). Dell's results are 61 percent positive, 10 percent negative, and 19 percent mixed.

189 *This has been especially reinforced by some literature*: Pete Blackshaw, *A Satisfied Customer Tells Three Friends, Angry Customers Tells 3,000: Running a Business in Today's Consumer-Driven World* (New York: Doubleday, 2008).

193 *The work of Jonah Berger and Katherine Milkman*: Jonah Berger and Katherine Milkman, "Social Transmission, Emotion, and the Virality of Online Content," December 25, 2009, http://ssrn.com/abstract=1528077, accessed December 20, 2011.

193 *The first has to do with human nature*: Tali Sharot, *The Optimism Bias: A Tour of the Irrationally Positive Brain* (New York: Pantheon Books, 2011). See also Tali Sharot, "The Optimism Bias," *Time*, May 28, 2011, http://www.time.com/time/health/article/0,8599,2074067,00.html, accessed December 20, 2011.

193 *Tali Sharot, a research fellow*: Tali Sharot, "Major Delusions," *New York Times*, May 14, 2011, http://www.nytimes.com/2011/05/15/opinion/15Sharot.html?_r=1, accessed December 20, 2011.

194 *TV news viewers and newspaper readers*: Andrew Ross Sorkin, "Lehman Files for Bankruptcy, Merrill Is Sold," *New York Times*, September 14, 2008, http://www.nytimes.com/2008/09/15/business/15lehman.html, accessed December 20, 2011.

194 *Two weeks later, as anxiety accelerated*: Carl Hulse and David Herszenhorn, "House Rejects Bailout Package, 228–205; Stocks Plunge," *New York Times*, September 29, 2008, http://www.nytimes.com/2008/09/30/business/30bailout.html?pagewanted=all, accessed December 20, 2011.

197 *But what about conversations*: "Advertising amid Crisis: Lessons from the Financial and Automotive Industries in 2009" was presented by Brad Fay and David Shiffman of the media agency MediaVest at the Advertising Research Foundation's Re:Think 2010 Conference on March 22–24, 2010. The presentation can be found at http://www.slideshare.net/gsweeton/advertising-amid-crisis-42010, accessed December 20, 2011.

199 *Worse, the company was perceived*: Hiroko Tabuchi and Bill Vlasic, "Toyota's Top Executive under Rising Pressure," *New York Times*, February 5, 2010, www.nytimes.com/2010/02/06/business/global/06toyota.html?scp=3&sq=toyota&st=nyt, accessed December 20, 2011.

199 *On February 24 he did so again*: Micheline Maynard, "An Apology from Toyota's Leader," *New York Times*, February 24, 2010, www.nytimes.com/2010/02/25/business/global/25toyota.html?scp=4&sq=toyota&st=nyt, accessed December 20, 2011.

201 *Impressively Toyota recovered*: Makiko Kiutamura and Yuki Hagiwara, "Toyota Stays Ahead of GM as World's Largest Automaker," *Bloomberg Businessweek*, January 24, 2011, http://www.businessweek.com/news/2011–01–24/toyota-stays-ahead-of-gm-as-world-s-largest-automaker.html, accessed December 20, 2011.

202 *Tim Morrison, a thirty-year Toyota man*: Personal interviews with Tim Morrison of Toyota, April 6 and June 1, 2011.

203 *Morrison's "Ask Somebody" campaign*: Toyota, "United States Operations 2011," www.toyota.com/about/our_business/our_numbers/images/USOperationsBrochureFINAL_4–1–11.pdf, accessed December 20, 2011.

203 *The company used the social media platform Digg*: Jon Fortt, "Toyota's Low-risk Dialogue on Digg," CNN Money, February 8, 2010, http://tech.fortune.cnn.com/2010/02/08/toyotas-low-risk-dialogue-on-digg/, accessed December 20, 2011.

205 *Saatchi's "return on marketing investment" team*: Personal interviews with Conrad Nussbaum and John Lisko of Saatchi LA, June 1, 2011.

206 *Marketers' fear of negative word of mouth*: Personal interview with Brett Hurt of Bazaarvoice, April 8, 2011.

208 *Certainly, that is the view of L.L. Bean*: The L.L. Bean word-of-mouth story was told by company CMO Steve Fuller at the Bazaarvoice Social Commerce Summit on April 5, 2011, in Austin, TX, http://www.bazaarvoice.com/blog/2011/04/21/social-helps-brands-keep-their-promises-says-l-l-beans-steve-fuller/, accessed December 20, 2011.

210 *By 2007, though, the company decided*: Personal interview with Alex Gruzen of Dell, April 15, 2011.

210 *The Word of Mouth Marketing Association and the Federal Trade Commission*: Suzanne M. Kirchhoff, "Advertising Industry in the Digital Age," Congressional Research Service Report for Congress, February 1, 2011, http://womma.org/diresta/2–10–11.pdf, accessed December 20, 2011. See also "Ethical Education and Oversight," Word of Mouth Marketing Association, 2011, http://womma.org/ethics/code, accessed December 20, 2011; "Guides Concerning the Use of Endorsements and Testimonials in Advertising," Federal Trade Commission 16 CFR Part 255, October, 2009, www.ftc.gov/os/2009/10/091005revisedendorsementguides.pdf, accessed December 20, 2011.

CHAPTER 9: IMAGINING A NEW SOCIAL MARKETING

213 *Indeed there are a remarkable number*: Chris Perry, "Let's Get Over Who 'Owns' Social Media," *Ad Age Digital*, May 7, 2009, http://adage.com/article/digitalnext/digital-marketing-owns-social-media/136481/, accessed December 20, 2011; Joseph Jaffe, "Who Owns Social Media?," *Adweek*, March 15, 2009, http://www.adweek.com/news/advertising-branding/who-owns-social-media-98655, accessed December 20, 2011.

214 *Even human resource departments*: Jaffe, "Who Owns Social Media?"

214 *In a 2011 survey of brands*: Internal WOMMA survey, quoted by permission of the Word of Mouth Marketing Association.

214 *In late 2010 Altimeter partner*: Jeremiah Owyang, "Social Business Forecast: 2011 the Year of Integration," LeWeb Conference Keynote Address, December 9, 2010, http://www.slideshare.net/jeremiah_owyang/keynote-social-business-forecast-2011-the-year-of-integration, accessed December 20, 2011.

214 *He also analyzed the management strategy*: The following are the definitions used by Altimeter in their report, as shown in Table 10.1. *Decentralized*: no one department manages or coordinates, efforts bubble up from the edges of the company; *Centralized*: one department (like Corp Communications) manages all social activities; *Hub and Spoke*: a cross-functional team sits in a centralized position and helps various nodes such as business units; *Multiple Hub and Spoke ("Dandelion")*: similar to hub and spoke but applicable to multinational companies where "companies within companies" act nearly autonomously from each other under a common brand; *Holistic*: everyone in the company uses social media safely and consistently across all organizations.

215 *Another Altimeter principal analyst*: Brian Solis, "Who Owns Social Media?," BrianSolis.com, August 20, 2009, http://www.briansolis.com/2009/08/who-owns-social-media/, accessed December 20, 2011.

216 *Another answer we've heard*: Sam Decker, "Who Owns Word of Mouth in an Organization?," *Social Media Today*, October 17, 2007, http://socialmediatoday.com/samdecker/110111/who-owns-word-mouth-organization, accessed December 20, 2011; John Bell, "Who Owns Word of

Mouth: The Athens Sessions," Digital Influence Mapping Project, October 13, 2007, http://johnbell.typepad.com/weblog/2007/10/who-owns-word-o.html, accessed December 20, 2011.

218 *Best Buy has long understood the value of conversation*: Personal interview with Barry Judge of Best Buy, January 11, 2011.

220 *We then consulted with General Mills*: Personal interview with David Witt of General Mills, February 14, 2011. See also "General Mills: Going Social," presented by David Witt at the Marketing 2.0 Conference in February 2010. The presentation can be found at http://www.slideshare.net/Insidebsi/general-mills-going-social, accessed December 20, 2011.

221 *CMO Addicks says that General Mills' journey*: Personal interview with Mark Addicks of General Mills, July 28, 2011.

221 *The character was created in 1921*: Dottie Enrico, "Top 10 Advertising Icons," *Advertising Age*, March 29, 1999, http://adage.com/article/news/top-10-advertising-icons/62929/, accessed December 20, 2011.

222 *Inspiration for one of General Mills' current programs*: "General Mills: History of Innovation, Bisquick," http://generalmills.com/~/media/Files/history/hist_bisquick.ashx, accessed December 19, 2011. See also "Seven Decades of Great Taste from Bisquick," *DVO* online, http://www.dvo.com/recipe_pages/betty/SEVEN_DECADES_OF_GREAT_TASTE_FROM_BISQUICK.html, accessed December 19, 2011.

223 *Fiber One bars are an example*: "General Mills: Going Social" was presented by David Witt at the Marketing 2.0 Conference in February 2010. The presentation can be found at http://www.slideshare.net/Insidebsi/general-mills-going-social, accessed December 20, 2011.

226 *In her humorous autobiography*: Tina Fey, *Bossypants* (New York: Little, Brown, 2011), 11–18.

227 *Kimberly-Clark executives believed*: Nancy Redd, Chelsea Krost, Tomi-Ann Roberts, and Aliza Lifshitz, "Break the Cycle: A Study on Vaginal Health," U by Kotex—Kimberly-Clark Corporation, study conducted August 3–19, 2009, http://www.ubykotex.com/downloads/pdf/u_by_kotex_real_talk_a_study_on_vaginal_health.pdf, accessed December 20, 2011.

227 *First launched in Australia in 2007*: Industry data provided by Claire Miller of Kimberly-Clark, June 28, 2011.

227 *Indeed U by Kotex was named Product of the Year*: "The Most Innovative Consumer Packaged Goods of 2011 Revealed at Last Night's Product of the Year USA Awards Ceremony," *PR Newswire*, February 9, 2011, http://www.prnewswire.com/news-releases/the-most-innovative-consumer-packaged-goods-of-2011-revealed-at-last-nights-product-of-the-year-usa-awards-ceremony-115630824.html, accessed December 20, 2011.

227 *In 2011 the Brand Power Index*: Caleb Melby, "What Brands Do Women Want? Harley-Davidson Tops List," *Forbes Magazine*, August 24, 2011, http://www.forbes.com/sites/calebmelby/2011/08/24/what-brands-do-women-want-harley-davidson-tops-list/, accessed December 20, 2011.

229 *Most marketing executives at Kimberly-Clark*: Personal interview with Tony Palmer of Kimberly-Clark, August 4, 2011. See also video conference with Michelle Froah, Claire Miller, Melissa Sexton, Sarah Freiburger, Jennifer Westemeyer, Joanna Klee, and Jay Gottlieb of Kimberly-Clark, Amy Carvajal of Organic, and Diana Littman of Marina Maher Communications on June 28, 2011, New York.

230 *The campaign itself was all about disruption*: Andrew Adam Newman, "Rebelling against the Commonly Evasive Feminine Care Ad," *New York Times*, March 15, 2010, http://www.nytimes.com/2010/03/16/business/media/16adco.html, accessed December 20, 2011.

231 *According to CMO Palmer*: Jack Neff, "How Kimberly-Clark Is Lifting Sales by Elevating Marketing," *Advertising Age*, November 7, 2011, 6.

231 *We worked collaboratively*: Personal interview with Marina Maher of Marina Maher Communications, August 9, 2011.

231 *Writing in her blog just after MMC won*: Marina Maher, "Breaking Barriers in Marketing to Women," *Marina Maher Communications: The Inside Scoop*, June 10, 2011, http://www.mahercomm.com/breaking-barriers-marketing-women/, accessed December 20, 2011.

233 *Thus the campaign is an outgrowth*: Personal interview with Claire Miller of Kimberly-Clark, August 5, 2011.

233 *In a July 2008 interview*: "Measured Thoughts: Tony Palmer, Senior Vice President and CMO, Kimberly-Clark," Marketing NPV Webcast, July 8, 2008, http://marketingnpv.com/content/measured-thoughts-tony-palmer-senior-vice-president-and-cmo-kimberlyclark, accessed December 20, 2011.

Index

Page numbers in *italics* refer to illustrations.

About the Authors

Ed Keller is the CEO of the Keller Fay Group, and has been called "one of the most recognized names in word of mouth." The publication of his first book, *The Influentials,* has been called a "seminal moment in the development of word of mouth." He is a past president of the Word of Mouth Marketing Association (WOMMA) and of the Market Research Council. He lives in New York.

Brad Fay is the Chief Operating Officer of the Keller Fay Group. Brad won the Grand Innovation Award of the Advertising Research Foundation for the development of Keller Fay's TalkTrack®, a continuous measurement system for all consumer conversations about brands and companies, both offline and online. He is a member of the Word of Mouth Association Board of Directors. He lives in New Jersey.